Dear Allison,
I love you,

xx-x

Advancing Sisterhood?

SHARON MONTEITH

Advancing Sisterhood?

Interracial

Friendships in

Contemporary

Southern Fiction

The University of Georgia Press

Athens and London

© 2000 by the University of Georgia Press

Athens, Georgia 30602

All rights reserved

Designed by Kathi Dailey Morgan

Set in Berkeley Old Style Book by G&S Typesetters

Printed and bound by Thomson-Shore

The paper in this book meets the guidelines for
permanence and durability of the Committee on
Production Guidelines for Book Longevity of the
Council on Library Resources.

Printed in the United States of America

04 03 02 01 00 C 5 4 3 2 1

Library of Congress Cataloging-in-Publication Data

Monteith, Sharon.

Advancing sisterhood? : interracial friendships
in contemporary southern fiction / Sharon Monteith.

p. cm.

Includes bibliographical references and index.

ISBN 0-8203-2249-0 (alk. paper)

1. American fiction—Southern States—History and criticism.

2.Women and literature—Southern States—History—20th century.

3. American fiction—Women authors—History and criticism.

4. American fiction—20th century—History and criticism.   5. Afro-
American women in literature.   6. Southern States—In literature.

7. Female friendship in literature.   8. Race relations in literature.

9. White women in literature.   10. Friendship in literature.

11. Women in literature.   I.Title.

PS261 .M65 2001

813'.5409353—dc21   00-041800

British Library Cataloging-in-Publication Data available

For my family with love

Contents

Acknowledgments

I would like to thank Helen Taylor, Richard H. King, and Pete Messent, who offered such insightful advice on the first draft of the manuscript. I would also like to take this opportunity to thank the anonymous readers whose reports on *Advancing Sisterhood?* were generous and energizing. I am indebted to my friend and colleague Richard Godden, who may not realize, not having read a word of this book, that it was he who gave me the impetus to finish it. Talking about the South with Richard Godden, Richard H. King, Peter Ling, and Helen Taylor is always a pleasure. Among friends, Sue Aldridge, Marie Cable, Tina Galloway, Lise Lavelle, Louise Palmer and Andy Spong, Pat Wheeler, and especially Jenny Newman and Dave Evans never failed to inquire how the book was going and offered me the chance to talk about it. My most grateful thanks go to Nahem Yousaf, as always.

Among the librarians I have consulted, I have very much appreciated the help of Neil and Karen Allen at the University of Hertfordshire. At the University of Georgia Press, I would like to acknowledge Malcolm L. Call, Marlene Allen, Erin Kelly, and, for her careful and professional editing, Ellen Harris.

Parts of chapters have appeared in the form of articles in the *Journal of American Studies* (Cambridge University Press), *Women: A Cultural Review* (Routledge), and *Overhere: Reviews in American Studies*. I acknowledge the editors and publishers for permission to reprint parts of those articles here.

Advancing Sisterhood?

Setting the Parameters

Women Writers and Interracial Friendship

In 1996 Rebecca Wells's *Divine Secrets of the Ya-Ya Sisterhood* became a runaway success, and Ya-Ya groups began springing up across the South. Published in Britain in 1999, the novel headed straight for the bestseller list this side of the Atlantic too. *Divine Secrets* is the story of a group of white "sister-friends"; it is set in Thornton, Louisiana, over a period of sixty years. Readers follow the friends—Vivi, Caro, Necie, and Teensy—from childhood scrapes through the anxieties of old age. Wells said that she created the Ya-Yas because "I wanted a group of friends like that."[1] The "friendship plot" has become so popular that not only does similar material appear in Wells's novel *Little Altars Everywhere,* but it can be seen to dominate novels by writers as different as Alice Walker and Belva Plain, Ellen Gilchrist and Ann Allen Shockley. *Advancing Sisterhood?* examines friendship—the most common human relationship but the least criticized—a relationship that is extraordinarily resonant in popular cultural productions. In recent years stories about women's friendship have enjoyed cinematic as well as literary popular success, from Whitney Otto's *How to Make an American Quilt* to Terry McMillan's *Waiting to Exhale.* Most often the "sister-friends" belong to a single racial or ethnic group, but notable amid such representations of friendship are those narratives which depict cross-racial relationships, and it is with these that this book concerns itself.

Bebe Moore Campbell, promoting her *New York Times* bestseller *Brothers and Sisters,* a depiction of a cross-racial friendship set in Los Angeles in the aftermath of the 1991 riots, asserted: "Despite all of the laws and quotas that have been passed to deal with race, in the final analysis it comes down to one-to-one relationships. . . . If we can't get past some of the barriers to friendship in this country, we're not really going to move forward on the democratic notion of racial harmony."[2] This liberal sentiment is clearly based in a belief in the individual as the basic component of political change. Feminist critiques of liberal individualism have charged the tradition with separating the private from the public and disengaging individuals from their social context. But in many literary representations of interracial friendship, social consciousness is the point of departure, as is the setting of the American South. Manning Marable has noted that many of "the most striking changes in public perceptions of race [have] occurred in popular culture," through the arts—fiction and the media.[3] Sometimes, in fiction and film, interracial relationships are presented as redemptive psychodramas or bizarre and dark comedies—Burt Brinkerhoff's TVM-feature *Jailbirds,* in which Dyan Cannon, a "cheap stupid small-town girl," and Phylicia Rashad, a "black college graduate who won't shut up," are on the run in Louisiana; and Joe E. Lansdale's crime novels featuring white and straight Hap Collins and black and gay Leonard Pine, in which the antiheroes fight the Texas Klan while maintaining the closeness of brothers.[4]

More often, interracial friendships work microhistorically to expose the context in which friendship may be seen as transgressive, trespassing the borders of what is socially expected or countenanced. In the south-ern context a brief list might include Alice Walker's *Meridian*; Rita Mae Brown's *In Her Day*; Ellen Douglas's *Can't Quit You Baby*; Dori Sanders's *Clover*; Connie May Fowler's *Sugar Cage* and *Before Women Had Wings*, the latter filmed by Oprah Winfrey for the ABC network; Kaye Gibbons's *Ellen Foster* and *On the Occasion of My Last Afternoon*; Carol Dawson's *Body of Knowledge*; and southern-influenced novels by writers from outside the South, like Sherley Anne Williams's *Dessa Rose*, and from those who have moved away, like Lane von Herzen, author of *Copper Crown*. Robert Penn Warren concludes his study of the racially torn South of 1956, *Segregation: The Inner Conflict in the South*, with the hope that, "because it has had to deal concretely with a moral problem" in a country where "moral identity is hard to come by," the South may of-fer the nation leadership if America is "to break out of the national rhythm, the rhythm between complacency and panic."[5] Writers, social commentators, journalists, and historians as different as Warren, Ralph Ellison, who famously avowed he would not "Jim Crow" his imagina-tion, John Egerton, Peter Applebome, and the African American histo-rian John Hope Franklin, head of Clinton's commission on race, have discussed the "southernization" of America. They posit the belief that the South, the nation's most visible crucible of national racial guilt, is, nev-ertheless, the nation's "best hope for racial peace."[6] Much is invested in the contemporary South's abilities to redeem the nation at the end of the twentieth century—the century W. E. B. Du Bois presciently predicted would be beset by the "problem of the color-line"—from articles in the national press to statements on national television.[7]

Advancing Sisterhood? considers the ways in which contemporary white writers buy into friendship as a way to "cement the political bonds of the community," to borrow Alisdair McIntyre's words in *After Virtue*, with the South as their setting. Via close readings, it examines the way writers imaginatively configure friendships and associations between black and white women, presenting as well a more general overview of novels and stories that foreground interracial friendships between women. The texts that are the focus of close readings have been chosen specifically to advance the critical study of contemporary white writing about race and about white racial responsibility. This is a field of inquiry that demands attention. Black women writers are examined throughout, since their works are often more direct in their confrontations with racism and their explication of anger and *ressentiment* in interracial friendships and encounters. One thinks immediately of Alice Walker's stories "The Revenge of Hannah Kemhuff" and "Advancing Luna and Ida B. Wells," as well as the Kentucky writer Ann Allen Shockley's "Home to Meet the Folks." In *Skin Deep: Black Women and White Women Write About Race,* Marita Golden remarks that the narratives written by black contributors "throb" with bitterness, whereas those by white writers "tellingly reveal" how their lives have been "enhanced and enlarged by their connections/ friendships/liaisons with black women and even their fantasies *about* black women."[8] White women in novels by black writers are rarely represented as conscious of racially defined contexts. Miz Millie and Eleanor Jane in Walker's *The Color Purple* are largely oblivious to their oppression of black women like Sofia. Eleanor Jane slowly learns the significance of her relationship with the older black woman, but her understanding is belated and underpinned by tragedy. Sherley Anne Williams's Rufel in *Dessa Rose* commodifies and sentimentalizes her "mammy" and is thrust into comprehension of the fact only when Dessa can no longer tolerate her relegation of another black woman to her service role. Dessa and Rufel do come together as friends, in danger and trepidation, but when they part they are unable to express their affection for each other outwardly: "We couldn't hug each other, not on the streets . . . not even after dark; we both had sense to know that. The town could even bar us from laughing; but that night we walked the board-walk together and we didn't hide our grins."[9] Williams eschews a completely happy ending because historically there is no social space in which the women can behave as equal friends: Dessa goes west and Rufel east to "some city didn't allow slaves." Williams avoids a utopian ending in a novel set in the 1840s South, but *Dessa Rose* is a rare example of a black writer proffering an interracial friendship that is successfully negotiated and that brings pleasure to both women. Dessa never meets the equal of Rufel again.

The idioms white protagonists deploy are frequently much more utopian and therapeutic—providing a soft-focus conciliatory perspective—in the way that Helena Michie describes the paradigms writers use when advancing ideas of sisterhood.[10] Sisterhood is itself a kinship term with a much more established history within black cultures than white, as Gloria I. Joseph and Jill Lewis and, more recently, Maria C. Lugones and Pat Alake Rosezelle discuss.[11] For white women its derivation is frequently the civil rights movement and white activists learning to call black and white women "sister."[12] The novelist Marita Golden describes friendship as "the way black women have survived" and adds, "When white women discovered that women could be friends in the seventies, I asked, 'Where have they been?' Friendships have been our psychic glue."[13] While black women writers often celebrate relationships between black women, white women writers more usually privilege the moral growth of their white woman protagonist through her relationship with a black friend. Interestingly, Marilyn Friedman, in *What Are Friends For?*, bases her definition of friendship on the "moral witness," so that friendship fosters "vicarious participation in the very experience of moral alternatives." This implies that when friends share the same backgrounds, it becomes less likely that they will afford each other the opportunity for radical transformation: "Friends who are very akin to each other could not stimulate each other's *wholesale* rethinking of deep moral values or principles."[14] Friedman does not extend her discussion to cross-racial friendships but her idea keys into an unresolved dilemma around friendship, race, and racism that both fascinates and challenges.

Texts that explore and expose a history of cross-racial association between black and white women tend to emphasize the difficulties and improbabilities of the association, looking back to slavery and to black rancor over white women's suffrage, where the empowerment of one group of women made manifest the disempowerment of another. From the titles of recent critical studies that discuss women's cross-racial associations, and in the central metaphors they deploy, it is clear that these historical tensions are beginning to be addressed. Minrose C. Gwin uses the scene from Faulkner's *Absalom, Absalom!* in which Clytie is rebuffed by Rosa as an inescapable motif in her study of black and white women in southern writing. When Rosa shudders at Clytie's touch, a powerful image of the guilty intimacy of southern race relations pulses through southern literature. But a startling and disturbing scene of this type actually occurs four years earlier in a novel written by a white woman, *Call Home the Heart,* by Fielding Burke (a.k.a. Olive Tilford Dargan). In this novel—based on the strike of cotton mill workers in Gastonia, North Carolina, in 1929—Ishma, a poor white Appalachian woman, saves Gaffie's husband, Butch, from a lynching. But when caught up in Gaffie's arms and called "Sistah," she is suddenly filled with "uncontrollable revulsion." She strikes out wildly at the black woman in "unutterable horror of herself" before stumbling away.[15]

Critics like Kenneth Warren have referred to Americans as "black and white strangers," strangers to each other's worlds, just as Minrose C. Gwin still deploys the trope of slavery as a peculiar institution to entitle her study of relations between black and white women in fiction "The Peculiar Sisterhood." The extent to which black and white women can each be described as protagonists or antagonists, and as collaborators or conspirators, is indicative of wider social relations in the United States, not just in the South. Women writers have approached this difficult terrain in novels set across the nation: Alice Adams's *Listening to Billie* in New York and Janice Deaner's *Where Blue Begins* in New York State; Jewelle Parker Rhodes's *Magic City,* set in Tulsa, Oklahoma, imagines the Tulsa race riot of 1921 via a series of violent and tragic events. In this novel Mary and Hildy strike up a friendship when brought together in fear and pain in the midst of racist violence. Michelle Cliff's *Free Enterprise* places a historical figure at the heart of the story. The black abolitionist Mary Ellen Pleasant's difficult relationship with white Alice Hooper is one feature of a novel that explores racial politics in the mid-nineteenth century and sees its protagonist supporting John Brown at Harpers Ferry. Similarly transgressive relationships are explored in Jewelle Gomez's *The Gilda Stories.* "The Girl," a runaway slave, becomes Gilda the vampire and loves and befriends women across racial and ethnic boundaries down the centuries, in a novel that moves from Louisiana in 1850 to New Hampshire in 2020 and closes with a return southward in 2050, with "The Girl" no longer fleeing for her life. Whether white like Deaner and Rhodes and or black like Cliff and Gomez, women writers are still as likely to talk of "A Peculiar Sisterhood" or "Divided Sisters" as of "Broken Silences" or "A Southern Weave of Women." This propensity mirrors recent sociological studies of race, like David K. Shipler's *A Country of Strangers: Blacks and Whites in America* and anthologies like the historian of "whiteness" David Roediger's important *Black on White: Black Writers on What It Means to Be White.*[16]

Writers of novels would seem to take up the challenge to find what bell hooks calls "integrating philosophies," in which bonds can be forged within and around difference. hooks has expressed her desire, in *Yearning* especially, to explore community and relatedness "on much deeper bases than 'in reaction to,'" as Rosa reacts to Clytie and Ishma to Gaffie, and they find themselves stifled and silenced by the reaction, unable or unwilling to articulate its meaning.[17] Like Eudora Welty's young protagonist in "A Memory," who peers at the world and at women through the restricted frame she makes with her fingers, one is tempted to delimit fictional ways of looking at black and white women. Certainly, Benjamin DeMott makes a convincing case in his 1995 book *The Trouble with Friendship: Why Americans Can't Think Straight about Race* for what he calls "friendship orthodoxy," whereby across film and television and by way of popular and neoconservative critical writing about race, amity and goodwill are expected to repair social ills.[18] Fictional representations are less uniform, but the seduction of utopian "happy endings" is still a powerfully motivating factor. In *Advancing Sisterhood?* black and white writers and critics are used in convergence and in counterpoint, and the project necessarily draws on the legacy of civil rights preoccupations with racial equality and the ramifications of feminist organizing, as well as recent preoccupations with community and communitarianism. Foregrounding southern white writers in this context acknowledges their contribution to writing about race relations and goes some way toward refuting the assumption that race is inevitably the primary theme of writers of color, their "proper" subject. A number of black women writers have professed their impatience with the burden of representation that makes them primarily responsible for inquiries into race and racism. But tensions also arise when white writers tackle representations of black characters. In Dori Sanders's *Clover,* white Sara Kate, who lives amidst a black community in rural South Carolina, is accused of seeking to commodify that same community: "The first thing you people usually do is write a book. So I'm sure you've joined all the other white Southern women writers. Eager to grab at the chance to say all the things you would love to say, but are afraid to say. . . . If you ever write like the others that our homes are dirty, our black men are shiftless, and dare use the word nigger, you'd better be prepared to leave Round Hill."[19] As this black writer implies, the territory can be a minefield, accommodating as it does issues of sameness and sympathy, antipathy and resentment, calls for justice, and hidden guilts and anxieties. This study opens up the ways in which contemporary white writers explore the racial landscape to depict the tensions between integration and segregation.

𝒵 Novels have been selected for the different ways in which they structure cross-racial friendships, interactions, and misalliances, textually as well as thematically. As James Snead shows, race works rhetorically in fictional forms so that the "characteristic figures of racial division repeat on the level of the phoneme, sentence and story."[20] A number of critics, Henry Louis Gates Jr. notably, have called for readers and critics to "examine how attitudes toward racial and gender differences generate and structure literary texts by us and about us."[21] This study examines and illustrates the means by which contemporary fictions are structured around race, formally and aesthetically as well as in content and context, in novels where white women create friendships between black and white girls and women. Feminist principles and motifs of sisterhood often inform the structuring of novels. For example, in Whitney Otto's *How to Make an American Quilt,* the quilting bee operates to structure the text via a ritual in which black and white work together. It recalls the scene in Margaret Walker's *Jubilee* where Vyry's family is finally supported by the white community in which they have come to live, and the women come together to quilt. The quilting bee is perhaps one of the most inclusive ways of combining different women in a text and context. However, I am much more interested in novels where problems of structuring a cross-racial relationship formally *complicate* that relationship rather than in texts where the structure—polyphonic in Connie May Fowler's *Sugar Cage,* for example—is left so open that it may incorporate any combination of women across a range of differences. Texts in which a single interracial relationship is foregrounded prove the most problematic, often as a direct result of the genre and form that is chosen to frame the pairing, and so they provide the main focus of this study. In this context the framed narrative would appear to be one of the most inhibiting of forms to employ when setting out to depict an interracial friendship; in my definition it is a story constrained by another story, held in parenthesis, if you will. An understanding of its ambiguities and formal ironies will inform my readings of novels by Kaye Gibbons and Lane von Herzen.

When I consider the formal qualities of the novels, I do so in the understanding that the formal elements never exist in total isolation from wider sociopolitical determinations. The narratives work to perpetuate—or to challenge—some of the dominant paradigmatic formulations of black and white women's associations that have held sway in literature, and sometimes actually do both simultaneously. Mikhail Bakhtin advanced the idea that "new images in literature are very often created through a re-accentuation of old images, by translating them from one accentual register to another." [22] Bakhtin, whose ideas inform facets of my close readings, goes on to exemplify a shift from the comic to the tragic plane. But I would extrapolate on his statement to note how many of what might be called southern signature relationships between women are mediated in self-conscious ways in contemporary fiction— the mammy and the daughter of the house; the black domestic and her white employer; black and white girls whose childhood friendship is lost in the racially separate spheres of adulthood. I do not celebrate particular novels as ideals against which others may be measured; the focal relationship remains ambivalent and problematic in each. But each novel I discuss privileges the playing out of a particular relationship as a friendship—constructs it, deconstructs it, and reconstructs it, contextualizing it against southern codes and southern culture. Each novel considers how black and white women are presented as different from one another within discourses about race and the history of the South; inevitably theirs is a historically contingent relationship, and it demands a broad historical understanding. It is with fictional representations and issues of fictionality that I am primarily concerned, however. Each chapter explores how different literary strategies are deployed to tease out the nature of a particular interracial friendship where the story of that friendship is made available in the intersection between two characters. Contemporary white writers are attempting to gain a better purchase on how black and white southern girls and women might collaborate by joining in friendship. They depict the tensions, the mistakes, and the compromises that the white characters make in the telling of their friendships. In this book I explore those texts that seem to fit the friendship paradigm but also examine the ways in which they fail to do so. I have purposely selected novels where the encounter is problematized, despite the utopian emphasis on feminist sisterhood that may underpin them, and where internal structural contradictions with subject matter work to circumvent the realization of friendship, sisterhood, and, ultimately, community and a politics of difference.

This book may be understood as taking off from where Minrose C. Gwin in *Black and White Women of the Old South: The Peculiar Sisterhood in American Literature* and Diane Roberts's *The Myth of Aunt Jemima: Representations of Race and Region* leave their studies of black and white women in the Old South and in the early twentieth century, based as they are in slavery and its aftermath.[23] Whereas in these groundbreaking texts the writers explore interracial friendships in well-known and often critically acclaimed fictions, like Willa Cather's *Sapphira and the Slave Girl* and Faulkner's *Absalom, Absalom!*, I have deliberately chosen very recent novels that have, as yet, received limited critical attention but which continue to examine interracial associations in the South and advance the discussion of race relations. It is certainly true that Faulkner, in novels like *Absalom, Absalom!* and *Requiem for a Nun* especially, succeeds in drawing out many of the tensions between black and white southern women. Diane Roberts notes this facility in the representation of the relationship between Temple Drake and Nancy Mannigoe, for example: "In their secret language, in their talks in the kitchen, in their friendship itself, Nancy and Temple expose some of the fissures and gaps in the southern social order."[24] Understandably, the contemporary writers I discuss continue to be influenced by Faulkner's preoccupations as well as his style, and this is very apparent in the writing of Ellen Douglas and Carol Dawson.[25]

There is to date no single critical work that foregrounds the dilemmas of commonality and difference among southern women that preoccupy the writings of so many contemporary southern women writers. In fact, a number of very interesting writers who open up what Mary Ward Brown has called "the whole Pandora's box of race, with all the conscious, unintended, even unrecognized withholdings of respect, status privilege, even insights," are yet to receive the critical attention their work merits.[26] In *A Southern Weave of Women: Fiction of the Contemporary South,* Linda Tate provides an introductory overview of contemporary novelists, including Ellen Douglas (*Can't Quit You Baby*) and Kaye Gibbons (*A Cure for Dreams*). Her project is based on the desire to celebrate the multiculturalism of contemporary southern fiction. My own book is a critique of the very ideas of nurturing and cross-cultural support that Tate sees as empowering since they are frequently undermined by the very structuring of the novels in which they are codified.[27]

When I began writing and thinking about Ellen Douglas, whose novel *Can't Quit You Baby* I discuss in chapter 4, there were very few critical appraisals of her work, despite the fact that she had published six novels and two collections of short stories. However, in 1995 the *Southern Quarterly* published a special issue dedicated to her writing. Kaye Gibbons, whose first novel, *Ellen Foster,* is the focus of chapter 2 and whose most recent, *On the Occasion of My Last Afternoon,* is discussed in chapter 5, has rapidly become an established southern writer, with six novels to her credit. Her work is the subject of a number of reviews and short pieces, but few detailed explorations of her writing exist at this time, beyond individual articles or parts of chapters, as in Linda Tate's recent study. Carol Dawson and Lane von Herzen are Texan writers; *Copper Crown* is von Herzen's first novel, and she followed it with *The Unfastened Heart.* Dawson's first novel, *The Waking Spell,* was something of a *succès de scandale* in her native Texas, since it was generally understood to be a roman à clef in which families she knew were exploited in a riotous family romance. The novel I discuss in detail, *Body of Knowledge,* is her second.

Barbara Christian, among others, has written of her desire to discover "new readings," to access contemporary critics' views on new writers, as well as their new thoughts on writers already valued and established by literary critics. Kenneth Warren concludes his study of what he calls mainstream texts in *Black and White Strangers* with the assertion that "the construction of black/white racial difference in the United States has been so central to our political, imaginative, and economic lives that it ought to be possible to trace the process of this construction in a variety of cultural places, many of them unexpected and not yet adequately examined." [28] I believe it is of value and of salient importance to read those books which are new, popular, and informed by contemporary cultural practices and pressures. Rather than make value judgements on texts that have not yet stood the test of time, I am far more interested in the ways in which contemporary novels can "introduce the kinds of questions one might bring to cultural criticism," as Joseph R. Urgo has recently expressed the act of scrutinizing novels. [29] I explore the relation of gender, race, and social position to the structure of subjectivity in southern contexts and for the extent to which a particular friendship is posited or played out. This book is not primarily "about" the writers I have chosen but explores how the novels can project ideas and apprehensions about southern culture and interrogate these ideas through formal strategies. Nancy Porter, writing in 1991, described fictions that depict cross-racial alliances as a small but burgeoning area of contemporary writing. [30] Since she detected this trend, there has emerged a striking number of novels of this particular type, where syncretic models are foregrounded. The impetus to map the ground they cover becomes, at once, more pressing and more engaging. This study will consider some of the patterns that emerge in contemporary fictions where the focus is on friendships forged across racial differences.

While Shirley Ann Grau believes that what she, writing about race relations and most specifically about the American South, calls "the black/white thing" had "exhausted itself" by the late 1980s, I would disagree. Grau won the Pulitzer Prize for writing about "the black/white thing" in the 1964 novel *The Keepers of the House* and professes to see race as one of the sources of conflict that will dramatize a narrative.[31] The writers discussed in this study explore relationships between characters of different racial backgrounds more self-consciously than exclusively or avowedly as a source of dramatic conflict. I would contend that interracial relationships in their many forms have consistently remained a popular subject for writers throughout the 1990s.

To examine, for a moment, novels published in a particular year: 1992–1993, for example, saw Steve Erickson's postmodernist epic of black and white America, *Arc d'X*, a highly imaginative exploration of Thomas Jefferson's relationship with his slave Sally Hemings; Marsha Hunt's *Free*, describing a white Englishman's love for a black American male in Pennsylvania in 1913; and Walter Moseley's *White Butterfly*, an Easy Rawlins saga set in a Los Angeles in which a white woman's death complicates the serial killing of black women. Susan Fromberg Schaeffer creates in *First Nights* a Garboesque silent-film star's friendship with her Caribbean maid, set in New York over the last years of her life. Also published that year were Nanci Kincaid's *Crossing Blood*, in which a white teenage girl finds herself strongly attracted to a black boy in 1960s Tallahassee, and Lynn Lauber's *21 Sugar Street*, in which a white girl and a black boy fall in love and have a child in Ohio in the 1970s. Janice Deaner's *Where Blue Begins* traces the childhood friendship of a black and a white girl in New York State, and Connie May Fowler's *Sugar Cage* explores two white families in Florida in the 1960s and the two black women who affect them deeply. Of the examples listed above, only two are written by black writers (Marsha Hunt and Walter Moseley). This is not indicative, nor is the list exhaustive; but the range of texts indicates the interest contemporary white writers have come to express in cross-racial alliances and friendships. Consequently, critics like Nancy Porter, Suzanne W. Jones, Elizabeth Schultz, and Minrose Gwin have begun to provide new readings of fictions that prioritize issues of commonality and difference in a historically biracial South.[32]

In exploring cross-racial friendships in contemporary fiction, and emphasizing the tensions that are raised through form and structure as well as content, this book sets itself directly against Grau's view that writing about race is passé. Necessarily, it also contends with the critical consensus that supports this view, as in Fred Hobson's *The Southern Writer in the Postmodern World* (1991).[33] In an informative study Hobson writes mainly of what he calls the third generation of southern writers, those writing during and after the 1960s, among whom he numbers William Styron, Ernest Gaines, Bobbie Ann Mason, and Anne Tyler. But he makes much mention of what would be a fourth generation, writing first novels in the 1980s and 1990s, the writers I discuss. He believes that "the old albatross of segregation" has been thrown off and that, consequently, novelists also cast off "the old southern subject" of race and racial conflict, "the old setting" of the rural South, and "the old theme" of community. He asserts that black writers are more likely to maintain an interest in these themes than white, though he admits there may be exceptions to his general thesis. In a book that derives from a series of lectures, it is inevitable that some broad generalizations will be forthcoming, but Hobson attributes a Faulknerian moral seriousness about human drama as racial conflict to Ernest Gaines alone and draws no other black or white writers into his framework. Michael M. Cass summarizes the argument in his foreword: "The younger writers are not writing with the 'burden' of racial guilt; they are writing about 'unburdened' characters. . . . recent novels still feature distinctively southern voices, but their characters apparently do not have the southern-consciousness and self-consciousness typical of a Faulkner character." Hobson is quite specific that most southern writers no longer look to Faulkner for thematic sustenance. He is assured in the belief that, despite contemporary fiction's exploration of postmodernist literary practices, the southern writer "essentially accepts, rather than invents his world, is not given to fantasy, does not in his fiction question the whole assumed relationship between narrator and narrative, does not question the nature of fiction itself."[34]

Hobson's map of contemporary southern fiction directly excludes writers like Lewis Nordan, whose *Wolf Whistle* is a surreal, postmodernist exploration of the circumstances surrounding the 1955 murder of Emmett Till, and Randall Kenan, Barry Hannah, and Barry Gifford. It also excludes much of what is important to the writers I discuss in this book. Ellen Douglas is important as a transitional figure between Hobson's third and fourth generations of southern writers and as such receives scant acknowledgement in a grid that divides the generations so categorically. Her invention of a self-reflexive narrator in *Can't Quit You Baby* is the mainstay of a metafictional investigation into a carefully racially coded and typically southern relationship; she quite clearly exposes the very nature of fictionality. Lane von Herzen creates a fantastical inquiry into race relations in early twentieth-century Texas, in a novel in which the development from the American romance to magical realism via ecocritical ideas is clear. Carol Dawson's *Body of Knowledge* remains highly influenced by Faulkner and by the "traditional" subjects and themes of southern writing, in the way that Michael Kreyling describes: "If the 'South' is a cultural entity, then 'Faulkner' is its official language."[35]

Neither Hobson nor I pretend to provide a complete survey of the preoccupations of recent southern fiction writers. But readers of southern fiction cannot help but be aware that, just as new subjects and styles abound in Bobbie Ann Mason and Lee Smith's popular cultural realism, or Lewis Nordan and Barry Gifford's postsouthern parody, many established literary subjects and styles maintain their hold on the imaginations of writers who explore those subjects in differently nuanced and often highly self-consciously literary ways.

When asked whether living in Mississippi prompted her to meditate on the interrelatedness of black and white women and men, Ellen Douglas was emphatic in her answer: "I had been thinking about that all my life. How could you not think about it if you were a writer and lived in the South?"[36] Bearing in mind the deleterious effects of segregation, Richard H. King raises the interesting idea that white American writers may behave as if they have, in fact and in feeling, a moral imperative to write about "matters African-American."[37] It is certainly the case that the fictions I have selected examine segregation and racism, ostensibly, from both sides of the divide and frequently celebrate black characters as they scrutinize whites. Morality has proved to be a testy but significant feature of southern writing, not only where issues of slavery and segregation and ubiquitous racial metaphors are addressed head on, but also in the moral surety and simplicity many writers have nevertheless ascribed to the rural and small-town South. This remains the setting for a number of novels I discuss in detail and for others discussed along the way.

In reading contemporary fictions by white American women who choose to pursue cross-racial cooperation in differently imagined southern contexts, I detect a trend, a moral imperative, even a distinct literary and cultural terrain, that may be mapped and explored. Geopolitically this terrain is southern. Geographically, the novels under review are set in the South and usually written by resident southerners; politically, those that are not quite "southern" according to W. J. Cash's design or Louis D. Rubin's, Richard Gray's or Michael Kreyling's—or, indeed, Fred Hobson's—may still be understood to reflect concerns and themes that are promulgated as *typically* southern.[38] Such themes are detected by white writers like Pete Dexter, a northerner who in *Paris Trout* writes a *typically* "southern" novel, and by African Americans Toni Morrison and Gloria Naylor, not southerners by birth but often expropriated as southern as a consequence of the novels they write and their southern ancestry. Henry Louis Gates Jr. has famously professed that all black Americans are southern, and academic interest in the southernization of America grows apace. Relations between white and black southerners are foregrounded in this study, as they tend to be foregrounded in the biracial literature of the South.[39] "The South" can be predominantly a South of the imagination, and Ellen Glasgow noted as early as 1931 how elastic the term *southern writer* can be: "It isn't necessary to be born in the South in order to become a Southern writer. It isn't necessary even to take the trouble to live here."[40] Her words may be tinged with a certain dry apprehension, but they demonstrate that the *idea* of the South works as a literary agent of creativity as much as, if not more than, the historical and regional intricacies of the area itself for a writer like Glasgow or Eudora Welty, for whom Jackson, Mississippi, is her "piece of the world." Southern writing in all its forms has secured readers not just in a sentimental tradition of moonlight and magnolias, but in a bitingly realist tradition, in meditations on history, and in the bizarre and gothic parody. Popular southern fiction is alive and selling well in all its forms.

Donald Noble agrees; writing in 1985, he believes, unlike Grau and Hobson, that "race will still be a major subject for Southern literature." But he forecasts change: "The stories of gross cruelty, lynching and brutality will be fewer and give way to more subtle examinations of race relations in an integrated society." The shift he perceives is an obvious and a natural one, albeit that Lewis Nordan in *Wolf Whistle* and Vicki Covington in *The Last Hotel for Women* revisit some of the most brutally racist historical moments in civil rights struggles against white intransigence in the 1950s and 1960s South. Somewhat contradictorily, Noble argues that a sense of community will be weaker. As he sees it, "strangers are moving in, and now probably not everyone residing in a small town was born there." For Noble, verisimilitude remains a basic requirement for representations of community in fiction.[41] What Noble fails to note is how often "family" and "community" are represented as strangers or social misfits coming together. Characters' experiences are often designed to reflect the evils, the pressures, and the prejudices in the society that has alienated them and that forces them to form different and often oppositional units. Recent examples include Barbara Kingsolver's *Pigs in Heaven,* which tests the boundaries of "family" on a journey from Kentucky to Oklahoma; Rebecca T. Godwin's *Keeper of the House,* in which women working in a brothel in coastal South Carolina become "family" to one another; and Cris South's *Clenched Fists and Burning Crosses,* where a group of marginalized lesbian friends come together as anti-Klan activists. The patriarchal family, traditionally a symbol not only of community but of its endurance and survival, is often either exposed or simply ignored in recent writing that imagines community. Communal and even familial relations are renegotiated in southern fictions as different as Gail Godwin's *A Southern Family* and *A Mother and Two Daughters,* Susan Richards Shreve's *A Country of Strangers,* Lane von Herzen's *Copper Crown,* and Carol Dawson's *Body of Knowledge.* All featuring a focal interracial female friendship as the basis of community, they renew the focus on equality that remains the unfulfilled legacy of the civil rights movement.[42]

I read contemporary fictions by southern women not only against feminist models of women's friendship but also for the extent to which they engage with ideas of imagining community in the American South after desegregation and pursue communitarian ideals and utopian projections, pushing these concerns further, toward ideals of national redemption as a result of racial justice in the future. Helen Taylor reminds us of the "political significance of fictional texts in the ideological construction of the South and its racial history."[43] This book involves the belief that fiction has a cognitive value and so considers the social and ethical questions fiction may help to raise, arguing that fictions may illuminate historical moments or preoccupations and may also work to reflect current critical debates. As Jonathan Culler observes, "We still do not appreciate as fully as we ought the importance of narrative schemes and models in all aspects of our lives."[44] Novels engage with ideas of what may be socially and politically desirable in women's friendships and coalitions. They strain toward democratic dialogues or a "dialogic communitarianism," to borrow Frazer and Lacey's phrase.[45] They begin to overcome what is mendacious and inequitable at the level of personal friendship and look forward to such friendships translating into social reform according to more egalitarian ideals. They do not look to the past in the hope of discovering a golden age that never existed; they imagine national and personal recovery through coalitions built with reference to the past and to civil rights reforms, but with faith in the future. However, none of the novels I explore in detail either achieves or fully imagines the desired transition from personal relationship to wider social change;

for different reasons they each conclude before such a stage is reached. I shall explore some of the possible reasons why the novels remain discursively locked.

Each novel under consideration, then, focuses on relations between blacks and whites in the American South, but the historical settings range from the very beginning of the twentieth century to the present. They were written in or just after what Manning Marable has referred to as the "post-reform period" (1982–1990) when, despite political protestations to the contrary, he adjudges that a central political characteristic was a conservative reaction to the "legacy of the civil rights movement."[46] These are the Reagan years, and Omi and Winant, in their study of racial formation from the 1960s to the 1980s, describe debates about race relations in this context as "a world of paradox, irony and danger."[47] Social schisms according to race have been deepening and widening since the 1960s, and this is quite clearly complex literary terrain, both ontologically and epistemologically. Attempting to express either the norms in American race relations or the breaks in the paradigms involves a careful choreographing of character and connections. For example, one of a medley of racially inflected stereotypes associates whites with order and rationality and blacks with disorder.[48] Bearing this in mind, Victoria's ordering of the black housekeeper Viola's story in *Body of Knowledge* would seem to pander to an assumption that the black teller will tell her tales haphazardly, while the white chronicler exudes ordered calm. Two factors undermine the playing out of this assumption in the novel, however: the white woman is finally unable to create order in a story about a white southern family, since disorder and disaffection dominate its history; and the chronicler is almost entirely reliant on the black storyteller for every scrap of information she craves. A similar narrative strategy operates in Kaye Gibbons's more recent *On the Occasion of My Last Afternoon*. So the dependency of white women on black, another paradigm, becomes wholly pervasive and is made entirely visible.

Racial attitudes and anxieties are multifarious, even schizophrenic. Texts like *Can't Quit You Baby* and *Body of Knowledge* reflect these levels of uncertainty through self-conscious narrators and in the structuring of the stories they tell of cross-racial relationships. In *Shadow and Act* Ralph Ellison declared, "I guess it's the breaks in the pattern of segregation which count, the accidents."[49] The writers I discuss, even when they stage the most paradigmatic and clichéd of relationships between black mammy and white child or black domestic and white employer, seek to break the pattern into which the relationships have been inscribed in order to explore the women's connection in elucidatory and revealing ways. Again, Ellison, in his assertion that "archetypes are timeless" whereas "novels are time-haunted," helps to articulate the creative possibilities present even in the rigidity of archetypal characters and via very specific contexts like racial segregation. Perhaps Ellison's "breaks in the pattern" are homologous with the "breaks in the text" that Terry Eagleton describes in his reading of Macherey.[50] Such breaks may be illuminating. In examining them a critic explores the lacunae in an ideology and consequently makes that ideology visible. This is, of course, of special import when the ideology is the basis of southern culture. Joel Williamson selects the word *placeness* as the one which most nearly bespeaks his sense of a South where everyone and everything is designated a place and space and where "because of the necessity of keeping blacks in their place, that quality is vastly exaggerated."[51] In literature about the biracial South published late in the twentieth century, the points are plentiful at which rigidly demarcated social roles are stretched to encompass a space in which friendships might be developed. Friendships are frequently lived out in highly structured settings, however—in white homes where black women work, and sometimes also live, and in the tight formal structures of the texts themselves.

This book determines whether contemporary fictions provide a space in which a certain nostalgic hope for the kinds of moral and social certainties that characterized civil rights struggles may be reasserted, or a space within which the social and moral dilemmas the struggles began to articulate continue to be critically and creatively explored. There were undoubtedly more women like Ellen Douglas's Cornelia in *Can't Quit You Baby* than there were white civil rights workers like Rosellen Brown's Jessie Singer or Alice Walker's Lynne and Luna. The novels I choose as my focus, whether set firmly in movement times or not, explore those girls and women whose conscious or unconsciously liberal sentiments underpin and motivate their relationships with black people, rather than specific and shared political goals. The depictions of both of these literary "types" of women are played out against the background of the movement, however, since each of the novels is contemporary, and the history and effects of the civil rights and women's liberation movements are conditions of the texts' existence as ideology and as fictions. The 1960s have been mythologized as a kind of "upfront moral formulation" of issues "which did not hurl us into quandaries of rhetoric," as June Jordan describes the memory of a moral high ground where "right" and "wrong" were meaningful items of vocabulary in a discourse of "unabashed moral certitude" and "righteous rage."[52] In the recent work of a number of writers there is a thoughtful reassessment of the relation of literature to politics, to social formation, and to activism, which often comes together in ideas and myths of the 1960s. Fictions often articulate a specific association with that decade's hopes and achievements, its reforms, and promises, deferred or unfulfilled.

Manning Marable has talked of a specter that haunts black America and can be seen to haunt the imaginations of a number of white writers too: "the seductive illusion that equality between the races has been achieved, and that the activism characteristic of the previous generation's freedom struggles is no longer relevant to contemporary realities."[53] This haunting obviously functions on very different levels. Marable is worried about how to combat the impression that can be created through rhetoric, and via a powerful media and the testimony of a minority of black middle-class professionals, that equality can be seen to have been achieved. Benjamin DeMott, in *The Trouble with Friendship,* an important book treated in more detail in my conclusion, believes it is the "personalizing, moralizing, miniaturizing habit of thought" that makes this seem possible.[54] In my view liberal white writers run the risk of being seduced by hope in democratic freedoms they associate with past decades. But unlike the examples from cinema and television that underpin DeMott's critique of a "friendship orthodoxy," in writing fiction novelists grapple with many of the cognitive and theoretical pitfalls inherent in upholding an orthodoxy.

✍ In this book I avail myself of a range of theoretical textual practices in order to approach a position where the aesthetic and the sociopolitical are seen as intermeshed in southern fictions, rather than as distinct and discrete cognitive structures. The theoretical debates and apparatus on which I draw are wide-ranging: postmodernism and poststructuralism, postcolonial and cultural studies. I recognize that literary traditions have often refracted "woman" as a distinct category but that the distinctiveness has masked differences according to race, class, culture, and ethnicity. Theorists like Mikhail Bakhtin express ideas that can share territory with a plethora of theoretical positions and inform them. His concerns are often anticanonical, and his ideas, as I deploy them in my reading of *Ellen Foster*, illuminate the problems of privileging a single character's voice over others. The emphasis placed on conceptualizing female subjectivity and agency in these novels, and the tensions deep-rooted in southern black and white women's communications with each other, points up how strongly the novels push toward social and political change. They push toward imagining possible and constitutive communities in the way that Audre Lorde, Adrienne Rich, and, more recently, Nancie Carraway have spoken of in feminist writings and T. V. Reed and Stuart Hall express in cultural studies.

Popular fiction, despite tendencies on the part of critics and readers alike to read it as if it invariably upholds dominant ideologies and orthodoxies, may also be the very site in which critical and oppositional perspectives may be most imaginatively explored. John G. Cawelti has pursued the idea that all texts contain inventions as well as conventions and that these have different, even contradictory, cultural functions. While literary and generic conventions help to maintain a sense of social and readerly stability, inventiveness can operate as a response to changing social and political circumstances explored in the realm of the imagination.[55] Feminist critics frequently argue that literature is the forum in which women first explore and define their political ideas. Some of the novels in this study, like Carol Dawson's *Body of Knowledge,* appear to rest securely within popular genres, the southern family romance or gently feminist fable, when in fact a reading of them may elucidate how interrogative and critical they also are of the status quo they apparently endorse.

It is clear that there has been an erosion of the boundaries between what had been designated "high" and "low," or "popular," cultural forms, and theory and politics. As Jay Clayton describes the contemporary situation: "Serious fiction regularly incorporates themes and techniques from detective fiction, science fiction, and romance, as well as motifs from nonliterary forms like TV, advertisements, movies, popular music, MTV, and more. This trend has diminished the aura of sanctity that surrounded culture in the modern era, making it seem more heterogeneous, democratic, and accessible."[56]

His words form part of a wider discussion taking place across the humanities that draws on ideas of democracy, morality, and social progress. The philosopher Richard Rorty expresses very similar views when he asserts that "the novel, the movie, and the TV program have, gradually but steadily, replaced the sermon and the treatise as the principle vehicles of moral change and progress."[57] When Virginia Woolf said, "Imagine a literature composed entirely of good books. . . . starvation would soon ensue. No one would read at all," she made clear the distinction between high and low forms of cultural production as they have been traditionally distinguished, apparently according to value and aesthetics.[58] Though questioning the emphasis placed on canonical works, Woolf nevertheless accepts literary value judgment as a sine qua non, according to the ideological determination of her time. Again, Clayton's sensible comments on the status of fiction in contemporary life help to elucidate my own position in this work. He argues that the power of contemporary fictions lies "in their participation in larger networks of discourse and in their ability to attract, to hold, and to shape particular communities of readers."[59] Like Rorty, he believes that terms like *literature* are no longer bound up with an unsatisfactory panegyric on the supposed literary qualities of a book but on their relation to wider ideological considerations and social ideals.

Novels that involve a quest for self-awareness and cooperation carry ethical implications. Self-help and collective recovery have become buzzwords in the contemporary climate and inevitably involve reassessment of the past circumstances and contingencies that make such recovery necessary.[60] The tension between American democratic ideals and undemocratic practices mediates against the ideal and idea of community whether one looks to the past or projects into the future. When Rorty discusses narratives, he emphasizes their potential as a means of articulating the connection of the present with the past and with utopian futures. The narratives I examine each follow this impetus to differing degrees.

"Theory" has traditionally been approached with a measure of cynicism and distrust by a number of American feminists and critics in southern studies. Emphasis on praxis and agency have tended to hold sway over highly theoretical and theorized discussion until recent interventions by Michael Kreyling and others. Theory has begun to be viewed interrogatively and creatively, as replete with possibilities that relate directly and lucidly into political and social praxis.[61] Theory can become a basis for creative exploration, and fiction an arena in which to explore and begin to theorize ideas of social change. Certainly issues are often raised through fiction that are painful to discuss in other forums or, at the very least, controversial: black men's exploitation of black women as approached by Alice Walker in *The Color Purple,* Toni Morrison in *Song of Solomon,* and Terry McMillan across her novels, for example; and black women's historical mistrust of white women's sexuality where it relates to black men, as in Walker's *Meridian* or Bebe Moore Campbell's *Brothers and Sisters.*

Southern studies' strong empirical and autobiographical tradition is based in southern history. Most of the writers I discuss ensure that the white characters' "whiteness" is historically specific: Cornelia in *Can't Quit You Baby* is of "Scotch-Irish" extraction, typical of white southern ancestry, and Cassie Sandstrom in *Copper Crown* is, by name, of immigrant stock in a town where Scandinavian settlers abound. Ellen Foster is a character who fits into a strong tradition of poor whites in southern fiction. The mystical and mystifying lyricism in much French feminist thought, like *écriture feminine,* has utopian qualities that I might have employed to enhance my discussion of the element of utopian longing in a novel like Lane von Herzen's *Copper Crown.* But the rhetoric inherent in essays like Cixous's "The Laugh of the Medusa" or Irigaray's "When Our Lips Speak Together" highlights how they function metaphorically, whereas in my readings southern women's identities as expressed in fiction are always encoded to reflect social formation—even in a novel that draws on the supernatural.

There are a number of critical investigations that combine empirical knowledge, identity politics, and critical theory in an effort to build an epistemological bridge between writer and reader, speaker and listener, and consequently enter directly into dialogue with others. In her long essay "Identity: Skin Blood Heart" Minnie Bruce Pratt produces a creative and theoretical exploration of identity and subjectivity that is open and interactive; it encompasses self-analysis, family and community, southern feminisms, critics, novelists, conferences, and support groups. A southern white lesbian, Pratt exposes racism in her own and others' experiences, and attempts to theorize abstract hopes and commitments into a project for coalition. The critical space she creates, however, is fragile: "I'm putting it down for you to see if our fragments match anywhere, if our pieces together, make another layer, a piece of the truth that can be part of the map we are making together to show us the way to get to the longed-for world."[62] The pieces and the map are signs in a system that contemporary writers and critics are using to explore ideas in theory and fiction. As Jack Butler declares in his contribution to *The Future of Southern Letters,* while critics map the southern coastline, the writers *are* the coastline, "which continually changes shape, and on closer resolution shows finer and crazier variation."[63] The "truth" that shapes a "longed-for world" is problematic for poststructuralists and pragmatists alike.

As this study will show, even the most concrete statements on coalition border on the utopian, partly because of the discourse available in which to express them. In the conjunction between a feminist project, an acknowledgement of how seductive utopian hopes and agendas can be in southern fictions, and an interrogative analysis of differences between dominant images of southern women, *Advancing Sisterhood?* begins to map the terrain. It examines the metaphors and tropes that conceive of relating across friendship as visionary and liberating. Many white writers are drawn by the lure of symmetry in black and white women's lives, but the topic of interracial friendships and coalitions involves many complexities, as my discussions of theories of friendship, sisterhood, and community in chapter 1 should reveal.[64]

Of the chapters that follow, the first provides a survey of theoretical and literary formulations of friendship. Since friendship is a relatively underresearched field of inquiry, it teases out the key tropes by providing a bibliographical overview of material that merits explication in light of the literary readings that follow. Chapter 2 focuses on childhood friendship and investigates the extent to which the bildungsroman form constrains the representation of a formative interracial association. Via Bakhtin and definitions of realism posited by Catherine Belsey and others, I explore representations of poor white southern girls who, in Connie May Fowler's *Before Women Had Wings* and most especially in *Ellen Foster,* draw their moral sustenance from the black characters who are their most reliable friends.

Chapter 3 opens up discussion of narrative strategies to consider recent interest in ecocriticism to understand the female southern pastoral. Via Louise Westling, Jane Harrison, and Lawrence Buell, I discuss some of the facets of environmentally aware contemporary fiction before going on to read Lane von Herzen's *Copper Crown* as a novel of interracial friendship influenced by a deep appreciation of the land. In chapter 4 Ellen Douglas's *Can't Quit You Baby* is the key text, but discussion of her self-conscious exploration of friendship between a white householder and her black domestic of many years' standing is prefaced by an examination of more conservative renditions of this archetypal southern women's relationship in the work of Ellen Gilchrist and others. Chapter 5 pursues the problem of updating another of the established southern signature relationships, that between the mammy and the white girl who is her charge. Jack Butler has divided contemporary southern writers into conservators, updaters, deniers, and futurists, and the writers examined in this study fall most clearly into the category of updaters.[65] The inevitable question Butler's category begs is whether an updating is also a reinvestment: to vary an old theme may be to run a new thread through an established pattern, but it may result in the pattern's becoming even more established. With special interest in Carol Dawson's sprawling family saga *Body of Knowledge,* I examine the extent to which writers create innovative variations on a traditionally southern theme.

In conclusion, *Advancing Sisterhood?* explores a subject that is often glossed over in southern fiction, the drama of black and white friendships between women and what white writers are trying to accomplish by playing out this drama in their novels and stories. Black and white women exist at the heart of southern mythology. We have long been familiar with Fiedler's visions of interracial social harmony between men as played out across American literature. In *Advancing Sisterhood?* I discuss the ways in which contemporary white women writers have stretched to imagine the conditions in which attachments between black and white women might form the basis of community at the end of the twentieth century.

CHAPTER ONE

Advancing Sisterhood?

Theoretical and Literary Formulations of Friendship

There is a distinct tendency in feminist theorizing to value most those friendships forged out of adversity or on difficult social territory. Critics value those relationships in which anger and resentments are expressed and worked through and where friendship is a site of contestation but ultimately proves enduring. The tendency can be detected across the critical spectrum—lesbian, radical, liberal, communitarian, white, and black—that "friendship in adversity, unity in the face of opposition have been hallmarks of the positive side of women's relationships."[1] Historically this comes about as a resistance to patriarchal distrust and patriarchal disapproval of women's friendships as subversive, transgressive, and even political. Literary exemplifications of such fears, so often discussed by feminist theorists, occur in texts as different as Kate Chopin's *The Awakening,* now canonized by feminist readings; Toni Morrison's *Sula,* a novel about a friendship that has been read by one critic as a model of lesbian bonding; and *Clenched Fists and Burning Crosses: A Novel of Resistance,* a radical lesbian feminist novel by Cris South. Anne Goodwyn Jones notes that an expectation of southern women's literature is to find female friendships featured very strongly. She recognizes that "the role of race," as she terms the nexus of race and power according to which southern women have traditionally lived, will affect the "perceptions, themes and styles of southern women writers."[2] Overall, the scope of her already full and informative thesis in *Tomorrow Is Another Day* and of Helen Taylor's in *Gender, Race, and Region,* where the acknowledgment of the significance of friendship in the representations of southern women writers is clear, precludes a detailed examination of specific formulations of friendships in the literature.

When one remembers that Aristotle deliberated upon types of friendship, distinguishing among the useful friendship, pleasant companionship, and mutual esteem, it may seem odd that there are, as yet, relatively few theoretical texts that explore friendships and relationships head on. The complexity of women's friendships as an area of theoretical and literary inquiry has been underestimated by feminists, social activists, and philosophers alike; by Simone de Beauvoir, for example, in her ideas of an "immanent complicity" between women and in her assumptions that motherhood is crucial to this complicity. For de Beauvoir women are more likely to share recipes and family gossip than opinions and ideas in "warm and frivolous intimacy." Despite enclosing women in a sphere of general inactivity and social ineffectiveness, de Beauvoir does hit upon the importance for women of creating a "counter-universe" to the one she visualizes men as inhabiting and controlling in her thesis on patriarchy. She also recognizes the significance of oral traditions in women's lives, but she goes no further to explore the dynamics of women's friendships, believing that women's "fellow feeling rarely rises to genuine friendship" in any case.[3]

Hannah Arendt is typically much more searching in *The Human Con-*

dition, where she assesses that friendship may be "a regard for the person from the distance which the space of the world puts between us, and this regard is independent of qualities which we may admire or achievements which we may highly esteem."[4] This is Arendt's definition of political friendship as a civic model (an issue also taken up later by Jane Mansbridge and Mary Dietz) rather than intimate relations. But one cannot help noting the detached quality of the "regard"; its significance is that, above all things, individuals maintain the ability to see their counterpart and to judge the nature of the connection. Theories of friendship that focus on Anglo-American women are thus relatively uneven and often underdeveloped. Friendship remains a neglected relationship, as Lillian B. Rubin has observed in *Just Friends: The Role of Friendship in Our Lives:* "Friendship in our society is a strictly private affair. There are no social rituals, no public ceremonies to honor or celebrate friendships of any kind, from the closest to the most distant. . . . Our language offers few possibilities for distinguishing among friendships, the word 'friend' being used to refer to a wide range of relationships with varying degrees of closeness and distance."[5] Rubin's is a very full and descriptive study, but it takes no account of the differences in background and experience that persons bring to a friendship and that infuse it and charge it as a creative struggle.

Although Rubin deals in abstractions, she does begin to discuss types of friendship. In her chapter "Best Friends," for instance, she emphasizes the promise inherent in and specific to a best friendship: "a promise of mutual love, concern, protection, understanding and, not least of all, stability and durability."[6] In each of the novels about friendship discussed in the chapters that follow, the friendship approaches that of "best friends," openly so in *Ellen Foster* and *Copper Crown;* uncomfortably in Douglas's *Can't Quit You Baby,* where the understanding is that Cornelia and Tweet do not acknowledge the depth of their interconnectedness until the end of the book, even though Tweet mourns Cornelia's husband in her stead at his funeral. Their intimacy can prove oppressive for Tweet to the point of intolerability, based as it is on a model of employer and employee. In Carol Dawson's *Body of Knowledge* the relationship between Viola and Victoria is somewhat different: whereas best friendships are usually formed between people of similar ages and interests, theirs crosses generations. Its durability is as much a product of circumstance and the circumscription of their lonely lives as of mutuality. Like Cornelia and Tweet, they are actually much closer than either finds it provident or easy to acknowledge. In each case the attachment is complex, whether self-consciously presented, as in *Can't Quit You Baby*, or emotionally intense, like Cassie and Allie's friendship in *Copper Crown*, or, as in *Ellen Foster*, framed so totally within the experience of one party that the other appears ethereal and barely present. Perhaps only in *Copper Crown*, of the novels I discuss in detail, does the attachment fully correspond with the abstract fantasy of Rubin's definition of best friends. Rubin's work is expanded in the recent study *Best Friends: The Pleasures and Perils of Girls' and Women's Friendships*, a book she endorses on the dust jacket, insofar as a psychotherapeutic study of women's memories about girlhood friendship and betrayal reminds us of the emotional importance of friendship for girls. Teri Apter, Ruthellen Josselson, and Jaimie Baron's collaborative exploration is an attempt to map the area by exploring the "psychology of women," and it does so through interview, anecdote, and recollection.[7]

𝒮♥ There do exist guardedly hopeful celebrations of women coming together. Consciousness raising (CR) sessions of the 1960s and 1970s and the call for dialogue and interaction that characterized women's studies in the 1980s encouraged the production of fiction and theory about how friendships develop and are maintained: "Women are gathering again—slowly, tentatively, unclear perhaps about the agenda, or the membership or the process, but united in the recognition of one irrefutable fact: much remains to be accomplished."[8] The intricate ways in which relationships are influenced according to the race, class, and age of the women concerned are often underexplored, however, even in studies that center on friendship as a model for feminism. The 1980s was, avowedly, a decade of "healing and consolidation": in what Reagan termed a "New Beginning," he "called upon the country to bind up its wounds, heal its divisions, and commit itself anew to shared traditions."[9] But the political ramifications of the decade, as previously noted, bear out other and very contradictory factors. In this period there was a strong capitulation on the part of both the major parties to a more "conservative and repressive social order," and a number of writers and critics wrote directly against this tendency in projects that examined the formation and the maintenance of friendships and feminist coalitions.[10]

Pat O'Connor's attempt to review and summarize existing theories of friendship in *Friendships between Women: A Critical Review* draws on much scholarship of the 1980s. In a primarily sociological study, O'Connor admits that issues of race, as well as class and age difference, have been summarily ignored in friendship theory, but she does not choose to address the reasons why this occlusion of key issues in women's relationships may have occurred. The text comments and inquires into the studies that exist rather than simply summarizes them, and the final chapter aims to discuss issues that the author feels should be addressed in future studies.[11] O'Connor pursues, to some extent, the idea of a friendship acting to "validate one's class position," and the importance of locating friendships within "a social structure which is class-based," and she assumes it will be a consideration of future studies. But she neglects to locate race or ethnicity as social realities of similar and inextricable importance, or as what she calls "situational factors," factors relevant to friendships as a structural basis for social change. The racial and cultural background of women is not addressed when O'Connor raises issues of inequality within friendships.[12]

My expectation is not that O'Connor *should* study interracial friendships but to note that in her important and wide critical review, she misses the range of materials available on cross-racial friendships. The ways in which attention to race as well as class may inform an understanding of friendship groups and dynamics are elided. This is a pity, since the focus of this otherwise very full and detailed study is Britain and America, both multicultural and multiracial societies. Silence on the topic of race as it affects women's friendship was famously critiqued by Adrienne Rich in the American context as long ago as 1978: "The mutual history of black and white women in this country is a realm so painful, resonant and forbidden that it has been barely touched by writers of political 'science' or of imaginative literature."[13]

O'Connor locates her study within certain debates of the 1980s, and she looks forward to the 1990s in her projections of future sites of inquiry on friendship. A study which addresses race and ethnicity in the way my own book tries to do must inevitably take note of very specific studies often not referenced in texts about friendship, like Trudier Harris's important examination *From Mammies to Militants* and Judith Rollins's *Between Women: Domestics and Their Employers,* as well as histories like Sara Evans's *Personal Politics* and Gerda Lerner's much-acclaimed *Black Women in White America.* In each of the above, economic and class-based differences pertain where race determines the social status and the dynamic between women who come together in work and who, at times, forge alliances across the very differences that divide their experiences.

Common Differences: Conflicts in Black and White Perspectives, by Gloria Joseph and Jill Lewis, combines the ideas and writing of a British with an American feminist, a white woman and a black woman respectively. Joseph and Lewis directly address sisterhood, dedicating their book to each other "in affirmation of difference, collaboration, commitment, and caring."[14] While such studies incorporate ideas on friendship and relationships, studies like Jackman and Crane's "'Some of My Best Friends Are Black . . .': Interracial Friendship and Whites' Racial Attitudes" provide an important contribution to the research. This is also true of Hazel Carby's "White Woman Listen! Black Feminism and the Boundaries of Sisterhood," a groundbreaking essay in which diasporic and feminist connections across nations and continents were reviewed and a call issued for comparable studies on women's networking and dialogues.[15] In the 1980s "networking" and "dialoguing" proved key feminist buzzwords, terms designed to connote the importance of mutual support between women in dyads and in groups, despite or because of the political climate. Gloria Steinem, one of America's most vocal feminists since the 1970s, when she was the founding editor of *Ms.* magazine, asserted in her 1982 essay "Networking" that women were creating forums and workshops over shared concerns and out of "women's ability to make bridges out of their shared experience," so that networking was "becoming to this decade what consciousness-raising was to the last." [16] It is hard to ignore the impact that consciousness-raising and dialogue have had on theories of women's friendships, their politics, and their struggles. The impact of feminist theory as praxis and the interest in democratizing models of friendship are significant developments in this field of inquiry. Feminists have often worked to build theories cooperatively, through dialogues and debates like those between Audre Lorde and Adrienne Rich, or Audre Lorde and Mary Daly. Their open letters are complemented by less well known but equally relevant discussions: the exchange between Elizabeth Abel and Judith Kegan Gardiner over issues of complementarity and difference as interplayed in representations of female bonding in fiction, or that between Minrose C. Gwin and Barbara Christian about white women listening to black women and learning to read themselves via black women's writing. [17]

There is no easy symmetry to be uncovered between women who become involved with each other across their differences, and theorists like Pat O'Connor recognize this fact. Audre Lorde's call for women to develop "new definitions of power and new patterns of relating across difference" still remains an area of feminist and literary study that begs inquiry. [18] O'Connor predicted that the 1990s would see the launch of new work in the area. Already feminist critics and literary theorists whose work has influenced my own thinking have published studies that focus on friendship in illuminating ways.

Rosemary Magee is a white southerner who, in a collection of essays and speeches, *Friendship and Sympathy: Communities of Southern Women Writers,* argues that there is a distinct tradition of writers, black and white, communicating and supporting each other, appreciating and reworking each other's ideas. She detects meaningful intertextual relationships as well as deriving meaning from individual friendships like that between Katherine Anne Porter and Eudora Welty. Like Thadious Davis, the black scholar and critic, she believes that writing about and appreciating southern women's writing necessarily involves understanding that it is "cross-generational, cross-racial, cross-class or socioeconomic status, and even cross-regional in a distinctly multiregional, diverse South."[19] Susan Tucker attempts to create just this sort of southern hybridity out of an essentially paradigmatic southern relationship in *Telling Memories among Southern Women.* Tucker succeeds in writing a nuanced study that combines interviews with domestics born between 1880 and 1965 and their white employers with her own memories and a store of literary exemplifications of the kinds of interracial relationships she unearths. *Telling Memories* builds on the work of Trudier Harris and Judith Rollins on black domestics. It emphasizes the inextricability of black and white lives and the rancor as well as the fondness that exists in women's memories.

In *Divided Sisters: Bridging the Gap between Black and White Women,* Midge Wilson and Kathy Russell, white and black respectively, begin by describing "an Arctic ocean" of tension that "too commonly exists between African American women and White women." They note that, according to their interviews and researches, few American women have close friendships with women of a different racial background from themselves. In a lively if somewhat generalizing overview, they exemplify what has been divergent in the histories of black and white American women and, via critics like Lois Scharf and Joan Jensen, conclude, unsurprisingly, that attempts at interracial cooperation failed during the first half of the twentieth century.[20]

In spite of the historical backdrop, writers continue to imagine and discuss the conditions out of which fear—and the ideological apparatus by which only those designated inferior are regarded as having racial identities—might give way to more self-conscious critiques of white as well as black identities.[21] Postcolonial theories and paradigms have augmented the critical vocabulary of W. E. B. Du Bois and Frantz Fanon when describing consciousness of race in theoretical terms as well as in praxis. Conceptually, the racial "other" has become salient in describing subjectivity and selfhood forged in a context where the dominating culture is white, and race and racism have affected and structured social formations.

Perhaps the most positive inquiry into harmony and relatedness to date is Janice Raymond's *A Passion for Friends: Toward a Philosophy of Female Affection*. Raymond asks if female friends are "equal to the task" of "building a creative and responsible friendship" and explores the possibilities in depth via her theory of "gyn/affection."[22] She advances an "integrating philosophy," to use bell hooks's phrase, but, as in all things, it is easier to state what should be done than to conceive of how it is to be achieved: "We cannot blur the distinctiveness of victimization by race or class or anything else [she has worked through aging and lesbian identity earlier in the text], thereby rejecting political and moral responsibility for the consequences of these distinctly different oppressive conditions of many women's lives. Yet by the same token, we cannot allow these distinctive differences to erase or extinguish our commonality as women who are oppressed as women, who bond as women."[23] The difficulty lies in how to make the next step and produce a framework through which the meanings of friendship may be interpreted. Too often in texts about women, there is the obligatory disclaimer in which race and class are noted perfunctorily and the writer moves on.[24] Raymond stays with it and begins to expand upon gyn/affection as an opportunity to initiate a political statement of purpose: "Female friendship is much more than the private face of feminist politics. Although politics and friendship cannot always go together, we need to create a feminist politics based on friendship."[25] Raymond's ideas here echo Hannah Arendt's formulation of a political friendship based on respect, but any potential for a "politics of friendship" must, in this book, be set alongside more utopian ideas of "sisterhood." These ideas inform the models of friendship I detect in contemporary literature as markedly as calls for a common politics of friendship that addresses issues of race, class, and identity.

✍ Within the women's movement, sisterhood has traditionally acted as a "powerful emotional bond, bringing to our political lives a warmth and affinity we usually reserve for what is private."[26] The word *sisterhood* pretends a homogeneity of experience that is difficult to prove or to imagine. As Audre Lorde points out, the need for unity "is often mis-

named as a need for homogeneity."[27] Helena Michie turns the word around to coin the term *sororophobia*, in a rare effort to contend with the problems that beset the term. Her starting point is the family and the sibling love and rivalry that characterize many autobiographies and literature by women, as with Christine Downing's *Psyche's Sisters: Re-imaging the Meaning of Sisterhood*, but there the similarity ends.[28] It becomes apparent that her intention is to apply the term to all forms of negotiated connections between women. Inclusive it is not, however, since her explorations focus on women of the same generation, studying as they do the competition she sees as inherent and endemic in alliances between women of a similar age. A personal as well as politicized literary investigation, Michie's *Sororophobia: Differences among Women in Literature and Culture* is one of the most insightful of the texts in this area. For my purposes here it is disappointing to note that among Michie's impressive range of texts, canonical and popular, filmic and televisual, she does not choose to work through a cross-racial alliance in any context, nor does she look at the maid or domestic "other" women in her exploration of different patterns of "otherness." Interestingly, though, she does cite Alice Childress's *Like One of the Family* as the work that "first forced me to think about the connections between family, race and exclusion in the ideology of the U.S." Childress's book sets out many of the problems of alterity and nonnegotiation that complicate womanhood as well as sisterhood—the exploitation of women by other women and the appropriation of another's skills as one's own—via her feisty narrator, Mildred, a black domestic in 1950s New York who refuses to allow her work to demean or debilitate her.[29] Although Michie does not seek pithy resolutions to the conflicts with other women in which a character like Mildred finds herself involved, or to the other conflicts her book poses, she finally decides that coalition building is the way forward to combat the intransigencies of sororophobia. Like Charlotte Bunch, she believes in "making common cause" by interactively confronting the fear and distrust that can atrophy attempts to break through the social lines that reinforce separation.[30]

Elizabeth Fox-Genovese, in *Within the Plantation Household: Black and*

White Women of the Old South, argues that white plantation mistresses denied sisterly attachments with black women, when their power, leisure, and status derived from their making common bond with their menfolk and from distinguishing themselves from black women. She denies sisterhood in all its facets across race and class lines. Like Eugene Genovese in *Roll, Jordan, Roll: The World the Slaves Made,* she assumes that cross-racial influences work in one direction only, and therefore there is no context for black women to appeal on the grounds of sisterhood to white women, not even on the grounds of a "peculiar sisterhood." The tendency toward individualism over coalition is a specific feature of Fox-Genovese's study, and it persists as the basis of her entire thesis in *Feminism without Illusions,* where important historical inquiry is, unfortunately, also marred by an arch-conservatism previously attributable to many of the plantation mistresses themselves.[31] There are, however, examples of profound and enduring relationships between plantation mistresses, their daughters and slave women described in diaries by Susan Bradford Eppes and Mary Ferrand Henderson, for example.[32] When one considers how very recently southern society sanctioned such friendships, it is all the more significant that antebellum women's interracial friendships should be revisited in contemporary novels like Rita Mae Brown's *High Hearts* (astutely criticized for its representations of race by Linda Tate), Sherley Anne Williams's *Dessa Rose,* and Kaye Gibbon's *On the Occasion of My Last Afternoon.* Contemporary writers remind us of how friendship or sisterhood could begin to develop even in a society where black and white women's lives were inherently unequal.

Within the "privacy" of novel writing and reading, stories frequently bespeak dreams of collectivity and mutuality that are utopian in their projections and desires. Anne Phillips argues that "no-one wants to be tainted with the utopianism of earlier decades," however; so how can novels by white women writers pursue in fictional form the hope in coalitions expressed by Phillips, Elam, Michie, and Bunch while also avoiding what has been viewed as naive utopian fantasy?[33] And if the 1960s epitomizes utopian ideals, why then does the decade continue to feature so prominently in contemporary literature? Is it to reinforce the importance of the political strides that were made back then or to reclaim and reinvest in a radical spirit unafraid to express utopian hopes?

The utopian impulse operates structurally and aesthetically in popular fiction. Rather than inevitably confirm ideological and social conventions, characters and episodes may function as coded aggregates of contemporary problems. I do not intend that the novels I have selected be read solely as a means to an end, whereby their dominant or only function is deemed to be to represent a willingness to address in fictional form the kinds of tensions that have characterized the American South and that have jeopardized contemporary coalitions between black and white. As Richard H. King and Helen Taylor point out, "Not everything that white Southerners write or think or paint or sing has to make reference to and make amends for the 'barbarism' of southern history."[34] But it is clear that there is a recognizably moral and utopian impetus behind much contemporary writing by white southern women, novels that examine past tensions and historical moments critically as well as imaginatively while drawing in contemporary ideas and debates.[35] It is also clear that a number of contemporary black and white women novelists reconfigure existing paradigms like those of maid and mistress, southern white child and black retainer or nurse, as this study shows. But they also write to establish pairings that have traditionally received relatively little literary attention, like white and black lesbian lovers in Carol Anne Douglas's *To the Cleveland Station* and Cris South's *Clenched Fists and Burning Crosses,* which confirm an erotic charge between black and white woman. Novels like Dori Sanders's *Clover* and Connie May Fowler's *Before Women Had Wings* explore a white mother's love for her black stepdaughter and a black woman's intelligent nurturing of an abused white child. Such novels may be read as contributing to the beginning of a project that may imagine in fictions the kinds of coalitions that feminist thinkers like Audre Lorde, Adrienne Rich, bell hooks, and Nancie Carraway have been trying to articulate and theorize in contemporary cultural criticism. Writers frame black and white girls and women in friendship, in anger and resentment, and in love, in contestation and in commonality. But in novels by white writers in particular, there is usually a moral and somewhat idealistic impulse that charges the narratives. This impulse is of special interest to me in this book.

It has been generally posited that a text, to qualify as utopian, should "apply to, if not directly concern itself with, the interactions of persons," because to conceive of utopia is to endeavor to "reconstruct human culture."[36] Models of friendship can form the basis of a utopian premise as a first stage in imagining new communities and lifestyles. Many critics have demonstrated the significance of utopia as a literary form at times of social crisis or change. This is not to say that utopias appear only under such circumstances, since dreams of a better or alternative way of life persist at all times as expressions of hope. But utopian writing is often specific to context insofar as it is "rooted in the unfulfilled needs and wants of specific classes, groups, and individuals in their unique historical contexts."[37] Utopian texts are political fictions in which dominant social and ideological forces, codes, and systems may be challenged on the basis of Mannheim's distinction between ideology and utopia, where ideology signifies the status quo directed toward closure and utopia represents the impetus for change and development. Tom Moylan uses this distinction in *Demand the Impossible* in order to describe utopia as "that unconquered power of the imagination which resists the closure of ideology."[38] But Moylan moves out from the initial binary opposition to introduce into his study utopian desires operating within ideological frameworks, in ways that I find reminiscent of Fredric Jameson's idea of texts as symbolic acts in which otherwise unwieldy and complex social problems, impossible to resolve satisfactorily in life, may be imaginatively resolved. My reading of a novel like Lane von Herzen's *Copper Crown* rests on the belief that utopian desires can coexist with, and be examined within, a problematic representation of an interracial relationship that strains against social structures and mores even while it upholds them. As a genre, utopian fiction is necessarily compromised by gaps and ellipses, between what one might hope to have or achieve and what it is possible to achieve, and between what one individual might see and hope and what another individual might strive for in the same context. Any investigation of popular fictions by and about women has to be grounded in an understanding that representation is political. As Diane Elam asserts, "Feminism necessarily upsets the way we think about politics because its activist political movement is inseparable from a critique of the history of representation."[39] The female protagonists of the novels under discussion and the friendships they develop are informed by contemporary ideas of race, gender, and class representation and the politics that underpin these representations.

Novels about friendship are almost inevitably works in which issues of sisterhood and community feature strongly. This is not to say that each novel studied here could be described as a "narrative of community"; but it is to recognize that encounters between women often operate strategically to comment on wider social propensities for denying or eschewing the kind of communities these novels posit or imagine. Sandra Zagarell identifies a genre of narratives of community by women writers, but the texts she uses to establish her formulation are preindustrial and nostalgic, and community is established and maintained rather than negotiated. Most of the novels I discuss, however, are in dialogue with the idea of community as a result of their focus on ways of interacting with others across differences rather than describing (utopian) communities at work.[40]

℘ There are a number of surveys of women's writing that establish women's friendship as an area of inquiry across a range of theoretical or critical positions. Janet Todd in a study of mainly eighteenth-century English and French literature, *Women's Friendships in Literature,* posits a number of types of friendship that she sees as deriving from the need for a confidante: sentimental friendships; erotic friendships, for which she employs Cleland's *Fanny Hill* and Rousseau's *Julie* to discuss the problem of manipulation within a personal relationship; political friendships, which "require(s) some action against the social system, its institutions or conventions"; and social friendships, which inevitably involve social support as well as interaction. In eighteenth-century texts, female alliances are usually secondary considerations to a romantic heterosexual involvement on the part of the female protagonist. The patterns of friendship are frequently broken, whereas nineteenth-century examples, as Nina Auerbach argues in *Communities of Women: An Idea in Fiction,* often move out to consider the potential for communal bonding beyond or outside of the realm of individual alliances.[41] Considerable work has been done on canonical literature in which female friendships feature, and the work of critics like Auerbach and Nina Baym provides an important feminist spin on the observations of Leslie Fiedler in his important study *Love and Death in the American Novel.*

Fiedler, an eclectic and controversial critic, is renowned for advancing the thesis that the nineteenth-century American canon employs a central, archetypal, and sentimental image "in which a white and a colored American male flee from civilization into each other's arms." Fiedler marks the beginning of an archetypal relationship that "haunts the American psyche": "two lonely men, one dark-skinned, one white" who "have forsaken all others for the sake of the austere, almost inarticulate, but unquestioned love which binds them to each other."[42] The relationship is homoerotic and redemptive; it recognizes, as F. O. Matthiessen allowed, "the terrifying consequences of an individual's separation from his fellow beings."[43] For Fiedler the white character, often confused and conflicted, is rescued by the redemptive black character. It is impossible not to consider Fiedler's thesis even when reading texts as recent and as integrally "about" women as the ones I discuss. Only *Copper Crown,* of those I explore in detail, could be said to pursue the idea of boon companions and to create a homoerotic interchange. But the redemption of the white woman through her black companion is paramount in each novel I examine. Consequently, the archetypal American interracial relationship Fiedler explicated continues to be recast in contemporary American writing.

Via Fiedler, Nina Baym exposes what she has called "the American critic's 'drama of beset manhood.'" Her project is to explicate how women writers have been traditionally excluded from the American canon and from male writers' analyses: "Stories of female frustration are not perceived as commenting on, or containing the essence of our culture, and so we do not find them in the canon."[44] The buddy-buddy formula so beloved of Hollywood is of course derivative of those same nineteenth-century models of intimacy that Fiedler discusses and Baym critiques. Ridley Scott's controversial road movie *Thelma and Louise* is often credited as the film that changed the direction of Fiedler's model, as played out in films like *The Defiant Ones* and more recently in the *Lethal Weapon* series, in the direction of female buddy-buddy movies.[45] Since *Thelma and Louise* Hollywood and independents like John Sayles have seen the box office potential in films that depict female friendship and sisterhood of all kinds, including the cementing of interracial friendships. The means by which an acquaintance develops into a bond in a narrative has been explored by Elizabeth Abel. In her essay "(E)Merging Identities," Abel distinguishes between commonality and complementarity in representations of friendships in recent fiction and considers how the nature of the narrative may require a certain differentiation between two women characters before they are drawn into identification and alignment. This is very much the formula in films like Percy Adlon's *Baghdad Cafe* and John Sayles's *Passion Fish*. In cinematic terms the differentiating principles tend to be marked via film codes like mise-en-scène and editing; in fiction they can be rather more subtly defined. For Abel the desire for identification, or the merging of separate identities into complementarity whereby one woman mirrors the other, is a "leitmotif of female friendship in fiction" nevertheless.[46] An intense desire to impose a coherence upon a relationship is evident in Lane von Herzen's *Copper Crown*, where a desire for symmetry informs the way in which Cassie, the white protagonist, sees her black friend, Allie; and vignettes in which they are encoded as visually similar abound, as they would in a film text.

Abel is following a psychoanalytical model of female subjectivity where the doubling of self as other and the elasticity of selfhood as experience prefigure a relational self-definition for the characters. It is this element of Abel's discussion that evokes one of Judith Kegan Gardiner's reservations in her critique and appreciation of Abel's important essay. Gardiner worries that psychoanalytical models lead to character criticism, which "reads the fictional friends on the therapeutic model very much as one reads case histories."[47] In fact, Abel is showing how such models, explored in their minutiae in examinations of paradigmatic female associations like mother-daughter, have been underused in exploring other equally important nonfamilial relationships; sisterhood and friendship are becoming as important as motherhood as models through which to explore women's lives. Most forcefully, Abel continues her work in the coedited collection *Female Subjects in Black and White: Race, Psychoanalysis, Feminism,* where psychoanalytical theory is deployed as methodology. As with Abel and Gardiner, the participants in this project are engaged in a process of debate in which interconnecting essays respond to problems posed by others in the collection, to incrementally engender an organic exploration of what Hortense Spillers has called "psychoanalytics," whereby political agency mediates a dominant literary discourse.[48]

Feminist critics have long debated the pros and cons of psychoanalytical criticism in feminist inquiry, as it tends to privilege theory over history and context, and have begun to consider how theoretical cultural work like poststructuralism and material feminism might combine with psychoanalytical models. Gardiner responds to Abel's "(E)Merging Identities" by bringing Toni Morrison's *Sula* into the frame and contextualizing Morrison's depiction of the friendship between Nel and Sula with regard to the First World War and the social and psychological damage that war precipitated. She also analyzes the racist patriarchy that leads to the formation of a community like "The Bottom," in order to refocus the terms of Abel's argument and critical method more broadly.

My own readings of novels tend to take the same sociohistorical bases as the context from which to explore friendships as fictional constructs rather than psychosocial models. In the context of the segregated South, as represented in *Copper Crown,* set in east Texas in the early twentieth century, the racial identities of the characters dictate the extent to which their subjectivities can merge, or indeed the extent to which they communicate at all.[49] At times the tendency may be to overplay the connections across difference, as if to blur the very differences of experience that have historically separated blacks from whites. For example, what

Alice Walker professes to admire about Flannery O'Connor's fiction is that she limits her treatment of black characters to their "observable demeanor and actions." Consequently, in Walker's view, O'Connor leaves her black characters free to inhabit another landscape in the reader's imagination. She feels this is a kind of grace on O'Connor's part, which successfully avoids stereotyping and recognizes the limitations on black/white connections in the segregated South via the ideologies of representation.[50] Psychosocial models risk overdetermining fictional friendships, as Gardiner notes, but her essay is a critical intervention into a discussion she values. It is this form of debate that characterizes much of the scholarship on literary formulations of feminist ways of reading as well as theorizing about female bonding.

Interestingly, the discussion that arises between Minrose C. Gwin and Barbara Christian opens out a range of critical and readerly positions that posit other models by which to read black and white women in texts. In 1988 Gwin published "A Theory of Black Women's Texts and White Women's Readings; or, . . . The Necessity of Being Other." This is a self-reflexive account of reading her own white womanhood in texts by black women and of her desire to consider "how we read and write biracial female experience."[51] The image of a white woman that recurs in the texts she reads is "The Breaker of Promises," the jealous and sadistic slave mistresses, and other white women who break their promises to black women. Instead of erasing her whiteness in the reading, as she is tempted to do to extricate herself from the implication of complicity, she engages with the image because "I want to be able to really hear black women and to hear black women I must confront and read my otherness in their texts, however painful that may be."[52] In her "Response" Barbara Christian steps back from the emotion that is honestly addressed at the heart of Gwin's critical engagement. But she joins a debate she obviously values, and she attempts to build on the theorizing inherent in Gwin's enterprise. She acknowledges that in the act of reading one may find one's sense of self disrupted, but she emphasizes the creative possibilities that reading texts which destabilize the category of "woman" may open up for readers.

To assume that only those who experience life as women can write about it or that only black people can, or should, portray black characters and black lives is ideologically dispiriting, when in fact, as Todd Gitlin has argued, "across boundaries, at least in complicated societies, people are always translating differences into mutually intelligible terms," as Gwin succeeds in doing.[53] When Zora Neale Hurston has Janie Crawford say in *Their Eyes Were Watching God,* "Yuh got to go there to know there," Janie's context is the creation of a black southern community, but she is also endeavoring to make her own individual story intelligible to Phoeby, her friend and ally. In contemporary American society, where identity politics continues to play such a major role in the way in which groups identify themselves, there is always the risk that differences may become congealed according to polarities. Fictions can help to facilitate a thinking through of which factors in American society continue to polarize lives. On the other hand, since so many white writers set novels about race relations in the era of civil rights reforms, there remains the pitfall of romanticizing black lives in lyrical and sentimental oversimplicity, in fables and parables that mine the highly mythologized drama of the 1960s.

Charles Fister makes an interesting point in his discussion of Ellen Douglas's *Can't Quit You Baby* when he questions "whether it is better to translate large issues like the history of race relations or Dr. King's death downward into domestic situations like the personal histories of two Mississippi women. When an author does this, is it merely to celebrate her own powers as a creative artist?"[54] However, his use of "better" and "merely" imparts a moral judgment that almost precludes "race relations" from the realm of creative writing. Deeming race special territory in this way corresponds to the worries Barbara Christian and Todd Gitlin express. Ellen Douglas explores the history of southern race relations, and in doing so she pays particular attention to the ways in which her white character begins to explore the meaning of her own racial identity as a white woman in the American South. Fiction allows her the space to think through some of the southern myths of white womanhood and to contextualize them as well as deflate them. Her fiction explores issues that feminist critics have been debating for some time and these too are "large issues," to reemploy Fister's phrase. For example, Adrienne Rich has written at length about the problem of white solipsism, and, following Minrose C. Gwin's start, Kathryn Ward and Missy Dehn Kubitschek also explore whether white women need to be silent and to listen to those who have been effaced by solipsistic feminist discourse. Ward's belief that white women need to be "silent for a spell, while they read, study, and listen to women of color" before honestly examining their own standpoints is her way of trying to combat what Adrienne Rich has called "the vast encircling presumption of whiteness."[55] There are, of course, amid the idealist tendencies, dangerous assumptions that a white woman can learn about her own racism, her own white identity even, from listening to black women. This may be one of Fister's worries about "translating down" from the history of race relations to personal relationships at a micro level. However, this is not the effect of Douglas's novel; the relationship between a black and a white woman is used as a model that draws as much on the debate about listening and hearing one another in which white and black women have engaged around race and awareness following the 1960s, as it does the history of race relations. *Can't Quit You Baby* looks forward as well as back in time; Douglas examines how American literature has traditionally represented black and white friendships within the crucible of race relations, and she experiments with postmodernist strategies in an effort to imagine new ways of presenting a historically loaded relationship in fiction. *Can't Quit You Baby* reminds us that what is often seen as socially peripheral—a relationship between women that takes place in the kitchen of one of their homes—can be symbolically central to understanding the South.

White writers and critics have begun to take very seriously the argument advanced by Ralph Ellison and taken up by Toni Morrison that the presence of black peoples in America has influenced the content, structure, and language of all American literature.[56] More recently, Kenneth Warren, in *Black and White Strangers: Race and American Literary Realism,* follows their lead by considering how racially inflected novels by Stowe, Howells, and James actually are, and Laura Doyle, in *Bordering on the Body: The Racial Matrix of Modern Fiction and Culture,* examines what she calls "the race aesthetic" across a range of predominantly modernist texts by black and white and British as well as American writers.[57] As yet, no one has sustained a critique of contemporary fictions as racially inflected; in the short studies that exist only one, Elizabeth Abel's, privileges issues of form and aesthetics over content in its discussion of Toni Morrison's short story "Recitatif."[58] Morrison presents a cross-racial childhood friendship as indisputably *reciprocally* ambiguous at the most buried and instinctual levels. Morrison's story is an ingenious depiction of two eight-year-old girls who share a room in a shelter for neglected children and who share distinct, yet quite irrational, prejudices. The ingenuity lies in the fact that, although one is black and the other white, it remains unclear which girl is which. One important effect of Morrison's story, like Douglas's novel, is to draw the reader's attention to the dominant paradigms within which cross-racial relationships have traditionally been, and in the main continue to be, described and circumscribed. Each of the girls is described by the very *absence* of literary devices that work to ascribe a racial identity. Abel, the only critic I have discovered who provides a detailed reading of the story, pursues the means by which Morrison succeeds in undoing racial hierarchies.[59] The discrepancies between individuals inform any representation of interracial coordination, and, once apprehended and conceived, visions of cross-racial social harmony involve reading diacritically across the silences between characters as well as reading that which is expressly stated. Such texts and the relationships they describe can prove as elusive as they are illuminating.

It has been argued, and most vociferously by African American writers and critics, that when a white woman enters a story it changes to become "about" her. In Thulani Davis's *1959* there is a discussion about stories that describe segregation and that use white women as a device. A black woman reading such a story declares: "A device! Since when was a white woman ever just a device! Honey, a white woman is a white woman. Once you put her in there, it's no longer about the Negro, it's about the race question, the ways of white folks and all that."[60] America has a complicated racial history, and white women have a complicated place within it, especially in the South. Lillian Smith tells of how she learned to believe in freedom but to evade her conscience and to ignore certain social realities in order "to glow when the word democracy is used, and to practice slavery from morning to night."[61] Smith, a moral objector, has written and spoken incisively about the contradictions between democracy and discrimination and the presence of white women within a discourse about race. The most durable symbols, for instance the southern white lady on her pedestal, relied indisputably for their symbolic cultural value upon controlling images of black men and women. Black men were carefully codified as rapists and black women as libidinous in direct correspondence to the white lady as the spiritual symbol of an inviolate South, despite being threatened on every side by groups who would impeach her morals and besmirch her example if they weren't kept in their place. Drawing upon W. J. Cash's assertions about the South's ideological requirements of the white southern woman as "a mystic symbol of its nationality," Kathryn Seidel follows Ann Firor Scott in writing about the white anxiety that fueled and promulgated these images. The African American writer and critic Sherley Anne Williams has described the "tired symbolism" she detects in representations of white women in many texts.[62] Contemporary writers inevitably respond to established images of white and black women when they write novels that focus on interracial friendships.

When we consider the images of the black characters, it is immediately clear that many are fixed into disturbing and seemingly unbreakable typologies, in the way that David Richards reminds us that "all images are partial but many masquerade as absolute or sovereign."[63] It is difficult to effectively break open such icons as the messianic mammy or the loyal and self-effacing domestic. Breaking apart the images may serve only to set a humorous or laconic spin on the character types, with the character traits of the original remaining the significant trace elements that instruct the audience in reading the new images. White writers working on this difficult terrain do not always succeed in developing new images; Ellen Gilchrist, as discussed in chapter 4, stays close to the original types. Other writers, as this book shows, push further forward to disturb the divergent histories of black and white women in southern fiction.

CHAPTER TWO

Between Girls

Friendship as a Monologic Formulation

Does identifying with the heroine or protagonist necessarily refuse the reader access to a second character whom the plot may
structure as auxiliary? The autobiographical narrative—or bildungsroman—is a staple of much fiction by women. It is a formal structure that denies dialogue in order to privilege the voice
or the interior reality of a single protagonist. How does the form
affect a novel when the focus is a developing friendship between
two characters? In this chapter I wish to raise questions about
the ways in which cross-racial childhood relationships are represented formally and aesthetically. There is often an understandable but troubling literary-critical impasse whereby black
girls are contained within the white protagonists' first person
narrations, which, while explicating the connection between
the girls, risk engulfing or subsuming the black "best friend."

I shall examine the extent to which this may be the inevitable result of the bildungsroman form and consider how the representation of the cross-racial friendship at the heart of *Ellen Foster* is modified in direct correspondence to the novel's structuring.[1]

The significance of finding a friend in childhood has been a salient feature of the bildungsroman and a notable feature of much autobiographical writing. Ralph Ellison has described the "mutual loneliness" that can draw children into proximity in his touching depiction of his own experience of a childhood friendship with a white boy.[2] It is noteworthy that in many fictions in which interracial childhood friendships occur, the tendency is also to create characters who are orphans or who feel themselves at a distance from familial or social groups, who are isolated or lonely and thus gravitate toward each other for companionability.[3] In Kaye Gibbons's *Ellen Foster,* a cross-racial friendship between an orphaned poor white girl and her poor black friend problematizes the very structure of the novel. This novel will form the basis of this chapter's close reading, after an elaboration of childhood friendships as played out in southern fiction.

Southern writers explore many of the traditional obstacles that have worked to circumvent cross-racial support, enterprise, and love beyond an early stage. Harmony and discord have long been the narrational nodes of story, but this particular instance of childish reciprocity changing to adolescent discord has proved a difficult if persistent subject in American literature across the nineteenth and twentieth centuries. In the South it has its antecedents in the slave system and is addressed in slave narratives and early sentimental novels. In *Incidents in the Life of a Slave Girl, Written by Herself,* Harriet Jacobs includes a scene in which two little girls embrace. They are a white girl and the black slave who is also her half-sister. The narrator focuses on the sorrow she feels at the "inevitable blight" that will befall the slave girl in specific and clear contrast with her white sister:

> I knew how soon her laughter would be changed to sighs. The fair child
> grew up to be a still fairer woman. From childhood to womanhood her path

was blooming with flowers, and overarched by a sunny sky. Scarcely one day of her life had been clouded when the sun rose on her happy bridal morning.

How had those years dealt with her slave sister, the little playmate of her childhood? She, also, was very beautiful; but the flowers and sunshine of love were not for her. She drank the cup of sin, and shame and misery, whereof her persecuted race are compelled to drink.[4]

The passage exhibits the emotive rhetoric of the slave narrative, intended as it is to "kindle a flame of compassion" in the hearts of readers as well as to alter their mind-sets.[5] It also establishes an absolutist dichotomy between the lives of white and black that reflects the codes of slavocracy: a Manichean opposition that attributes happiness and moral goodness to the white girl, while allotting the black girl grief and moral degradation.[6] The embrace they share is "an illusion of an embrace," to borrow a phrase Tillie Olsen uses in her depiction of an interracial childhood friendship.[7]

Novels that have had central canonical place in delineating black/white relations have traditionally featured children as salient; *Uncle Tom's Cabin* provides a prime example in the relationship of Little Eva and Topsy. More recently, Shirley Ann Grau's award-winning 1964 novel, *The Keepers of the House,* includes a description of Abigail, the white protagonist, at age eight playing with her grandfather's mixed-race children, his second family, who are of a similar age. Abigail's childhood relationship with Nina and Crissy is complicated. Friendly connections are severed after childhood, despite belonging to the same family. Integration of an interracial family within a racist society cannot operate to the benefit of its black members, and so they remain at a distance from "home," and home is left in the keeping of the white adult, Abigail. The relationship between the girls is situated within the long history of slavery in Wade County, Mississippi, and its repercussions into the twentieth century. Kaye Gibbons's *Ellen Foster,* itself a reworking of a particular literary classic of childhood, *Huckleberry Finn,* also relies upon the Manichean oppositions encoded in earlier texts to locate the relationship between Ellen and Starletta. But the novel is also complicated by its form; the reader gleans what she can of Starletta, the black child, through Ellen, the white child, whose story frames their association. Like the other novels in this study, *Ellen Foster* is a novel of self-realization and self-definition for the white protagonist as well as a novel about a friendship. In each case the white protagonist embarks on a process of self-comprehension that for much of the text supersedes her role as friend. This is even the case when the novel is read according to a discernible "friendship plot," as I shall read *Ellen Foster*. It is contingent on the problematizing of the friendship through the novel's form and structuring, and there are distinguishable "formulaic restraints," to use Nina Baym's term, when one comes to identify a typology of fictions about friendship.

Ⓛ In the work of contemporary writers who explore the racial and social geography of growing up in the American South, fleeting encounters between white and black girls abound, but enduring friendships prove to be more problematic to represent. In *Ellen Foster*, Ellen and Starletta's association stretches across the novel, whereas, more frequently, the points at which black and white women converge and relate are brief and transient, as in Toni Morrison's *Beloved,* where a heavily pregnant and fugitive Sethe is aided by poor white Amy; or in Thulani Davis's *1959,* where the brief kindness of a white woman is remembered as a significant, if fleeting, gesture.

Landscapes of childhood are received rather than chosen, and contemporary writers often explore the ways in which the young black and white girls gravitate toward friendships with each other but become victims of the structuring of the southern societies the novels seek to reflect. Their roles are important as markers of the boundaries that southern society sought to maintain and to stabilize via childhood identity formation under racial segregation. Ruth Frankenberg's recent study sees the "social geographies of race" as the organizing principle of the childhoods of the white American women she interviews, for whom unofficial demarcations according to race still persisted, wherever and whenever they grew up. This is an examination of racial geography that refers to the "racial and ethnic mapping of a landscape in physical terms, and enables also a beginning sense of the conceptual mapping of self and other with respect to race operating in white women's lives."[8]

This facet of southern culture fascinates writers; there are many autobiographies and memoirs in which writers explore childhood friendships within the crucible of race and segregation. Lynn Bloom has described race as that "touchy subject . . . that permeates twentieth-century southern childhood autobiographies and distinguishes them, as a group, from other American childhood autobiographies."[9] The "touchy subject" is also inescapable in fictions that seek to testify to and explore the searing effect racial division could have on young girls in the South. There is a marked propensity in fiction and in film to fix representations of cross-racial relationships of all types in earlier decades, when social roles were fixed and black characters had little space to maneuver outside an established paradigmatic formulation (white child/black nurse; white mistress/black domestic; white employer/black chauffeur).[10]

The meeting between a white girl and a black girl in contemporary fiction is frequently represented as a profound and meaningful encounter, an epiphany. It is this propensity that seems to underpin most fictional delineations of cross-racial childhood associations. Dorothy Allison in *Bastard Out of Carolina* and Nanci Kincaid in *Crossing Blood* each delineate southern landscapes of childhood and pursue the idea of cross-racial relationships as transgressive.[11] For their young white girl protagonists, meeting with a young black girl constitutes an epiphanic moment, a moment that carries much in terms of the text's meanings as it illuminates the white girl's progress toward adult understanding. Meaningful as the affiliation may be, however, such a relationship cannot and does not endure in either novel. In *Ellen Foster* Kaye Gibbons relies on such binary oppositions to explore in a more developed way the relationship between Ellen and Starletta. Starletta is Ellen Foster's only friend, but she is firmly fixed as auxiliary to Ellen, since Ellen is driven by an intensely personal quest to reestablish family and order in her life. The reader is appalled by the situation Ellen finds herself in, is compelled to follow her quest to find a new and safe home for herself, and admires the pragmatic determination with which she intends to achieve her ends. This is the basis of the reader's engagement with Ellen's personal narrative. In this respect Connie May Fowler's *Before Women Had Wings* forms an interesting comparison to Gibbons's novel. Poor white Bird Jackson, beaten by an abusive drunken mother and grieving for her dead father, escapes into a silent world of her own making, in which she is Jesus' "girlfriend." Most significantly, it is a middle-aged black woman, Miss Zora, who coaches her past her fear: "Otherwise, it will grow bigger and bigger every day until finally when you look in the mirror . . . you'll be looking at some other little girl, someone who lost her way." [12] Living in a trailer on the edge of a motel outside Tampa and making do, Bird's mother disapproves of "that crazy colored woman," and of Bird's most treasured and sustaining friendship. She deems it out of bounds until Zora succeeds in creating a friendship with her too, and finds a way to help mend Bird's broken family.

Ellen Foster also believes the adult world will judge her association with her black friend, so she begins, consciously and systematically, to differentiate herself from Starletta at every turn. As with Bird, disorder has ruled Ellen's life; her family falls apart, her home becomes unsafe as her drunken father lurches around it, so Ellen concerns herself with order and cleanliness and fixes Starletta as her opposite in order to judge what those characteristics might be. Starletta is inextricably linked into the dialectic of order and cleanliness versus disorder and dirt that preoccupies Ellen. Her first comment on seeing Starletta in the church at her mother's funeral focuses in on this most precisely: "I see Starletta and she looks clean" is immediately followed by the statement "Starletta and her mama both eat dirt." [13] Her observations bespeak a social conditioning, according to southern design, whereby poor white people learned to differentiate themselves at any and every level from poor black people. Gibbons doesn't attribute to her young protagonist this level of interpretative understanding, but Fowler does. Bird enlists a series of debilitating images to confront the racial stereotype of "white trash" that delimits her life chances and stirs her mother into disapproving of a black neighbor: "It would be years before I could pin all the right words to the sickening feeling in the pit of my stomach. . . . there's no forgetting when you're white trash—smirks, stares, stolen glances remind you at every turn that you're not worth squat. . . . And we females—girls and women alike— can't find enough strength in our battered souls to escape, so we birth our boys into legendary scoundrels, characters made better in the cross-hairs of half-truths. . . . We're still trapped." [14]

Both Bird and Ellen—and Bone in Dorothy Allison's *Bastard Out of Carolina*—battle against the circumstances that reduce them to "trash." One of the directions they take is to sustain or imagine enduring child-hood friendships. In Allison's novel, for example, a fleeting encounter occurs in which anything more than a swift exchange of glances between two girls is forestalled. Nevertheless, the mutual recognition contained therein combines apprehension of the stigma attached to both "niggers" and "white trash" and the gaping loss that is the impossibility of getting to know each other as friends. Bone says: "I wished that girl would come out so I could try to talk to her, but she never did more than look out the windows at us. Her mama had probably told her all about what to expect from trash like us." [15] The impossibility that the white protago-nist, Bone, perceives for one designated "white trash" to claim sorority with one who is black dominates the encounter. [16]

In contemporary fiction white girls are frequently fascinated with their black counterparts and pursue connections with them even under the strictures of segregation and even when rebuffed. But the constraints placed upon cross-racial childhood friendships are perhaps best exem-plified in the much earlier autobiographical writings of Lillian Smith, who interrogated the ideological apparatus that tried to ensure that friendships that crossed "the color line" would be dissolved when the girls reached the threshold of adulthood and introduction into their ap-propriately different places in southern societies. In 1943, before the Fel-lowship of Southern Churchmen, Lillian Smith spoke out against racial segregation and exposed the detrimental impact of post-Reconstruction controls upon black and white children. She spoke of her own childhood in the 1900s specifically, but also of systems still in effect at the time of her speech: "No colored child in our country, however protected within the family, is being given today what his personality needs in order to mature fully and richly. No white child, under the segregation pattern, North or South, can be free of arrogance, hardness of heart, blindness to human needs. The bitter and inescapable fact is that our children in America, white and colored, are growing distorted, twisted personalities within the frame of this segregation which our fears and frustrations have imposed upon them."[17]

Smith spoke out forcefully against the "frame of segregation" in her speeches, and much of her autobiographical *Killers of the Dream* is dedicated to explicating and exposing the false sanctity of white skin that was inculcated into children in the Georgia of her youth.[18] One incident in particular that Smith "forgot" for more than thirty years is wrenched into comprehension. It concerns a little white girl who is discovered living in "Colored Town" and is removed by the white townsfolk, with the aid of the town marshal, from a black family who are deemed "ignorant and dirty and sick-looking colored folks" and who must have kidnapped her. She goes to live with young Lillian's family, and the two become firm friends until it is realized that, despite her white skin, Janie is "colored" and must be returned. She will not be allowed over to play, and the dictate that "white and colored people do not live together" is played out to emotional effect in both girls' lives. Lillian feels guilty at having broken a clear social taboo by sharing her bed and her friendship with a girl who she discovers is black. She shuns her: "And like a slow poison, it began to seep through me: *I was white. She was colored. We must not be together. It was bad to be together. Though you ate with your nurse when you were little, it was bad to eat with any colored person after that.*"[19] Young Lillian and Janie share an intimacy that is subsequently shattered and distorted and even obliterated from Lillian's memory in the need to adhere to the racial geography of her day.[20]

The girls have engaged in a border crossing which, if it is allowed to continue, will destabilize and disrupt the map of social relations for which they are to be prepared. The episode Smith recounts is especially powerful in its playing out of the "rules" and the "frame" of segregation. After the social structure was legally dismantled, it was still deemed reasonable, even natural, that black and white children should play to-gether before school age. It was the onset of adolescence that marked the point after which their intimacy should be dissolved.[21] This "sorting," entrusted to the institutional jurisprudence of schools, proved insidious but effective and largely unassailable. The girls are maneuvered out of particular friendships as a result of the inflexibility of racial and social biases.

𝒞♥ It is, indeed, striking that white writers who have deemed cross-racial childhood connections significant, in that they have chosen to rep-resent them in their fictions, have simultaneously often left the black girl unvoiced and inactive in the encounter. One writer who does explore a relationship in which both parties strive to be vocal and actively equal participants is Susan Richards Shreve in *A Country of Strangers*. A short consideration of this novel may help to quantify exactly how it is that the friendship in *Ellen Foster* remains stifled and trapped within its struc-ture. It may also serve to illuminate that, whether couched in a mono-logic or dialogic framework, interracial childhood friendships typically do not endure beyond childhood in contemporary fictions, whatever their form. The two novels are structured very differently, but the prob-lems that arise in maintaining a cross-racial friendship beyond childhood association are present in each. Shreve locates a childhood friendship as one interracial connection amid many, but she features it centrally; in fact, it is the closest the novel comes to positing a successful cross-racial alliance.

Kate and Prudential meet in northern Virginia in 1942, and their en-counters are mediated through a third-person omniscient narrator who assesses each character's motives and feelings, whereas in Gibbons's novel Ellen may only assess her own. The girls' relationship begins in unequivocal aggression and antagonism, and Shreve retains a startlingly clear image of their differences, while maneuvering Kate and Prudential toward recognition of the elements that connect their lives. Kate imme-diately detects Prudential's hatred of her as representative of "white girls." The hatred is translated into a succinct and memorable incident in which Prudential, feeling a profound urge to spit at Kate, decides to urinate on her instead. She pees from way up in an elm tree, "a long thin stream, straight as a pencil through the branches. Bulls eye on top of her silky hair."[22] It is, in the scuffle that follows, Kate who spits in Prudential's face. Prudential describes this fight as a "conversation" and it is represented as the most honest exchange that the girls can muster in the first instance. Prudential is thirteen, pregnant by her father and angry. Only when Kate is abused at school by a boy who forces her head toward his erection, and she spontaneously confides the incident to Prudential, is their friendship sealed. Prudential does not reciprocate with her own experience of abuse, but her shocked "I had no idea that kind of misfortune could happen to a white girl" (111) belies her conditioning, historical and cultural. The white girl may have similar problems.

The girls are edged into contiguous and unforeseen symmetry: "Their bodies touched along the arms and thighs, their bony knees aligned as if such order in presentation were intentional" (110). Shreve patterns their commonality into each evocation of their daily lives in an interracial household in which they are the only members to overlook difference in favor of cohesion: they lunch together, sit closely side by side, and exchange secrets, except for the one alluding to the father of Prudential's baby. Their circumstances are not the same, but their desire to be friends is mutual, for much of the novel. It has been said of Shreve's work in general that "when her characters are not making grand gestures or being quietly introspective, they are usually talking with each other, most often interpreting and evaluating each other's lives."[23] This general tendency is significantly abridged in the case of Kate and Prudential's reciprocity, in that actions figure more than words; just as their first fight was a "conversation," so they go on to demonstrate their mutual support in deeds and actions. Kate buys Prudential a dress as a mark of appreciation, and Prudential fights Kate's battle with the schoolboy oppressor on her behalf, exacting revenge in a secondhand retaliation for her own as well as her friend's sexual distress. On only one occasion, and very untypically, does Prudential underline their equitable camaraderie in words: "It's like we were born together, halved out of the same eggshell" (129). The image serves to conjure up the fragility and precariousness of an association such as theirs in rural Virginia in the 1940s.

Kate and Prudential exemplify a spirited endeavor to elicit honesty and comfort from a cross-racial childhood friendship, but theirs barely persists beyond the age of thirteen. However a writer may choose to structure her novel—as bildungsroman or melodrama, through a dominant central character and voice, or in short narrative passages or scenes that coalesce as an exploration of relationships—the outcome tends to be the same when one focuses directly on the cross-racial childhood relationship. Very few withstand social or indeed personal pressures or remain as close, if they persist at all beyond adolescence, as they clearly had the potential to be in childhood. In *Meridian,* a novel set in the aftermath of the civil rights movement that engages with lost hopes and failed coalitions, Alice Walker has Meridian's grandmother declare that in all her life she has "never known a white woman she liked after the age of twelve."[24] In fact, writers do not tend to push much beyond the onset of adolescence, fixing the girls within a framework that reinscribes the repeated breakdown of cross-racial friendships or never allows them to become truly dialogic encounters in the first place.

 In *Ellen Foster,* Kaye Gibbons inscribes the girls' social experiences as racially different, their futures as ultimately separate, and their friendships as almost impossible to maintain. The structuring of the text separates the girls and keeps them separate, despite their friendship. Black girls are often framed and constrained within the white protagonists' first-person narratives in bildungsroman or biographical novels; and this form of narration, typically featuring a single narrating voice, fixes the black girl as auxiliary, as an emblem to signify a stage (or stages) in the white protagonist's personal development and rites of passage. The first person–narrated bildungsroman, described by Richard Gray as one of the South's "familiar regional narrative types and structures," is also a monologic form that silences other voices that might otherwise disrupt the monologue or deviate from its flow.[25] It has, of course, also been judged one of the most bourgeois of novelistic forms; classically realist, it privileges the individual (eponymous in this case), her psychology, and her character to the extent that Catherine Belsey has stated that "character, unified and coherent, *is* the source of action."[26] Kaye Gibbons unfixes some of the conventions of the form in her depiction of a poor white girl whose class and language clearly set her outside of a bourgeois formulation.

Nevertheless, the bildungsroman structure envelops the speaking protagonist in a kind of impermeable membrane and functions to divert the reader's attention away from characters who are positioned on the outside. This means that the black friend is not recognized with a space for speech, as she could be in a text in which more than one social discourse is represented. It is not the emphasis on Ellen's development that is disturbing but the inclusion of Starletta as an apparently major spur to Ellen's personal development, while rendering her mute and muted in the novel in all circumstances. She never becomes a speaking subject. This results in the aporia, or internal contradiction, in the text, that I read as the gap between the friendship, clearly present in the novel, and the organization of the novel as a monologue. This severely limits the representation of that friendship.

The disjunction between white and black characters in a text that can be read along an axis of friendship constitutes what I shall call a fault line in the text. This fault line splinters the friendship, since the friendship is ultimately only the casing or framework according to which the content of the text may be said to operate. Cross-racial cooperation, apparently of representative importance to the novel under discussion here, risks being undermined by set literary structures and paradigms deployed in the construction of black characters and in representations of black voices that inevitably function to segregate or "other" them, even to silence them completely. Gibbons creates a white girl whose epistemology derives from segregated situations but for whom even a radical ideological breakthrough of the kind she undergoes in the novel is contained within a narrative structure that, although it necessarily privileges her, denies agency to the "other" character on the friendship axis, Starletta. No matter what Ellen may think *or* feel about her friend at the end of the novel, the monologue form cannot disclose the voice or "I" of Starletta, since Ellen is the only developed subject of the text and it is her evolving consciousness that prevails.

Kaye Gibbons generally writes novels in the form of first-person monologues, since her intention is to create southern women characters who will appear to tell their own stories. She has indicated that she begins "her conceptualization of a work with character and voice, not with plot and abstract ideas. . . . In her writing, interior experience is more important than surface experience, and language is the important interpretative mechanism for bringing that to the reader, even concerning memories of surface experience."[27] For "surface experience" I understand social actions and interactions and the "abstract ideas" mentioned here I read as political as well as philosophical and existential considerations. In this, Gibbons's first novel, it is particularly the case that details of region and society receive attention only so far as Ellen "chooses" to articulate her child's understanding of wider issues. Ultimately, whatever does or does not transpire in the novel is circumscribed by Ellen, as Gibbons has her rationalize herself as an autonomous and coherent self. This is clear from the sheer number of times that Ellen repeats the phrase "my own self," so central to her idiom and idiolect. Her monologue is the self-analysis that her child psychologist tries unsuccessfully every Tuesday at school to extract from her. In this way Gibbons leaves little room for the interactions, dramatic confrontations, and emotional and violent exchanges that may be enacted in a more melodramatic text.

Ellen Foster is a self-celebratory monologue in the voice of a child who has not yet fully discovered that human experience is necessarily dialogic and collaborative. Ellen's monologue has, to employ Bakhtinian terms, a "centripetal" and a "monologic" imperative and force in which Starletta's silence is as necessary as it is disquieting. It is hard for Ellen to consider anyone else in any depth while she is in the process of self-formation, as is indicated when she takes the name Foster, a new name (the reader is never made aware of her family name). Ellen mistakes the term "foster family" for the family name of her "new mama" and appropriates it as a signal of her wish to cut the ties with her old life and with a "worn-out" name in order to make herself anew. The link she preserves with Starletta is really the sole connection she actively seeks to maintain with her old lifestyle; Starletta is her chosen and designated "other."

Ellen begins to reconcile herself to her *own* illogicalities in the way that Elizabeth Abel has discussed in another context when she notes that to (re)construct a friend is to (re)view the self so that the friend acts as an alter ego that "refines and clarifies the narrator's self-image."[28] In the final pages of the novel, Gibbons dramatizes the complex negotiations of racial social geography in which Ellen is involved, but solely in terms of Ellen's character. Starletta is sidelined even in the final pages, and her silence remains. Gibbons has implied that she was unaware of this factor until she got to the end of the book and "realized she hadn't talked." Significantly, though, rather than interrogate the motivation behind this feature of the text, and its effects, as Ellen Douglas does openly in *Can't Quit You Baby*, Gibbons provides a get-out that legitimates as it disclaims: "I said, 'Kaye, you've got to say why this girl has not said a word and I said, well she stutters and doesn't like to talk.' I took care of that real quickly."[29] Shirley M. Jordan, interviewing Gibbons, does not pursue the issue, but effectively disabling Starletta, disempowering an already disempowered character, does not "take care" of the discomfort and disappointment a reader may feel in having Starletta simply act as a silent witness and accomplice to Ellen's most forceful engagement with life. In Ellen, Gibbons creates a character whose strength, vitality, and creative good sense go some considerable way toward undermining a tenacious image of a "poor white" girl as hopeless, as does Fowler in *Before Women Had Wings*. Her creation of Ellen's black counterpart is all the more disappointing as a result. Starletta remains a plot function in spite of Gibbons's general engagement with issues of race and representation in her work, as discussed in chapter 4.

A more theoretical focus on the constitution of the subject is described by Tzvetan Todorov in his elaboration of Mikhail Bakhtin's aesthetic of otherness. For Bakhtin, self-consciousness as consciousness of self can only be realized "through another and with another's help," for "every internal experience occurs on the border, it comes across another, and this essence resides in this intense encounter. . . . Man has no internal sovereign territory; he is all and always on the boundary; looking within himself, he looks *in the eyes of the other or through the eyes of the other.*[30]

These ideas include the condition of self-existence as reliant on the other, so that existence becomes dialogical in principle. Bakhtin is interested in the writer or artist's relation to the characters he or she creates, but here I foreground the interrelationship between characters in an application of Bakhtin's ideas, in order to clarify how a novel that *ostensibly* values the mutuality and interdependency of friendship can nevertheless remain monologic in form by denying dialogue. In Bakhtinian terms: "Ultimately monologism denies that there exists outside of it another consciousness, with the same rights, and capable of responding on an equal footing, another and equal *I*. The monologue is accomplished and deaf to the other's response; it does not await it and does not grant it any *decisive* force. Monologue makes do without the other; that is why to some extent it objectivizes all reality. Monologue pretends to be the *last word*." [31]

Extrapolating from Bakhtin, I would argue that a monologic outlook dominates *Ellen Foster,* not simply as a result of Gibbons's own acknowledgment that Starletta's voice was of no particular concern but as evidenced in the formal structuring of the novel itself. Starletta is finally little more than a device circumscribed by a monologic textual exploration of the protagonist. Robert Stam points out the dangers of "pseudo-polyphonic" discourses, whereby certain voices are disempowered because they are marginalized, so that the "dialogue" that takes place is really between a voiced individual and a "puppet-like entity that has already been forced to make crucial compromises." [32]

In many ways Starletta is the puppet in the text; her reality is objectivized. Starletta figures only as a component in a series of elements in Ellen's life that Ellen is trying to fix in some order. The picaresque quality of their encounters as nodal points in a linear model bears this out. The construction of Starletta's character and of her silence comes perilously close to the construction of African American characters as foils in an "American" literary tradition—a construction that has been noted by Toni Morrison, and by Richard Wright and Ralph Ellison before her. If Starletta's silence is read as accommodation, she becomes an accommodating black presence in the novel. In *Playing in the Dark* Morrison describes black characters operating as a "control group" in a white American literary experiment and in the formation of white American national culture. Her idea can be extended in an analysis of the black characters in Gibbons's novel as they operate in Ellen's reformulation of her personal identity. For Morrison, "Africanism is the vehicle by which the American self knows itself as not enslaved, but free; not repulsive, but desirable; not helpless, but licensed and powerful; not history-less, but historical; not damned but innocent; not a blind accident of evolution, but a progressive fulfilment of destiny."[33] Morrison discusses nineteenth- and early-twentieth-century texts, as the language of her analogies indicates; ideas of individualism and freedom were inextricable from those of oppression and slavery; but *Ellen Foster* has most frequently been compared with *Huckleberry Finn* by reviewers, and its philosophy is distinctly Emersonian. Ellen's idiosyncratic first-person narrative commentary is replete with southern speech patterns reminiscent of Huck's, and the motif of self-reliance so strong in Twain's novel is clearly present in Gibbons's, from the epigraph from "Self-Reliance" to the end of the novel. Both Huck and Ellen escape alcoholic and abusive fathers and are orphaned, but, whereas Huck suffered the informal maternalism of the Widow Douglas and Aunt Sally, Ellen is immediately tied into the decisions of court welfare hearings and regular monitoring by an educational psychologist. Despite the obvious differences in context, the course Ellen is set upon in the novel involves her primarily in a progressive articulation of her own identity, and Starletta is, like Jim for Huck, the only other character present throughout the text who services this end. Gibbons is clearly aware of the American literary tradition, most clearly explicated by Leslie Fiedler, in which African Americans and Native Americans have functioned as subordinate and peripheral sidekicks to white individualistic protagonists. In *Ellen Foster* she retains the basis of this binary intact as she negotiates such a relationship for her protagonist.

🖉 In *Ellen Foster* the speaking protagonist records the period of her childhood in which she begins to identify herself as separate from her parents and as an active force in shaping both her environment and her future in the contemporary South. Starletta, her black friend, is the only character featured throughout the text who remains a constant presence despite the changes in Ellen's life. Ellen's mother's suicide precipitates Ellen's advance into the wider world; Starletta is present at Ellen's mother's funeral at the beginning of the book, and she is the first and the only person from Ellen's former life to visit once Ellen has established herself in a new foster home. But Ellen's efforts to lift herself out of what she understands to have been an ill-starred start in life quickly become indivisible from what she deems the clearest means of demonstrating herself to be a young lady of clean habits and reasonable, moderate behavior: she sets herself directly against what she deems to be the "standards" of the black members of the southern community in which she resides. Not only does Ellen seek to restore what order and routine she experienced while her mother was alive; she also embarks upon a related quest to ascertain her individual needs. Simultaneously, she discovers that she and Starletta are united by more than what divides them, and she wishes to maintain their connection in the new life she is in the process of mapping for herself: "I feel like she grew behind my back and when I think about her now I want to press my hands to her to stop her from growing into a time she will not want to play" (97). This realization is slow in coming, but it forms the trajectory of what is clearly a friendship plot. Before this discovery, the novel is punctuated by scenes in which Ellen expresses her wish to fit herself into quite conventional images of girlhood. With the intention to become a Girl Scout, Ellen signals her desire for a new and widely acceptable image. Her full school uniform is a source of pride and satisfaction as it marks her out as a good student.

Much of the time Ellen is groping toward a new identity, even though she couches her intentions in highly conformist terms and her narration is cluttered with concerns about the impression she makes on others. Ellen invests time and effort in herself, as made manifest in her attention to clothes and the outward presentation of self, but her determination to reassert herself in this way does not leave much time to devote to her own psychological recovery from the traumas that beset her, or to consider the meaning of her friendship with Starletta. This would involve considerable self-scrutiny, and Ellen's unceasing and at times breathless monologue belies a concerted effort to be outwardly self-confident rather than inwardly self-searching. Her bid to create a coherent sense of self, the express goal of the bildungsroman form, excludes a more open and problematic engagement with the facets of her character that are not immediately assimilable into this particular discourse of the self.

Ellen's prejudices and judgements about black people are disclosed along with her other feelings. Starletta is her friend, but she will not eat in Starletta's home nor will she drink from the family's utensils, despite having decided that they live "regular"—her shorthand for "like white folks." Her joy at the Christmas present she receives from them is re-doubled with "Oh my God it is a sweater. I like it so much. I do not tell a story when I say it does not look colored at all" (38). These and other indicators clarify the chasm that separates her own place in society from Starletta's, despite the way this directly contradicts her personal experi-ences. Ellen feels that her most safe and comfortable retreat is the black family's home. She escapes there on the occasion when her drunken fa-ther mistakes her for her dead mother in the dark, and she sleeps there in security, the like of which she has never experienced at home or when forced to stay with her own grandmother.

Initially, I felt that Gibbons might be working to create a different effect—or misprision—in her codification of race relations from that created in much previous American literature where the white protago-nist is mirrored or shadowed by a black companion. The reader is en-couraged in the belief that Ellen's sharp and pragmatic self-reliance is her most valuable asset. For the most part, she demonstrates an uncanny ability to slice through hypocrisy and etiquette and to catch people in a few words, as can be seen in her debunking of psychoanalysis and the court system. She disdains the child psychologist's tentative explanations that she may be suffering from "identity problems" following the traumas of her early life: "I hate to tell him he's wrong because you can tell it took him a long time to make up his ideas. And the worst part is I can see he believes them" (103). Similarly, the studied homilies of the judge who presides over the case for Ellen's guardianship are recognized for what they are; Ellen astutely reconciles the illogicality of his decisions in such a way as to preserve herself from the full force of their impact on her life:

What do you do when the judge talks about the family society's cornerstone but you know yours was never a Roman pillar but is and always has been crumbly old brick? I was in my seat frustrated like when my teacher makes a mistake on the chalkboard and it will not do any good to tell her because so quick she can erase it all and on to the next problem.

He had us all mixed up with a different group of folks. (66)

Despite such perspicacity, Gibbons shows that the social etiquette of race relations is much more difficult for Ellen to penetrate. She has Ellen revise her assumptions and come to understand that the criteria she employed to judge a black family as inferior were mistaken. But finally, the codification of the primary relationship does not differ significantly from paradigmatic depictions in earlier novels. In fact, Ellen refers to Starletta as "the baby" for much of this novel and describes her as hers, almost as a doll might be hers to keep and to love. Starletta is a kind of talisman for Ellen, certainly a touchstone in the sense of a comfortable place that she can return to at points on her journey of self-discovery and in her monologue. Each time the two meet there are examples of Ellen's tendency to feel that she may own her black "buddy": at the cinema, "Starletta was the only colored girl at the movies and she was mine" (60); on the bus, "I need to tell the driver first thing that I'll be having a extra passenger on board this afternoon. She'll be getting off at my house. She's colored but don't act like you notice. And she'll be sitting right up front with me. And she'll be getting off at my house" (142).

There are other black characters who are minimally drawn and who form part of Ellen's environment. Initially, they seem simply auxiliary figures playing bit parts, but they come to serve most importantly as an alternative locus for Ellen's desires for home and security. Starletta's parents are only an extension of Starletta, unnamed and described solely in terms of what they do for Ellen. They are a collective presence, but when Ellen goes to live with her grandmother and is set to work in her cotton fields, she meets Mavis, one of the cotton pickers, and she spies on black homes and communal home life from the bottom of "colored lane" with a half-acknowledged loneliness and envy. Her homelessness is the key to Ellen's mire of conflicting emotions, her psychological and existential predicament, the predicament she confronts only in her pragmatic assessment of her own needs. She comes to know Mavis, who protects her from the heavier work and who confides that Ellen's mother was her childhood friend and that she knew her "good as I know my own self" (76). Although the pairing of the young white girl and older black woman lasts only a short while, unlike the relationship between Bird and Miss Zora in *Before Women Had Wings,* it would seem to have a specific bearing on Ellen's reassessment of her own position with regard to Starletta, and Ellen's dawning apprehension that a "home" is of limited value if unsupported by wider social affiliations that can help to make it a shared space rather than a lonely sanctuary.

✌ By the end of the novel, Ellen feels the need to "straighten out" things between herself and Starletta so they can become "even friends" within the space of her new home. But this "evening out" does not include the need for dialogue with her friend, since Starletta's speech is never represented. Ellen does begin to seek physical intimacy with her friend rather than disdain it—"I wonder if Starletta would let me take a bath with her" (141)—and she sings her name inside her head all morning, looking forward to Starletta's weekend sleep-over. The language certainly registers love and desire, but Starletta is clearly the *object* of Ellen's affections. Ellen, Gibbons makes clear, is awakening to the wonderment and significance of a friendship from which she has derived comfort while denying its full import in her world, and in so doing she begins to desegregate her mind and her understanding but fails to dismantle the strategies of containment through which she has embodied Starletta. Consequently, there would seem to be a tension between the form of bildungsroman and the idea of representing a cross-racial friendship within it, particularly when for her author Ellen is "a child who thinks first and then feels."[34]

Ellen makes what she affirms is a revolutionary gesture and statement about her friend; she has Starletta to stay in her home as a special guest when "every rule in the book says I should not have her in my house, much less laid still and sleeping by me" (146). The novel ends on a clear note of social reconciliation, but it is primarily Ellen's reconciliation with her "own self" via Starletta, in a confession that facilitates an advance in Ellen's independent assessment of her life and her future but that does not permit response or debate: "Starletta I always thought I was special because I was white and when I thought about you being colored I said to myself it sure is a shame Starletta's colored. I sure would hate to be that way. . . . now I remember that they changed that rule. So it does not make any sense for me to feel like I'm breaking the law. . . . if they could fight a war over how I'm supposed to think about her then I'm obligated to do it. It seems like the decent thing to do" (146).

The attitudinal shift has come about as a result of the accumulated experiences of living in a biracial community that Ellen undergoes in this picaresque tale, staying the night in Starletta's home and picking cotton in her grandmother's fields, for example. The reader is also reminded during Ellen's confession of Huck's crisis of conscience over slavery and whether he should inform Miss Watson of the whereabouts of her runaway, Jim. Where Huck confounds his sin with not upholding the codes of the slavocracy, Ellen harbors no such paradoxical contradistinctions, but, lightly ironic, Gibbons has Ellen luxuriate in the magnanimity and munificence that integration with Starletta brings to her sense of self by having her draw on the Civil War and on civil rights history to create an ending in the manner of the old stories (and *Huckleberry Finn* may be one of them) that Ellen loves to read. This is dryly done. But, it nevertheless conforms to the convention of narrative closure that one expects in a classic realist format where the protagonist's maturation and self-discovery is the end and this ending forecloses on any further irony or deeper interaction with others.

It is disappointing, therefore, that, despite the threshold of ideological understanding the character may be said to reach by the end of this novel, and despite her belated acknowledgment that this is largely as a result of her friend, she still cannot see the importance of listening to Starletta, finding out what she thinks and might wish to say. In this I would disagree with Jay Clayton, who reads *Ellen Foster* as a narrative of racial reconciliation and who asserts that "the plot culminates in Ellen's *successful* efforts to make amends for former slights to her best friend" (my emphasis).[35] Clayton implies that the novel plays out its utopian possibilities, whereas I argue that they are left unfulfilled and that the ending remains far too ambiguous to be a culmination of all the ideas raised by the plot.

Arguably, Starletta remains silent because the text to be read is Ellen herself, and the textual lacunae in the representation of Starletta are the inevitable result of structuring the novel according to the principles of the bildungsroman, which serves on the one hand to emphasize and on the other to retreat from what I have termed the "friendship plot" in *Ellen Foster*. The friendship is plotted along an axis, the line about which the figure of Ellen may be understood to revolve. The novel is plotted around the friendship that helps to coordinate the trajectory of Ellen's life and progress, and this draws on the sense of alliance present in some definitions of the word *axis*. A friendship axis is clearly present and can be traced specifically via a series of incidents in the girls' relationship that structure the writing as a developing friendship for Ellen: a Christmas spent together, shopping together, a visit to the cinema, and Starletta's visits to two of Ellen's foster homes. They go to the same school, and, although they are in different classes, their connection is maintained, largely it seems because Ellen makes no particular friends in her own homeroom, as Starletta does in hers. The childhood friendship operates strategically to point up the relationships between institutions like school and the Girl Scouts, small-town life and family life, that are such socially powerful forces against which the crises of friendship contend. This is especially the case for an interracial friendship when, for example, there is no integrated, or segregated, Girl Scout group for Starletta to attend.

Gibbons leaves Ellen Foster on the threshold of a new phase of development, but the subordination of Starletta in the text does not offer much in the way of hope for sisterly connection. If one wishes to detect hope for the association, nevertheless, it may be present in the way in which Ellen has come to realize that Starletta has an existence independent of her. She has her own friends and ideas, and she may decide to drift away from their association, something Ellen intends to try to prevent by becoming an "even friend":

> Something tells me inside that one of these days soon she will forget me.
> So I have to make a big very big good time with her that she will not forget. . . . I know for a fact that I would not ever forget her but you can never be sure about how somebody else thinks about you except if they beat it into your head. At least that is how I am worried about Starletta who never has said much good or bad to me but before long I will have to know I am in her head like she is in mine. It is good to have a friend like her. (99)

This passage seems unusual in a novel that focuses so exclusively on the protagonist; it shows Ellen as she begins to appreciate that Starletta acts independently outside and apart from herself, but it also remains typical in its self-involved emphasis on Ellen's own fears and needs. Ellen remains consistent in her utilization of Starletta as a standard against which she may measure her own progress. Even her invitation to Starletta to stay in her new home acts as a celebration of how far *she* has progressed or of how far *her* world may be differentiated from Starletta's: "She would think back on me and how she stayed in the white house all night with Ellen" (99).

She says quite a lot toward the end of her monologue about her dawning understanding of the social order that kept her prejudices and assumptions in place and about the possibilities for a more open acknowledgment of differences between races. Certainly, Ellen has learned some important lessons about where she fits and where she may choose to place herself within a southern scheme of social relations. However, as the novel closes, she is resting comfortably in the image she has fashioned of her own magnanimity in reconciling her new, carefully integrated self with Starletta. Finally, individualism overrides the friendship plot in *Ellen Foster*. The friendship plot informs the composition of the text, but only so far as it helps to situate a self-made American individual on the threshold of a new phase in life.

The cross-racial childhood friendship in southern literature about girls is a palimpsest wherein the complexities of race and gender may be collapsed into a single unitary relationship when the complexities begin to intersect with the young girls' lives. This is not to say that each representation is a social protest or is reformist in some sense—Belva Plain's *Crescent City,* for example, is clearly neither[36]—but rather that the history of segregation restricts representations of a childhood friendship that seek to incorporate realism in their form or credibility in their content. Toni Morrison has said that there is always something "more interesting at stake than a clear resolution in a novel," and, unlike Jay Clayton, who feels there is a sense of culmination at the end of *Ellen Foster,* I believe that important ambiguities remain.[37] It is left ambiguous whether Ellen's developing self should finally be understood as essentially self-reliant or her sense of identity owes much more to group experience and to a salient cross-racial friendship. Such ambiguities are the crux of Ellen's monologue and of her story.

CHAPTER THREE

Envisioning Sisterhood

Eco-Utopian Romance and the Female Pastoral

The dream of creating a communitarian feminist politics based in friendship can, of course, be more nearly created in a fictional world than in the actual or, for that matter, in the realm of contemporary American feminist politics. Novels may work to compensate for a lack of hope in feminist movements, for a dearth of political activity, and for lack of faith in contemporary society, and may bring to the reader an awareness of such feelings through what Daphne Patai describes as an "implicit moral ideology."[1] A facet of that moral vision includes the pastoral and the project that Ellen Moers, Annette Kolodny, and Louise Westling have discussed: metaphoric female landscapes and the ways that women writers often "identify with and draw strength from symbolic landscapes."[2] From Emerson and Thoreau through the literary critics Lawrence Buell, Greta Gaard, and Patrick Murphy, writers have set their work against binary divisions such as culture/nature and incorporated nature and, most recently, eco-feminism into the broader spectrum of literary criticism.[3] Southern writing has long been associated with the land; the South is the dispossessed garden of Eden, as Lewis Simpson calls it, and writers like Eudora Welty and Ellen Glasgow affirm southern landscape in and through their attention to women's domestic activities. Patterns of violence and calm, assault and recuperation are punctuated with domestic ritual in southern stories like *Delta Wedding* and *The Golden Apples.*[4]

Most recently, fictions like Connie May Fowler's *River of Hidden Dreams,* set in the Florida Everglades, and *Before Women Had Wings* incorporate the ecological struggle and pursue the appreciation of flora and fauna, place and region. Fowler cites Zora Neale Hurston and Marjorie Stoneman Douglas, whose love of the Florida landscape inspires her work. In *Before Women Had Wings,* Fowler's young protagonist, Bird, on arriving in Tampa, gets to know the lay of the land by naming all the flowers: "As I named the bounty of the field, I began to feel responsible. Not as if I owned the place, but that these wildflowers, red birds, skinks were my brothers and sisters—as if my peace of mind depended on theirs."[5] It is when she feels her individual responsibility to the land that she meets Miss Zora, the bird-keeper, who comes to care for the poor white girl. Miss Zora dedicates herself to preserving her environment; this black woman, whose home borders on a motel park, manages to maintain a cottage garden. She first appears almost ethereally in the novel, as if part of the landscape: "I heard a gentle flutter of wings, and then she quickly disappeared down a path overgrown with wildflowers and thorns. The smell of the sea skittered off as well."[6]

A primary feature of the novel that is the focus of the most detailed reading in this chapter, Lane von Herzen's *Copper Crown,* is the healing properties of the land, but the controlling conception in Lane von Herzen's novel is the friendship between Cass Sandstrom and Allie Farrell, white and black respectively, in rural east Texas at the beginning of the twentieth century.[7] Lane von Herzen may no longer live in the South, but, like Sherley Anne Williams, Toni Morrison and Pete Dexter, non-southerners who have written southern novels, she too finds the South the center of her creative focus. She constructs a South out of her own southwestern ancestry, three generations of Texan women, and out of a literary tradition that has succeeded in establishing a pastoral version of the South in the imagination. Von Herzen writes in the tradition of the Deep South Texas writers Katherine Ann Porter, William Goyen, and William Humphrey, for whom blacks and whites living on the land, farms and plantations, cotton crops and the sharecrop-lien system, and— as James W. Lee describes—"moss-hung oaks, pine-covered hills, rice fields and sandy beaches" are as representative of Texas as the "branding iron, a marshal's badge, a ten-gallon hat, a six-shooter, a rattlesnake and a wagon wheel."[8]

Von Herzen's Texas, like Fowler's Florida, is imbued with a strong ecologically based appreciation of the land and nature. But *Copper Crown* is set in the past. Fowler reflects the beginning of the ecological movement in the 1960s via Miss Zora's concerns (writing letters to President Johnson, urging him to stop the war in Vietnam and to enforce civil rights legislation, she emphasizes the need to ban pesticides), and in the contemporary setting of *River of Hidden Dreams*, Fowler's ecological critique becomes much more pointed and urgent. The river journey through the waters of Ten Thousand Islands and the Gulf approaches Daytona: "Herons pierce the sky effortlessly, as if they cannot imagine the wilderness could ever be destroyed. But they should, for they are forewarned. Nearby are lands clear-cut and trailers sit placidly, side by side, like endless rows of giant coffins under a relentless sun." Thinking back through her ancestors, Cherokee and Seminole, African American and Irish, protagonist Sadie Hunter fears they would "gasp at our boldness and arrogance as we take nature by the neck and spit in her face." Although such high-handed offenses against nature may be likened, sadly, to the slaughter of the buffalo in the previous century, this form of ecological damage is unethical in other and quite precise ways, spawning "developments" with "filled-in marsh to create pesticide-rich golf courses" and condos with "toxic wall-to-wall carpeting" and windows that don't open.[9]

Von Herzen must deploy different models in a novel set so early in the twentieth century. In her most recent study of landscape's association with the feminine, *The Green Breast of the New World*, Louise Westling describes how the American literary landscape can become a "magical female space of pastoral *otium*." [10] *Copper Crown* can be read according to this gendered metaphorical model and Cass as reminiscent of a tradition of southern women characters who are deeply associated with the land: Scarlett O'Hara in Margaret Mitchell's *Gone with the Wind*, Virginia in Ellen Glasgow's novel of that name, and Dorinda in her *Barren Ground*, to name a few examples. As for Glasgow in *Barren Ground*, it is the seasons that mark the time line of *Copper Crown*, but whereas Dorinda Oakley battles to control the land, the Texas soil responds to Cass like a lover fulfilling her needs. But Cass, like those before her (Scarlett with Mammy and Prissy, Dorinda with Fluvanna) risks underestimating the needs and the significance of her black woman companion.

My reading concentrates on how the novel functions in its exploration of race relations and on what it anticipates via its utopian ecofeminist impulses. It seems to celebrate a limitless potential for cooperation between women that can transcend differences and even death in an imaginative foray into interracial configurations and negotiations. In its reworking of an American pastoral tradition, it genders the landscape in ways that Annette Kolodny, Elizabeth Jane Harrison, and Louise Westling have discussed. Even the sexual violence of the novel (rape and attempted rape), which follows a tradition in southern writing established in Faulkner and Welty, for example, is abated by the peace earned by women at the novel's end. Harrison argues that white writers are "less able to envision racial equality among characters" and that they seem less likely to operate within the set of conventions of the female pastoral than their black counterparts. [11] She uses Glasgow and Cather in her analysis, but in recent fiction cross-racial cooperative projects are as visibly the projects of white writers like Connie May Fowler, Barbara Kingsolver, and von Herzen and are frequently more utopian than those that Harrison discusses.

Copper Crown is what I would term an eco-utopian romance. It follows Cass through her formative years, but while Gibbons's *Ellen Foster* conforms to the realist conventions of the traditional bildungsroman form, *Copper Crown* involves incursions into the supernatural and magical realism in order to envision a friendship that survives a community's devastation and even the fact that Allie's brother murders Cass's sister. Eco-utopianism presents itself as a discernible feature of *Copper Crown*, but I do not suggest that von Herzen takes up this position in polemical or intensely critical ways. Rather, her environmentally sensitive romance is pastoral and utopian in its commitment to the land. It renders the land magical: bell trees never go out of flower, a few saplings planted on barren land by those who love the land become a forest in a matter of weeks. Von Herzen makes the ordinary strange but always in relation to nature and natural phenomena: "Lily Mark came to us by way of fire" (17) is a rendering of her family's home being lost to fire because her father was smoking in bed. It is the ordinary—the quiddity of things—a sense of the loveliness of nature as well as its dangers, and trust in its diurnal round, that make the novel feel almost Romantic. Von Herzen creates a self-revealing and self-renewing world, with spirit places and the ultimate ecodream, the forest, at its heart. In death Cass is set to become a bell tree at the center of the forest: "My branches would arch in their heaven" and crack the false walls society has constructed (240).

By drawing upon a range of traditionally southern genres and styles, von Herzen creates an ecofeminist space, her imagined Texas. *Copper Crown* also owes much to the tradition of southern gothic; Lynette Carpenter and Wendy Kolmar describe the conventions of the female gothic novel as "a series of themes and images—of women victimized by violence in their own homes, of women dispossessed of their homes and property, of the necessity of understanding female history, and of the bonds between women, living and dead, which help to ensure women's survival." [12] Von Herzen deploys many of such themes and images to create a ghost story in the text, one of the most popular derivations of the gothic romance, as Leslie Fiedler points out, while deploying the romance form as a means of developing a utopian sense of commonality between women in the face of violence, social ostracism, and death. [13]

As Richard Chase has argued in *The American Novel and Its Tradition*, the romance places the emphasis on individuals pitted against other individuals in a realm of good and evil and mysterious forces. The romance is not tied to the ordinary or the quotidian; it combines the psychological and the gothic, and both these elements allow for supernatural manifestations. In fact, the American romance has developed over the twentieth century into magically realist forms and structures, as Wayne Ude argues, most particularly in ways that respond to problems of how to continue to imagine frontier and wilderness experiences.[14] It is in this specific context that von Herzen begins to create an ecofeminist romance. Both the American romance and the slave narrative, the conventions of which also inform the opening section of the novel, involve their protagonists in a flight from society. Like Huck and Jim, and, more recently, Sethe in *Beloved,* Cass and Allie "light out for the Territory." They take flight from Copper Crown, although it continues to exist in their dreams at night. Their walk through the gauntlet of trees along Valley Road, from which the lynched black members of their community hang, associates their flight with an escape from the violence of the Reconstruction period that persisted into the twentieth century. It signals that their new start is weighted with the psychological burdens of guilt and memory, but, whereas the men in Copper Crown put the land to use to facilitate murder (Oloe's body is hidden in water, and a line of trees is used to hang black bodies), the fleeing women reaffirm their forest setting as a sheltered space and the alluvial east Texas soil as their wilderness-garden.

The east Texas landscape, as delineated by William Goyen before her, provides the mystical pastoral against which von Herzen plays out her relationships. As Goyen has summarized: "The landscape of my stories, generally East Texas, is pastoral, river-haunted, tree-shaded, mysterious and bewitched. Spirits and ghosts inhabit it: the generations have not doubted their presence, their doings. Here and there exists the local splendor of simple people who 'wonder' and 'imagine'. Some heartbreak is here, too; and something of doom."[15] Von Herzen's ecological message in this novel is mediated through the pastoral and the romance form. "Less committed to the immediate rendition of reality," as Richard Chase succinctly put it, the romance may "more freely veer toward mythic, allegorical," and symbolic forms.[16] This is the case when one examines the period in which the novel is set. Each section of *Copper Crown* is prefaced by a date, so that events are ostensibly contained within the historical time span of 1913 to 1932, incorporating the years that saw the height of Ku Klux Klan activity and millions of Americans unemployed.[17] The First World War acts as a prism through which is refracted what von Herzen characterizes as a war between the races in the South, whereby white intransigence continued to deny blacks the freedoms they might have otherwise experienced after Reconstruction. Consequently, the war abroad operates allegorically. The terrors of the Reconstruction period and its aftermath figure more strongly; up to and during the 1930s, mobs lynched thousands of black people in an atmosphere of racial and sexual terrorism.[18] In these years there were racial confrontations all over Texas, like the uprisings in both Brownsville and Houston in 1919, attesting to the fact that, as Angela Davis has discussed, "Texas could claim the third largest number of racist mob murders committed throughout the Southern states (only Georgia and Mississippi could boast of more)."[19]

In *Copper Crown* it is the white patriarchal order from which most of the violence in the novel emanates; from Jensen the plantation owner and the men he employs, from Cass's own father, and from Skeet, who tries to rape Cass. In this way it turns on the effects of the Reconstruction period and its failure to redistribute power, its reinvestment in whiteness, and the demise of the plantation system. Black violence tends to occur in retaliation or self-defense, but, whereas the ever-present threat of racially or sexually motivated violence is an important component of von Herzen's "usable past," she imbues it with hope, as her characters pit themselves against violence, understanding and forgiving it or refusing to collude with it. By the end of the novel, Jensen, who initiates much of the violence in Copper Crown, is dead, and his plantation is turned over to the black workers who were the victims of the plantation system. In this *Copper Crown* echoes Sherley Anne Williams's *Dessa Rose,* in which a neglected plantation becomes the center of labor, sustaining blacks and whites on the edges of the slave system. Runaway slaves and a white woman abandoned by her plantation-owner husband begin to work cooperatively in the 1840s South. *Copper Crown* features an agrarian backdrop with sharecroppers working the twilight years of the plantation system. This is a notion of rural peasantry, a typically southern thematic concern, whereby the natural is magnified and prioritized.[20] The first steps toward such change are the planter's own—Jensen's deferred guilt over years of abusing his power over black men and over women like Allie's mother—but it is Allie and, by extension, Cass who transform his guilt into economic sustenance for the black workers in a cooperative system.

The novel's hopes lie with a mutually sustaining cooperation between women that characterizes Anglo-American feminist thinking at the end of the twentieth century much more than at its beginning, when the novel is set. Despite its time span, and white American women's battles for suffrage coming to fruition in 1920, there is little sense of wider political struggles. *Copper Crown* is not a historical novel, but it is historically sensitive to its setting and to its time of production. Von Herzen purposefully chooses a period in Texas's history when interracial violence peaked and a time when, on the world stage, war colored views of history. She does not, as Welty did in *Delta Wedding,* deliberately choose as a backdrop to her explorations of domestic life a point in a state's history when few specific internecine conflicts are recorded.[21] If the relationship between Cass and Allie seems anachronistic, largely peaceful and reciprocal in the midst of violence and hatred, this is the very point from which the reader begins to question the wider effects of von Herzen's exploration of the potential for interracial harmony.

✍ The cross-racial friendship between Cass Sandstrom and Allie Farrell is the *focus* of the narrative and the location of its impetus and hope. Cass and Allie grow up together, and they leave the small fictional town of Copper Crown together in 1914, after a series of rapes, murders, and lynchings—white on black violence leading to bitter retaliations—destroys their relatively stable biracial community. They are only fifteen years old. They head out on the open road and begin to establish a new and much smaller community, sequestered in the backwoods many miles from their childhood home, in a manner that goes some way toward imagining Lillian Smith's and Adrienne Rich's ideas of "disloyalty to civilization" and Louise Westling's idea of "renegades from civilization."[22] The community that slowly evolves rests upon the nurturing reciprocity of its founders, and the friendship between the two girls persists once they reach womanhood and, the reader is given to understand, will endure even beyond death. The ghosts of Copper Crown follow the girls into the woods: Oloe, Cass's sister, killed by the black men who raped her, one of whom was Allie's own brother; Lily Mark, Cass's cousin who died in childbirth and whose child, Ruby, is being brought up by Cass and Allie. More ghosts follow—white and black, men as well as women; some of those left alive after the racist inferno also arrive, like Allie's sister-in-law Maggie, the wife of Allie's dead brother Clyde, and her son, whose father was a white rapist. It was this violent act against Maggie that unleashed the storm of hatred that consumed a town.

Leaving Copper Crown does not extricate the girls from the pressures of male violence. They begin working for Skeet, who in his racism ignores Allie but whose feelings for Cass fester until they are made manifest in an attempt to rape her. In a scene reminiscent of Dessa's saving Rufel from rape in Williams's *Dessa Rose,* Allie prevents the rape, and in the struggle, during which the women defend themselves, Skeet dies. After his death the women take over the running of his restaurant, having pooled all their savings to buy it in auction. Allie's culinary skills provide the economic base for the two women's new start. They follow the scripts of femininity—domesticity, household skills—but they make them pay: their homeplace is, as Helen Fiddyment Levy defines, "an ideal pastoral domestic setting,"[23] but theirs is a segregated restaurant, for white diners only. This fact, among others, cuts right against the prevailing vision of harmony in a utopian haven where even the dead and the living inhabit the same temporal plane.[24]

For von Herzen it is imperative to find a place where a cross-racial friendship may be sustained, as well as a context in which to prove that it would have been subject to social disapprobation. This tension is central to the novel but ultimately pulls it apart. Von Herzen provides a vision of sisterhood, but the imperfections and injustices of the Copper Crown community are ultimately the more enduring: the passages that describe them are much more memorable than the descriptions of the community the women subsequently create, despite the lyrical reveries on landscape. The novel is, after all, named after the town that forms the women. The restaurant at 137 Halliday Road, Victoria County, remains otherwise unnamed and hence retains an ethereal quality and utopian nonspecificity. An enduring and unassailable sisterhood and community remains within the province of hope but unrealized except in the imaginary world of the novel's final pages.

At the beginning of the novel, von Herzen establishes a version of rural Texas grounded in a sense of female culture continuing into perpetuity in a novel dedicated to mothers across four generations of her own family, "borne by Texas and bearing her again." She configures this symbolically throughout, in terms of the significance attached to the soil, the land cultivated by Cass and loved by all members of the community.[25] In *Copper Crown* the existence of a female culture relies intrinsically on the diverse domestic talents of the women involved: Oloe displays precious skills as a seamstress; Allie, with her culinary prowess, creates sumptuously ambrosial meals from the purest of natural ingredients; and Cass cultivates the land. It is a regenerative landscape. She plants the forest that surrounds their communal home, and her prodigious talent is described as the ability to "bury a jewelweed and coax it to come up a peach tree" (101).[26] The women's talents are inherited from their mothers, passed on as Allie's mother passes to her daughter the recipe books she borrows from the kitchen of the Jensen plantation, where she works. As the girls inherit the skills of the mothers, the generations combine in a facility to see Texas's past and to prepare for its future.[27]

The woman-centered inclusivity the novel reflects a consciousness about issues of equality in diversity that have increasingly prevailed as an area of feminist exchange and speculation since civil rights legislation and the sociopolitical gains of the 1960s. *Copper Crown* attempts to negotiate issues of sameness and difference in relationships in a way that is inherently bucolic and hopeful. Consequently, a most important consideration is whether Lane von Herzen inevitably produces a "sentimental" community and/or one that could be read as "constitutive," to employ Michael Sandel's typology.[28] The group that gathers to celebrate Cass's birthday and to comfort her at her impending death at the very end of the novel does so in a spirit that claims unreal as well as utopian connections and coalitions, despite racist and sexual violence, anger and jealousy, and death. Each of these factors is becalmed and ultimately refocused into a spiritually nurturing context in which lessons have been learned and transgressions forgiven.

In order for the community to be read as constitutive, it must be viewed as a possible and viable alternative to individual rancor and desire, on the one hand, and to the dominant and established practices of the larger community from which it sets itself apart, on the other. Communitarian ideals thus prompt an expression of utopianism in the novel, but it remains doubtful that utopianism might activate social change. That the community is secluded and sequestered in a rural enclave behind a high wall, away from the social turmoil that has characterized the first third of the novel, demonstrates its fragility. This romanticized rural community lies outside of institutional and political practices and thus cannot be considered other than historically untenable and unsustainable, even within the symbolic economy of the novel. So what von Herzen most successfully creates is an ecofeminist fantasy, a dream world.

Copper Crown ends with Cass peacefully preparing for her death, with the living and the spirits standing quietly by, encircling her as she listens to "the sound of peace in the trees" (239). The vision is of communal love in an unspoiled natural setting. Hope through sisterhood as evoked in the novel is the most important foundation upon which this community—and indeed the novel's success or failure—rests. Too much is invested in a single problematic relationship, however, since it is intended to carry the utopian impetus across the entire narrative. Von Herzen explores her black and white women characters' ability to recognize what is different in their social circumstances and their ability to see each other for who they really are, in the context of southern race relations.[29] However, the problems Cass and Allie encounter in their friendship are never resolved. The novel posits a model of mediation for the two women, but its working out stops short when the emphasis changes to a wider community of friends.

Von Herzen's community gains its power in the mind of the reader who has what Iris Marion Young has called "the ideal of community" at the center of a reading that rests on an illusion of coherence and cooperation but eschews the foundation of the communitarian ideal: the family. Young has warned feminists that communitarian ideas involve their own prescriptive roles for women within the institutions of family and home, as well as in a wider social realm. But in *Copper Crown* family units have been destroyed and individuals come together to renegotiate alliances out of their society's failures. This highly imaginative coming together precludes the potential to be socially as well as personally transformative, since its impetus can only be derivative of the central crossracial friendship between Cass and Allie. The concept of sisterhood, according to Elizabeth Fox-Genovese, "has given form to a dream" for genuine equality and harmony between women;[30] but it is a dream that many black and white working-class feminists have mocked, as a result of the exclusion black women have suffered, generally and historically, from white, middle-class feminist movements.

In her study of utopian fictions of the 1970s, Angelika Bammer notes that issues of race and class were excluded or remained peripheral in "what passed as feminist utopianism." She goes on to argue that fictions of the 1980s (and, significantly, Bammer singles out novels by American "women of color") involve what she calls an "anticipatory pragmatism": "a stance that is able to accommodate the vagaries of change because it thinks of change in concrete and practical terms, a utopianism in which the intense focus on the here and now draws the future (and the past) into the radius of its gaze."[31] Writing in 1991, von Herzen may be said to *approach* the trajectory of Bammer's line of thought and to create a novel that may be read against a developing genre of feminist utopias, but not unequivocally so.[32] Von Herzen draws on the past in her representation of an ideal polity that might inform the future of feminism, in the way that Alice Walker's formulation of the ideal of womanism, as yet only tentatively taken up by others, might open the philosophical gates to a more inclusive communitarian feminism.[33] She draws on the sense of impending crisis that drives environmentalists back to the land, but she goes only so far, since setting provides a haven, little more. If *Copper Crown* can be described as a feminist utopian fiction, it should be understood to begin to involve and welcome social development, rather than foreclose change in its own state of static perfection. Ultimately, the novel cannot stretch this far. For Bammer, the utopian is based on "people's longing for a more just and human world" founded on "their belief that such a change is possible, and their willingness to act as a basis of that belief."[34] Allie and Cass come closest to this when they acknowledge that the plantation Allie inherits should be owned by the black people who worked it for so long.[35] They translate this idea into action, and in this context principles become praxis.

The space between utopian rhetoric and feminist polemics proves a difficult space to negotiate in story; characters and episodes function as highly symbolic examples of a community-in-the-making. Von Herzen does not choose to confront the implications of a community in which men and women might form egalitarian relationships; men are not excluded, but, somewhat suspiciously, they are old or dead or *remarkably* peaceable. Lloyd, Maggie's son, is positively beatific; Humberto is an old man "too wise to take an anger to him for permanent" (90), while the spirit of Cass's grandfather is shy and gentle. The shift from cross-racial violence to gentle rustic peace is seductive but cannot reconcile the fact that social unrest still exists. The character of Warren, Allie's husband, is significant here. Warren remains angry about the cards society has dealt him and is unwilling to keep the peace for the sake of a status quo. Once murdered, he is not reclaimed as a member of the world of the spirits who, together with the living, have place within the new community that is forming. Warren has bequeathed his anger to Allie, who continues to feel that the racism at the heart of their bucolic world has yet to be addressed. What defies *Copper Crown*'s peaceful community is its inability to address what has deferred its unity.

The call for inclusivity in feminist enterprises has been confounded by problems of "speaking for others," to use the phrase that Linda Alcoff employs for speaking another's reality.[36] Von Herzen shows the terrible and tragic consequences of Oloe's and Maggie's silences in the text through the ways in which the patriarchal ideology of white womanhood denies Oloe a voice and the violence of race hatred forces Maggie to stay silent after she is gang raped. But she fails to work issues of silence and appropriation through so clearly with regard to the central relationship between Cass and Allie.

Oloe, Cass's older sister, lives at the Jensen plantation, where she works as a seamstress. The owner, her uncle, uses her as a tool through which he may gain a pretext to chastise his black male workers for supposedly slacking in their work. When he alleges that one man, Carlyle, was looking at his niece like "something fresh for his eyes to get a hold of" (46), Oloe knows he is wrong, but she does not speak out; she is afraid, and Carlyle is punished. Maggie is paired with Oloe at this juncture to play out the white South's double standard, which "presumed it the white woman's duty to preserve the purity of the race, while it gave white men free license to insult and assault black women."[37] Maggie is beautiful by everyone's standards, and as a result she is brutally raped. A gang of Jensen's white workers, whose insults she has bravely fought off for some time, "take" her "with a hate that made their hands tremble" (64). Maggie too remains silent, even after she discovers she is pregnant: "Maggie knew if she had told any of it to Clyde, he would've lost his life in the madness that was likely to take hold. So she kept her crying at the inside" (65). When baby Lloyd is born white, "not a mark of Clyde on him" (63), Clyde and Carlyle seek revenge and find it in the person of Oloe, through whom they know they can hurt Jensen. What begins as one rape for another ends in Oloe's death, since the men know that "black touching white was the same as setting rope for the hang" (66). White male power and the black men's revenge are inscribed on the bodies of the two women, black and white, and in the violence and lynchings that follow, all black men in Copper Crown from the age of fifteen to thirty-five are hanged. Seventeen men, fathers and sons, die: "People were saying that colored men would be laying down white women everywhere without a lesson to teach their kind different" (69).

Von Herzen re-creates the kind of circumstances that brought the Association of Southern Women for the Prevention of Lynching movement into being in 1930. Jessie Daniel Ames, the association's founder, a Texan crusader against lynching and mob violence, mobilized white southern women in an effort to break the silence of those like Oloe in this novel.[38] Southern society's claims on Oloe's youth and femininity in the name of "the chivalry of lynching," as Lillian Smith termed white men's "race-economic exploitation," are carefully wrought.[39] White men like her uncle can deny Oloe a voice, when all that is necessary is her physical presence to allow Jensen to exert his power over his black workers and allow her a voice if it is to cry the names of her black attackers, so that they may be publicly punished, within the law or outside of it.[40] Oloe's tragedy is finally the result of racial codes that entrap her, inflame others, and precipitate the spiraling repercussions of Uncle Jensen's sadistic power. Maggie, whose abused body is black, will remain unheard should she cry for legal redress. She can, however, prove a useful scapegoat for both communities in Copper Crown in their efforts to nullify the pain and the blame and the guilt in which they are all embroiled: "All the killings that came after on were God's judgment for a single Jezebel. Whites and coloreds the same said her soul was too dirty to rest your eyes on. Little children, taught by their mamas, threw stones at her when she walked the town" (98). Black and white are ironically brought together in their shared condemnation of this "dirty" woman whose job it is, ironically, to work at Olsen's laundry and wash the dirty linen of the whole town.[41]

Reading Maggie and Oloe is crucial to any understanding of how race and class affect sex and power when they are combined with violence in this novel. As Eve Kosofsky Sedgwick has explained the issue in her discussion of the representation of rape and sexuality in *Gone with the*

Wind: "It is of serious political importance that our tools for examining the signifying relation [of sex and power] be subtle and discriminate ones, and that our literary knowledge of the most crabbed or oblique paths of meaning not be oversimplified in the face of panic-inducing images of real violence, especially the violence of, around, and to sexuality."[42] In Margaret Mitchell's novel a black shantytown settlement is wiped out in much the same circumstances that von Herzen replays in *Copper Crown.* Scarlett is assaulted by a black man and a white man who seek to rob her of her purse, not to rape her, but the incident is retold as an attempted rape by a black man with no reference to his accomplice. The Ku Klux Klan and Rhett Butler alike act to punish the whole black community. Mitchell raises the issue of sexuality and its relation to race, and her playing the incident out shows that the absence of a rape makes no difference to the repercussions upon the shantytown settlement. The incident provides a significant commentary on the mores of the society Mitchell creates; the issue of Scarlett's responsibility for crying rape leads to the deaths of both black and white men and is a crucial element in any reading of the incident. In *Copper Crown* the dialectical relationship between sexuality and the violence that is meted out according to the southern rape complex and a southern race plot is the controlling ideology that underpins the entire plot. The counterpointing of Oloe and Maggie is effectively patterned into the novel, and the similarities and differences in their experiences are astutely and powerfully described. But the ambiguities of the novel come to the fore in the pairing of Cass and Allie.

As in *Ellen Foster,* Cass's emotions dominate any reading of the friendship through her first-person narration. Allie's words are reproduced in Cass's narration early in the novel when she recounts the history of her family, and her opinions often guide Cass and inform the narrative line. But it is Cass's voice that carries the tale. The first-person narrative form acts to impose a grid on a novel by excluding the black character from narrative agency much more than does the third-person form Ellen Douglas chooses to tell of her interracial friendship in *Can't Quit You Baby.* So, on the one hand, von Herzen's narrative strategies open up possibilities by subverting aspects of realism—employing pastoral mythical settings in which people are balanced with nature to landscape the backdrop for her interracial friendship—but, on the other hand, she closes down the possibility of reciprocity in the narrative form itself, schematizing the friendship through racial codes.

Cass speaks for Allie and refuses to see Allie's reality except as her friend and her boon companion—her ally—and it is with Cass's ability to see, to discern, that von Herzen concerns herself. Significantly, the preliminary reference to Allie from the narrator, Cass, is that from a distance she does not "look colored" (9). This reference to her mixed racial heritage is accompanied by an intimate description of Allie that compares with a lover describing the loved one, as in the biblical Song of Solomon; it focuses on her hair, her bosom, her skin, and her breathing. It implies the underlying fantasized intimacy between black and white inherent within southern culture, but it also demonstrates von Herzen's propensity to overdramatize the relationship, dressing it up with imagery and symbolism.[43] The description is followed by a much more uncharacteristic, because concrete and matter-of-fact, conversation between the two fifteen-year-old friends that bespeaks their visibly different social positions in Texas in 1913. Allie offers to cook at Cass's wedding, whenever she may choose to marry, "seeing as how I won't get invited no other way." Cass, in turn, denies she would omit to invite her should the situation ever occur, although "me and her both knew that colored girls didn't get invitations to the weddings of white girls. At least not in Copper Crown, even if they did somewhere else" (10). A situation that might reasonably apply in the girls' lives is mooted lightheartedly, and Cass chooses to focus on the strength of their friendship rather than allow Allie's pragmatism to hold sway.

The narrator's initial observation that Allie may not *appear* black, coupled with the underlying recognition of their intrinsically different experiences, foreshadows the complex balance of oppositions that Cass will gradually come to reconcile with regard to how she "sees" Allie. Allie too is forced to explore such oppositions in terms of her own comprehension of Cass as a white woman, with the distance that bespeaks, and as a sister, with the closeness that entails. Janice Raymond ponders the complex balancing act inherent in many women's friendships when she calls for an informed inclusivity: "We cannot blur the distinctiveness of victimization by race or class or anything else, thereby rejecting political and moral responsibility for the consequences of these distinctly different oppressive conditions of many women's lives. Yet, by the same token, we cannot allow these distinctive differences to erase or extinguish our commonality as women who are oppressed as women and who bond as women."[44] Von Herzen examines the commonalities that these two women share and simultaneously acknowledges the differences that frequently create obstacles to reciprocally supportive connections between women of their backgrounds. However, she does so through Cass, a character who actively seeks to blur what distinguishes herself from her friend. Ellen Foster accepted her learned superiority over her friend until very late in Gibbons's novel, with Ellen's regrets manifesting only in a very partial reconciliation with her friend. Von Herzen has Cass ignore the issue of difference for most of this novel too. In her desire for friendship and community, she puts aside what is irreconcilable about the differences in her own and Allie's lives, despite what has happened to Oloe and Maggie. The comradeship Cass desires is not unproblematically attainable, and in her recounting of events, von Herzen often has Cass unconsciously accept the racial segregation that divides the girls.

Initially, Cass and Allie's divergent positions are indexed quite literally by the separate paths they are set to follow; visiting the Jensen plantation to see Allie's mother working in the kitchen and Cass's sister living in the main house, Cass "took the path to the front door and Allie took the path to the back" (25). By the end of the novel's first section, though, in the aftermath of the violence and hatred that ricochets around Copper Crown, they find themselves "walking away to the same direction" for similar reasons (71). Each of their families, black and white, has been decimated. Allie's mother is dead, and Cass's father's part in the lynchings, and her cousin Lily Mark's death in childbirth, have broken apart her family, leading her to leave Copper Crown at her distraught mother's behest. So the coming together of Cass and Allie on Valley Road is nei-ther simple nor celebratory. They come together in sorrow and adver-sity, and their convergence coincides with their passing through the "Valley of Death" (72), the first time that they see the spirits of the dead following in their steps. The ghosts of Copper Crown are not buried, but remain syncretically present in the way that they project their meaning forward. The circumstances that dictated their deaths have been ad-dressed neither by the girls themselves nor by the community they leave behind; nor can they be adequately buried. The jagged and painful past continues to haunt the southern landscape, and it impinges on the friendship that is the focus of the novel's concerns.

Cass and Allie derive a sense of commonality, both specious and real, from their identification with Copper Crown—the codes and conven-tions that dictate their differences, as well as the town's history—and with each other's histories from their early years. This idea of common-ality is primarily constructed through the first-person narrator, however, and through Cass's declaration that "we all of us [she includes young Ruby] had been shaped by the same life, I guess, and the sameness showed" (182). Her bid to focus on what is the same about herself and her friend is (over?) reinforced by the text functioning as a "socially sym-bolic act," in Fredric Jameson's terms, and this feature draws on elements of what I call the ecofeminist romance. For example, both women are colored copper by a "red-dun dust" for nearly two days on the road and "couldn't decide whether we'd lost our colors or found them for true" (78); and when they have their photograph taken, their sepia skins make it seem that "we might have been related," because they are "the same aching yellow shade as the earth" (182). The young women are in fact cousins, as they discover when the identification of Allie's white father as Cass's Uncle Jensen is uncovered, but von Herzen pursues a common-ality that is essentially human and natural (nature-given) rather than strictly familial, and she risks pushing it too far.

In her reliance on nature and the positive and democratizing proper-ties of the environment, she has a tendency to employ pathetic fallacy, anthropomorphism, and heightened symbolism in all its devices; consequently, a relationship otherwise so carefully described risks abstraction. In one of the many visual vignettes of the novel in which nature is reflective of human feeling, the two silver saplings that Cass and Allie plant braid together, their arms clasping one another as a mark of the friendship wherein the two women's lives are enmeshed. The narrator begins early with her repeated "me and Allie," intertwining their lives and presenting them as encircling each other at every turn: "She put her arm circled around my back" (100). Consequently, the lexical level of the text is reinforced at the level of the symbolic to the extent that von Herzen risks overemphasis and sentimentality. She patterns their connectedness deep into the story, so deep that while the lyrical, natural descriptions and unfettered romance may cradle the reader during the act of reading, it is impossible not to be aware of their intrinsic function to trace the threads by which the author braids Cass and Allie's lives and seals their connection.

The literary device of doubling supports the symbolic meaning of Cass and Allie's relationship. It is this feature of the text that posits the novel as a model of mediation that might act as a starting point for a more developed understanding of the factors that determine any cross-racial accord in difficult and violent times. It is Allie, whose job it is to clean, who steps in for Cass in Skeet's kitchen, and who cooks the meals that fill his restaurant with satisfied customers. Each night he stands at the back of the kitchen speaking love and lusting after the figure he believes is Cass, until one day his lust leads him to reach out, and he finds himself touching a black woman: "When he saw her, really saw her— saw the dark stones of her eyes, the curl-wisps of her hair, the thick trembling at her lips—he dropped her as suddenly as if she was the devil wrapped up in a woman's form" (111). Unable to tell the white woman from the black, he punishes them both: Allie by substituting lye for soap so that when she starts cleaning her black skin is burned and blistered; Cass with the rape that results in his own death. Depicting and mediating their relationship according to what may appear similar in their circumstances provides a place in the novel from which they might begin to start really understanding each other. But the narrative progresses so that the differences between the women friends, which they have failed to address, become all the more marked and difficult to reconcile after having been buried for so long.

𝒮♥ In many ways von Herzen sets up a perfect friendship in order to unbalance it. The conditions for a shared understanding between Cass and Allie have been carefully concocted via Cass's configurations of sameness in their experiences. But in her idealization of the friendship, Cass's need for a friend allows her to accept an incomplete picture of Allie's reality. The friendship breaks down. Whether this is melodramatic or owes more to an exploratory exposé of Cass's unquestioning idealism and Allie's silence is not entirely clear. The section of the novel in which the threads that have bound them are unpicked begins interestingly, but by the end the utopian fervor that impelled the depiction and direction of the relationship has reignited. It is surely significant that von Herzen does not frame the experiences of Cass and Allie within a social movement. This is one of the reasons that the burgeoning rift that separates them, following the racist murder of Allie's husband, Warren, is so shocking to them. Apparently beyond the pale of many wider social interactions since leaving Copper Crown, they have consciously or unconsciously evaded recognition of many of the sociopolitical forces that operate to divide them, despite their apparent unity: "The two of us, we were so kind one to another for so many years, and then it seemed like all the kindness just dried up and blew away overnight. Seemed her preferences turned coloreder and my preferences turned whiter, and all we could do was gape at the skin on the other one like it was the worst surprise we ever got. How could we have not seen how God had made us so different from the get-go?" (197). Cass asserts that the basis of their separation after a lifelong friendship is not prejudice but "personal" (197), but her sudden recognition of the meaning of their different racial origins in this society echoes Skeet's shock at confounding a black woman with a white woman.

Once hurt, Cass too falls into musing on what Mark Snyder has called "self-fulfilling stereotypes," whereby she believes that race determines and constrains behavior.[45] She searches for some way of justifying the rift between them and opts for a theory constructed out of racial difference in an effort to avoid examining her own behavior toward her friend. Cass reaches for the quickest and easiest reference point for her feelings, and in denying Allie's pain after her husband is murdered, she denies her own humanity and friendship in her self-involvement. This is played out in the manner in which Cass mourns and misses Allie on returning to Copper Crown, when Allie, in an uncustomary peroration against her friend's blindness to her grief, asks her to leave. Cass moons around the house hearing Allie's voice, just as in *Can't Quit You Baby* Cornelia "hears" Tweet. But Tweet comforts and sustains Cornelia as she wanders New York at the very juncture in her life when she most needs to find a way to strengthen her resolve to live, whereas Cass tries "to be deaf" to Allie, returning her letters, but worrying that Allie "doesn't care for me any more." Her reaction to all these feelings resembles that of a jilted lover more than a rejected friend:

> So I tried to get shut of my caring for her, too. I tried to pass an entire day without me thinking on her, and there were a couple of times when I almost did it. I left all my pictures of her and me back at the restaurant, so that I wouldn't have to be looking on them to jar my remembrance. But still in my mind I knew all the pictures that were ever taken with us two in them— some of them with Ruby too—and they stood up in front of my eyes when I woke in the morning and then through the rest of the day. (p.197)

It is, therefore, possible to detect an erotic romanticism in this codification of a woman-identified relationship that is intensely quixotic and fanciful but which is also incredibly selfish on Cass's part. When Cass evades Allie's grief for Warren, she does so in the unstated hope that their own relationship will replenish Allie, since she will be entirely free to devote all of her time to it. She has felt excluded, relegated to the farthest point of a triangle in which she perceives the three of them are contained. In one scene the choreography is such that Cass silently and jealously watches and listens as Warren encircles Allie in his arms. He stares meaningfully over her head at Cass while trying to persuade Allie to buy Cass out of the restaurant. Cass excludes herself from their sympathy, jealous of the closeness they have found but also silent on the issue that holds meaning for them: that neither Warren nor Allie, nor their black friends, can eat in their own restaurant. Cass not only negates the full import of Allie and Warren's love but also the reasons he died, the political and personal reality of race hatred and racial violence. Warren is killed for having accidentally injured a white man at work. Cass's inability to see or understand this is reflected in her oversimplification of the situation, "I guess she forgot that Warren had been a man with plain limits," and it was "like she was nursing some private anger that nobody else could taste" (190).

Cass measures all situations as "personal," as if they stand outside of wider social discourse. She feels shut out, first from the marriage and second from the mourning of its passing. Her silence over the injustice of Warren's death and the fact that his murderers could be the very white men Allie cooks for and Cass serves at table quietly evokes the way that white women's silences frequently undermine black and cross-racial communal struggles. Cass's silence, and Allie's own for much of the time, about the segregation they practice in their restaurant, in an effort, it is to be supposed, to maintain its economic viability, is perhaps most pertinently described by Lillian Smith in a speech in 1957: "We were taught, in the South from early childhood, never to speak up against segregation. Now, when we do so, we feel anxious; we fear we may be wrong; our judgment may be bad. . . . certainly we'll lose our usefulness. So we grow anxious; we become hysterically mute. Most of our moderation is nothing but mutism."[46] Cass has never taken the time to consider any other way of interpreting her own life and the lives of those around her. The unpleasant realities and inequalities of southern life in a small town made Allie and Cass "so different from the get-go," but although the quotidian persistence of these factors may be left behind when they leave Copper Crown, the realities themselves cannot be escaped. Racism, fear, and social inequities follow them into the woods.

𝒮♥ Von Herzen explores the extent to which the claim to sisterhood and the vision of its success can be realized in this fiction. When Melissa

Walker reads the story of another interracial relationship, Sherley Anne Williams's *Dessa Rose,* she sees Dessa and Rufel as "a metaphor for the integration of society on a personal level."[47] It is of course possible to interpret the African American writer's novel in this way, but Williams's epilogue tells us quite markedly that Dessa went West as Rufel went East. Ultimately they separate, and any integration remains at the level of the imagination, as discussed in the Introduction to this book. When Allie can no longer stand coexisting with Cass, who cannot be her equal in sorrow or anger, she says, "You got to go your own way for awhile and it's got to be a separate way from mine" (191). In the American South the personal will always be confounded by the social, by slavery and segregation, in texts that take as their settings northern Alabama in the 1840s, in *Dessa Rose,* and Texas in the early twentieth century, as does *Copper Crown.* Von Herzen, finally, has Cass begin to address what is personally political in her painful split with Allie. Inherent within her confession is her overwhelming desire for the dream of egalitarian harmony in sisterhood that ultimately remains a vision, and that has both overwhelmed her ability to see the differences in her own and Allie's lives and prevented her from seeing what Allie shared with Warren:

> Even though I didn't want Warren hurt, I was hurting him all the while
> in my mind—turning him into a nothing, a nobody, an absence. I wanted
> things to be like they were before he ever came—when you and me and
> Ruby didn't know any divisions amongst us, when we didn't know any hurt
> or spite from each other that couldn't be mended with a laugh. And to my
> mind Warren was always putting himself in the way—always bringing up
> differences where I wanted there to be sameness, always bringing up injuries
> where I wanted there to be healings. (230)

Any vision of harmony between the protagonists comes at a price. For Cass to simplistically conflate her own and Allie's experiences, and to universalize them as indivisibly women's experiences, delimits woman as generic and abrogates the distinct subjectivities of both the women involved. Cass here functions to indicate the dangers of an incomplete vision of sisterhood in the way that Audre Lorde and Janice Raymond have warned: "There is a pretense to a homogeneity of experience covered by the word sisterhood that does not in fact exist."[48] A reading of *Copper Crown* as an example of eco-utopianism must rest on the ways in which von Herzen envisions and represents Cass's and Allie's relationship, through the initial visualization and "naturalization" of their sameness and the gradual, cumulative shift toward an emphasis on the differences between them, with their finally finding hope in their continued connectedness. Von Herzen imposes an apparent coherence upon their relationship by reiterating their sameness through the first two-thirds of the novel, drawing the women into alignment both physically and mentally against a rural backdrop. Elizabeth Abel considers this issue in terms of a young girl's choosing a "best friend" as "an extension of the girl's own ego, identical with her in respect to age, interests, and desires" in order to feel "doubled" and strengthened.[49] The strains of initiating and maintaining a relationship on these terms are emphasized in this novel. When young, Cass and Allie do tend to replicate one another's concerns, but this "doubling" is increasingly complicated by their unequal experiences as they grow older, and by Allie's displacement to secondary status via Cass's narration.

The tendency in fictions for the narrator to construct her friend as an alter ego can engulf or subsume the identity and the experiences of the friend. We have seen this at work most specifically in *Ellen Foster* through the monologue Gibbons deploys. In *Copper Crown* Allie is not silenced, but she is *conveyed* almost entirely through Cass's narration. Only on one occasion is Allie's voice heard for a sustained period: in the one short italicized section separated from the dominant narration, when she relates the story of her brother and sister-in-law's courtship and love (49–52). This story is enfolded within the text and contained within Cass's own memories of her own development, so that the novel's hermeneutic code remains predominantly that of a white woman's experience. In *Can't Quit You Baby* a self-conscious narrator exposes the dynamics and problematizes the friendship, but in *Copper Crown* the reader picks her way through the circumstances that dictate the dynamics of the friendship and is caught out of step when the issue of community overtakes the story of the friendship. The development of a new community out of the fragments of another comes about directly because of the success of the two women; their close cooperation has been crucial in its formation. The house at 137 Halliday Road is not a consciously chosen society but the result of a succession of circumstances: the girls leaving Copper Crown, Skeet's death, their subsequent taking over of the restaurant, the successful application of their skills to make the restaurant thrive. Each of these circumstances relates directly to the two characters in this novel who determine the future after Copper Crown. Cass and Allie's friendship is the model for a community that seeks to reconcile itself to a bitter and feuding past in the hope of a more harmonious future in the rural South. That community's resilience is called into doubt, however, when any clear resolution to problems that continue to beset the women is withheld.

In novels about heterosexual women's friendships, it is quite usual that the marriage of one of the pair proves a significant factor in eliciting change in the friendship. In Toni Morrison's *Sula,* a novel in which the highs and lows of female friendship are explored, Sula has an affair with her friend Nel's husband which, even as it breaks up the marriage, forces Nel to review the inextricability of her connection with her friend.[50] In *Copper Crown* it is Allie's marriage to Warren that seals her difference from Cass. Cass prefers to ignore Allie and Warren's marriage. She observes warily how they are together, and Warren perceives the challenge embodied in Cass's possessiveness, but Allie believes that both relationships can coexist in her life. She is always openly accepting of Cass's relationship with Ruby: Cass is, after all, in the position of a virgin mother, never having consummated her relationship with Murray, her childhood sweetheart, and raising his and Lily Mark's daughter, Ruby, as her own. Allie stretches to understand her friend's motherly role, but Cass, never having experienced the romantic love that Allie and Warren share, cannot finally surmount this difference. It overrides their commonality.

The two women's social experiences are inscribed as racially different, the "whites only" restaurant a reminder of the anomalous position Allie finds herself in every day, but their emotional axes are also differently formed, with Allie balancing her love for her female "family" with love for her husband, while Cass invests all her emotion in women. Warren sees Allie as exceptional, as singular and independent of her connection with Cass. He serves to magnify Allie's otherness for Cass and to clarify Allie's reinvestment in, and affirmation of, what is specifically black about her experience; she reopens the restaurant for black people and cuts her "prices down to where all of them could pay" (213). Warren's partnership with Allie and his consequent positioning in the iconography of the text interrupts the sequence of doubling that has reinforced pairs of women in relation to each other for most of the novel.

Ultimately, Lane von Herzen creates an uneasy equipoise between Cass and Allie in *Copper Crown*. The uneasiness comes about when a friendship that is broken is retrieved in the face of Cass's early death at thirty-four, and Allie, together with her sister-in-law Maggie, become Cass's nurses. The two black women tend to Cass in her last days. This points up for the reader that Allie has ever been Cass's carer and protector; she stands in for her at the restaurant, cooking the meals that Cass had been employed to cook, to earn enough to keep the two of them and little Ruby; she saves her from Skeet's assault; and she protects Cass from her anger by sending her away from Halliday Road. Through Cass's fatal illness von Herzen waives a period in which the women, as members of a wider community, might resolve issues that have divided them. Instead, there is a short and simple apology for all that has gone before, in which both women address their jealousy of each other but neither discusses the effects of race politics and violence on their lives. So much is left unsaid and unaddressed about the women's relationship that the novel almost becomes a failed love story in the typical American tradition. It is a story in which failures and society's fault lines are left largely unarticulated and unexplored. Cass is made ready for the party at which she presides over those of the novel's characters who have been brought together to form the new and secret ("It was a shame that none of the world knew we were here," p. 239) interracial, intergenerational community of the living and the dead. Their faith and forgiveness have empowered the author's vision of harmony, but their cohesion is not to be put to the tests of the outside world.

Having combined eco-utopian dreams with ghost story, *Copper Crown* is finally expressly antirealist, despite its attention to dates and the connotations of setting. Primarily, it is a romance with sentimental themes, and, consequently, von Herzen need not resolve apparent contradictions of form and content. The alliance of the supernatural with the historiographical has become of itself a genre popular with contemporary American women writers, who create versions of the past as they project forward with hopes and visions of the future. Von Herzen's moral and ethical vision in *Copper Crown* fuses feminism and environmentalism with an exploration of racism, but the lyricism finally overbalances issues of polity. *Copper Crown* has a happy, hopeful ending that involves a partial resolution of difficulties in the microcosmic model of a friendship where differences cannot be transcended but must be take into account. A charming magical story, it posits such ideas via a central interracial friendship that still leaves much unsaid and it overreaches itself in its desires for community on this basis alone.

CHAPTER FOUR

Across the Kitchen Table

Establishing the Dynamics of

Interracial Friendship

Literary representations of relationships between white employers and black domestics endure beyond the historical point
by which the connection was no longer emblematic of the
power structures of segregated race relations. Jeanne Noble
claims that the image of the black domestic, whose color immediately encodes status for the white family that employs her,
is "woven into the very fabric of America, especially in the
South where the role was perfected." Patricia A. Turner asserts
that "successful civil rights protests of the late 1950s and early
1960s liberated black women not only from the backs of buses
but also from the white kitchens." [1] Though statistics may bear
out Turner's view, it seems to me that black women characters

have not yet been liberated from the kitchens of white women in contemporary fiction. This is not to imply that all white women writers are naively unconscious of the historical complexities of black and white women's relationships or that they consign their black women characters only to representation within domestic frameworks, but to note that writers like Ellen Gilchrist have been criticized for reiterating stereotypes of the black maid who takes care of her white mistress. Conservative reiterations of mistress-maid formulations are in danger of seeming little more than racist holdovers from texts like *Gone with the Wind* and Sara Haardt's "Baby Chile."[2] The question is whether the black characters are sealed imperviously within such situations or whether the writers choose to grapple with the cultural hermeneutics that underlie the association.

It would seem difficult to remain uninterrogative, for those aware of women's movements on any level are cognizant of efforts to free them from white solipsism with regard to race and inattention to issues of class. But there remains a tendency for contemporary white writers to consign their black women characters to representation within the kind of domestic relationship that denies them social agency. Fictions by black writers that depict house slaves, black maids, or domestics are often so infused with black militancy, particularly following the civil rights activism of the 1950s and 1960s, that the image of the benign, long-suffering family retainer is turned around. Slightly earlier and outside the South, in Ann Petry's 1946 novel *The Street,* Lutie Johnson's life is ruined as a direct result of her finding work only in white women's kitchens. Her pent-up anger at second-class citizenship and poverty is vented in her killing of the pimp Boots Smith, a member of the Harlem community. The images in her head as she kills him, however, are of the hated white world: "the insult in the moist-eyed glances of white men on the subway . . . the unconcealed hostility in the eyes of white women. . . . she was striking at the white world which thrust black people into a walled enclosure from which there was no escape."[3]

Barbara Woods's "The Final Supper" can be read as an attempt to explicate Petry's metaphor of the walled enclosure historically and to relate it to black militancy. Written out of the context of black activism, it locates the struggle's beginnings in slavery with the earliest fighters for freedom.[4] The story is set close to Richmond, Virginia, in 1800. Rosa Lee poisons the Thanksgiving dinner of the family she cooks for and slits the throat of the master who has abused her and sold her children. She derives no support at all from her white mistress, who, overcome with bitterness at her husband's penchant for slave women, blames Rosa for his behavior. In a story set against the slave rebellion of 1800 led by Gabriel Prosser, Nanny, Prosser's wife, is slit from throat to stomach by white vigilantes. The narrative is trammeled with violence.[5] Woods's depiction of a resistant slave woman many years before abolition has been followed by depictions of maids and domestics in the twentieth century still flying in the face of white containment. Alice Walker's Sofia in *The Color Purple,* set in Georgia chiefly in the years between the two world wars, is a woman who resists oppression, whatever its source; she escapes abuse from the males of her family and brooks no attempt from her husband, Harpo, to make her "mind" by using his fists: "I'll kill him dead before I let him beat me."[6] But it is a white woman's assumption that Sofia would be honored to be her maid and her husband the mayor's slap across Sofia's face when the black woman's answer is most firmly in the negative that precipitates Sofia's physical assault on the mayor and her own demise. Sofia is so badly beaten by police that she is almost unrecognizable physically and mentally. She spends more than a decade in jail and as an enforced maid to the mayor's wife. Walker finds little to distinguish between the severity of the two forms of sentence.

A shift toward recognizing and representing forms of resistance in the behavior of black women working in white homes is not so discernible in white-authored literature, where the modifications to the mammy image and its contemporization tend to affect the *physical* characterization of the domestic. The women who populate the kitchens of white women's texts are no longer embodied as the "mammy" or Aunt Jemima figures that saturated American literature and popular culture. However, as recently as Robert Mulligan's 1988 movie *Clara's Heart,* a young and slim Whoopi Goldberg still resonates with unmistakable connotations of the traditional role.[7] Similarly, in Diane Johnson's novel *The Shadow Knows,* the misshapen and supposedly aggressive Osella, the domestic who was once a mammy, is replaced by the much younger Ev, live-in housekeeper and "ally" of her employer. But the introduction of Ev into the text follows the same recognizable troping of the domestic: "She is humming and scuffing her shoes around the kitchen, meaning she is comfortable and at home. She has a polka-dotted rag tied around her hair; her hair is going back, that's her big worry."[8] This is a novel that investigates the paranoia of the white woman in whose voice such descriptions are narrated, and consequently they can be understood in this framing. There are examples where the protagonist can be seen to lean on the comfort and safety of reading her domestic companion according to the image of a nurturing, reliable, and untroubled black retainer, despite the fact that it is made clear that Ev has considerably more to worry about than the state of her hair. This is a complex novel, but its complexity derives from the presentation of its white protagonist rather than those who surround her in her nightmare of crime and human loss.

It is not primarily with these early post–civil rights examples that my analysis rests in this chapter; more recent fictions exemplify the ways in which the paradigms still operate. Shirley Ann Grau continues to write black and white southern characters, and frequently maids and housekeepers. In her 1985 work *Nine Women,* the domestics are Greek, Guatemalan, and Irish, as well as black southerners, but it is telling that the images that codify the black domestic require and receive the least explication, embodying as they do a shorthand: "a large black woman who presided over greasy black stoves that were never cleaned and large black pots."[9] The woman is almost indistinguishable from her utensils, like Dinah in Stowe's *Uncle Tom's Cabin,* and as swiftly encapsulated as the domestic on television's popular cartoon *Tom and Jerry.* She is recognized by her spreading feet and exasperated tinny voice alone—a stale, clichéd characterization. One white writer, Josephine Humphreys, acknowledges this phenomenon in a more complex manner in her 1984 novel *Dreams of Sleep.* Humphreys's protagonist is a white girl, Iris, living in a predominantly black housing project in Charleston, South Carolina.

Since her own family has broken up, she comes to love and rely on her black neighbor Queen, a domestic. Queen is keenly politicized but described by the third-person narrator in terms of the feet and shoes on *Tom and Jerry*. A possible strategy behind this description becomes clear only when the reader learns that "Iris sees Queen whole, this mattress sinking under Queen's weight, no cartoon but a real, loved, blessed body."[10] Queen's identity is dependent on how she is viewed by the white protagonist, whatever secondary images may intercede upon the viewing. The dominant effect is not of the trope reinscribed but of the *Tom and Jerry* image undergoing critique as an anachronistic index of current attitudes. Any pairing that includes the black woman as domestic runs the gauntlet of a series of images and tropes before their friendship or relationship can be rendered particular.

The novels of Ellen Gilchrist and Anne Tyler span recent decades, and in them black women feature almost exclusively as housekeepers and maids. As early as *A Slipping-Down Life,* with her description of Clotelia, Tyler tries to recast the image of the domestic in particularized ways. Clotelia refuses any affinity with the family she works for. After four years she remains "an indifferent stranger kicking dust puffs with the toe of a cream suede high-heeled boot. Other people would have turned into members of the family by now."[11] She is self-contained and rarely says goodbye when she leaves work at the end of the day. Clotelia refutes any intimate connection with the white home in which she spends her days, usually watching soap operas. No employer/domestic relationship draws her into changing her mind. In Tyler's *The Clock Winder,* also set in the 1960s, Alvareen seems to herald a return to the domestic as grotesque, "a black hulk of a woman in a gay uniform," a caricature of a wayward servant who takes dubiously regular sick days, and with whom her employer will never admit any connection beyond the pragmatically businesslike. Alvareen fades out of the novel—which is primarily an exploration of the Emersons' relationship with their young *white* housekeeper anyway—but only after the narratorial voice has pointed out that "it wasn't just *work* that [Mrs. Emerson] paid Alvareen for, it was her presence in the house, something to drive the echoes away."[12] What exactly echoes in Mrs. Emerson's house is unclear: voices from the past echoing in the silence perhaps, her family having grown and living away for the most of the time, or the clamor with which the voices of 1960s civil rights activists press for change for those like Alvareen, whose presence in the house Mrs. Emerson believes testifies to her own status as a southern lady.

The larger implication is that the maid is her work and that she lives and knows nothing else. The domestic role is just beginning to be critiqued in these two novels by Anne Tyler, but outside of the framework of a key cross-racial friendship between women. Ironically, segregation in southern society had prevented blacks from being able to share the space allotted to whites under Jim Crow, yet all the time black women continued to share that most intimate of white spaces, the home. The domestic was deemed to safely occupy this space, since she was objectified as having no context outside of the family's requirements. In actuality, she was frequently the repository of the family's, and most particularly the mistress of the house's, tragic and personal secrets, as Toni Morrison recognizes in creating Ondine in *Tar Baby,* who lives with the knowledge that her mistress physically abused her young son for years. Anne Tyler explores this idea tangentially in *Searching for Caleb.* Caleb Peck disappears from the wealthy family home in Baltimore in 1912, and the tale is taken up in the 1970s when his elderly brother finally begins to search for him. It is, however, the family's maid, Sulie Boudrault, who has held the key to Caleb's whereabouts through all the intervening years but who is never considered worth questioning until 1973, when a private detective begins to logically follow all the leads in the case. It is assumed that Sulie can have no information of any use outside of her duties as a maid. What Sulie knows becomes her plot function. Tyler declines to critique the matter further, but the novel has drawn attention, through its emphasis on a plot-driven narrative, to the extent to which the maid or domestic is traditionally marginalized in terms of character, plot, and significance, and all but rendered invisible.

The idea seems to be explored more fully in Ellen Gilchrist's *Victory over Japan* via a close relationship between maid and employer. Crystal is conveyed exclusively by her maid, "Miss Crystal's maid name Traceleen, she's talking, she's telling everything she knows."[13] Traceleen knows a lot, and she begins with "the worst thing that ever happened to Miss Crystal" and plots her deterioration into histrionics. Traceleen professes to love Miss Crystal, who "has been as good to me as my own sister." She is entrusted by Miss Crystal, in a psychiatric hospital after a suicide attempt, to tell her story. Despite the fact that she is given the power of interpretation, Traceleen is still inexorably contained within her responsibility to the white family, and to Crystal in particular. References to her own life, to her husband, Mark, or her "auntee Mae," are fleeting and contextualized only in terms of Miss Crystal's needs; as auntee knew the family's past, she knows their present. In remaining the sole port in the stormy lives of "her" white family she exemplifies to a T Trudier Harris's idea of a maid forced to compromise her self in order to exist in this family's world.[14] This is demonstrable not least through the distinctive linguistic system within which Gilchrist keeps her contained, as clichés of ineluctable servitude trip from her tongue and Crystal—"a diamond all these different sides to her"—is reflected without irony with regard to the one side of her that is completely missing: Traceleen shoulders all childcare and domestic burdens. Traceleen is the responsible side of Crystal's character, and since it is Crystal's character that is ultimately disclosed, Traceleen is literally self-effaced; most of the individuality of the character is expunged in her role as interlocutor, interpreting the foibles of the mistress she knows at her intimate best and worst, the southern belle in decline.

These examples may be read as beginning to expose the internecine intensity of the mistress/maid dyad but solely in terms of the position of the white woman being explored and the black woman's function in explicating her. This forms a common pattern across a number of Gilchrist's novels. In *The Annunciation* Lavertis is the maid who becomes Amanda's best friend and ally: "Amanda and Lavertis loved each other from the start."[15] Lavertis, whose name indicates she may be read as a teller of truths, forces her mistress to confront truths in her own life and supports her through stopping drinking and securing a job. But she is supplanted by Kate, the woman Amanda meets on the very day of Lavertis's wedding and who accompanies her as her guest. Kate is white and mirrors the protagonist more nearly in her role as suitable best friend. Lavertis is therefore married out of the role as maid and confidante, but only once she has served her purpose, convincing the reader of Amanda's overall liberal standpoint on issues of race and class. Amanda's character as a southern white lady is again mediated through her black maid. Gilchrist recycles her characters, the white women specifically, as with Rhoda and the whole Manning family saga, and the black maids in terms of their roles if not their names. By *Net of Jewels* Gilchrist's fading belle Rhoda Manning seems no nearer to understanding her own and others' positions within the southern scheme of things than she was in earlier narratives, but in the last twenty pages of a long novel, she is finally precipitated into broaching the politics of gender and race when her maid, Klane Marengo, is put on trial for manslaughter. Rhoda charges off to help Klane, but the help she offers is complicated by guilt at having herself killed a friend's son while driving under the influence of drink and pills. Klane is her opportunity to make amends: "I'll make up for it now. I'll save Klane and that will make up for it"— although she does stop off at a dear friend's for waffles and Mahler on the way.[16] Rhoda does at least demonstrate some sense of the workings of the law in northern Alabama in the 1950s, when she worries that, since Klane is six feet and in Rhoda's view looks fierce and may be a Watusi, "a jury might convict her of anything." Klane hangs herself, and Rhoda's reaction, self-centeredly weak and pitiful as always, is, "What did I think I could do?" She has lost her chance to use Klane to atone for her own mistakes; she loses the opportunity to measure her own humanity according to her treatment of her black domestic.

The tempting conclusion to draw via Gilchrist's work is that no matter how acerbic and ironic she may be in exposing the faded southern belle, the relationship between mistress and maid is formulaic, reiterating that the mistress and slave are obverse images and that the southern lady is secure in oppositional status to the black woman. The relationship foregrounds the merits and demerits of the employer, with the white mistress garnering much of her moral and ethical as well as social status from the existence of the black domestic in her life. Other writers—Ellen Douglas and Kaye Gibbons, for example—do succeed in reconfiguring in ways that refuse to forestall or obviate the complexities that the relationship entails for *both* parties.

Kaye Gibbons's *A Virtuous Woman* is a study of marriage and bereavement structured via the memories of Ruby, who dies of cancer, and of her husband, Jack, who discovers he is out of step in the world after her death. Jack, in an effort to reorder his life, goes in search of a housekeeper and finds Mavis Washington, but his stereotyping of Mavis as someone who will be able to "make biscuits the kind you dream of" is undercut when she habitually arrives late and ruins his clothes with bleach.[17] His assumption that Mavis will conform to his needs is proved false and outmoded. The most telling and exploratory passage of the novel forms part of Ruby's narration, however. Ruby's childhood memories include numerous mentions of the family maid and housekeeper, Sudie Bee, influential in Ruby's understanding of women's roles. She expected to find a Sudie Bee in her adult life who would help her to pass for a responsible woman, but she does not. Ruby exists for much of the time below the poverty line as wife to a drunken itinerant and then to Jack, a sharecropper. Ruby finally comprehends the dependency culture that women like her own mother reinforced: "Somebody like Sudie Bee covers for people. Having her in my kitchen would've been no different from those commercials you see where the husband says, 'Mmm, Mmm, this sure is good cake. Tastes like you made it from scratch,' and the wife just winks at the camera and wiggles the mix box behind her back. It's not any different from that at all."[18] The analogy Ruby draws resonates with the presence of Aunt Jemima smiling from the pancake box and Aunt Delilah of "Delilah's Delights," in John Stahl's 1934 film version of *Imitation of Life,* in whom the iconography of capitalist aesthetics merges with the actual production of labor.[19] The image incorporates white women's leisure as inextricably incumbent upon black women's skills. Gibbons's exposé of the elemental features of domestic relations is more radical than the exploration of friendship in *Ellen Foster.* The precise means of production that render the image powerful are elucidated in microcosmic detail:

Mam'd baste a turkey that Sudie Bee had chased, caught, killed, scalded, everything. She'd tap more salt into the pan dressing Sudie Bee had made, and I'd come in when everything was basted, salted, and garnish the turkey, put napkins in rings. I put the finishing touches on mama's finishing touches. I was twice-removed from the real work. . . . But I had it in the back of my mind that mama was capable of doing Sudie Bee's jobs, and that she just didn't do them because she needed to be free to do other things, like sitting down at the kitchen table every morning with her cup of tea and a notepad, making a list for the day, then going upstairs to bathe, read, rest, embroider, then coming back downstairs to check on how things were moving along, do some of her finishing touches and split a RC Cola with Sudie Bee.[20]

Both Ruby and Jack inherit the expectation that a black women will bring order and calm into a white home, but Ruby begins to analyze the depths to which that order could go for the white women who set the modes of production. Splitting a can with her domestic is a small but significant detail to connote Ruby's mother as a kind and reasonable taskmistress, but she remains parasitic upon her maid. She splits the cola in the final stages of production and in so doing falsifies her share in that production of domestic perfection even further. These small "kindnesses" themselves became a trope by which mistresses were prepared to let themselves be known to their servants. Much earlier Lillian Smith explored in *Strange Fruit* how white women's kindnesses to black women who worked in their kitchens could exacerbate the oppression already entailed in the relationship. When her character Bess seeks to leave the kitchen of her employer, she encounters one of the strongest axes of power in the interchange—her employer's polite kindness: "She hedged you in with it, made you prisoner and walled herself from you as the kindnesses mounted."[21] This walled-off politeness—more subtle by far than the unconcealed hostility that Lutie Johnson noted—ensures that no common connection is allowed to breach the separate worlds in which white mistress and black maid are enclosed. In the same novel Laura is about to broach a sensitive subject with the black protagonist, Nonnie, when she "forced herself back into the conventional attitude of white mistress and colored maid."[22] The moment would have irrevocably altered the status quo for each of them, and on the final page of the novel Bess, Nonnie, and Dessie are still setting out at 6:30 A.M. to work for "their" white families: "Everything would be the same as it always was."[23]

In Gilchrist's stories things have remained the same and remained so without the barbed critique that Smith provides. Gilchrist is renowned for her sharp satire, yet this facet of the southern world she creates is surprisingly unmediated by irony. Across Gilchrist's stories the domestic relationship between black and white women remains comfortably within its conservative frame. Even when Gilchrist appears to break the frame, as with Rhoda and Klane in *Net of Jewels,* the power axes remain unchallenged. When Klane is imprisoned, a male friend declares: "We'll get your maid back. Don't worry about it." And when Rhoda's feelings are scrutinized, even the ironic lens through which she is viewed fails to lift the association beyond the superstitious and retrograde: "She stood up and I put my arms around her. She smelled like the night, dark and forlorn. I held her gingerly at first and then something happened to me, maybe it was the hangover or the Dexedrine I had taken. . . . maybe I just went crazy, but all of a sudden I was able to really hold her in my arms, all the long tall black body, all the history of her people, the majesty of the Watusi, spear and lion, ancient warrior race."[24] Immediately Rhoda disentangles herself from the black woman, Klane refers to her as "ma'am," and Rhoda's reaction to Klane's plight is simply to tell others to do something about it. This signature relationship is little changed by a single embrace and beyond shaking one's head at Rhoda's naïveté, Gilchrist gives us little pause for thought.

✍ Ellen Douglas is one white writer who has consistently pursued the meanings and deflated the myths of southern race relations, especially in *Black Cloud, White Cloud, The Rock Cried Out,* and *Can't Quit You Baby.*

Her project has included an examination of the complex ambiguities of friendship, from the passionate sisterly relationship of Corinne and Judith in *A Lifetime Burning* to the unwieldy dynamic of Cornelia and Tweet in *Can't Quit You Baby*. She has described the novelist's job as "to see and to show," not to provide answers to perennial problems like those of how to relate intimately across differences.[25] She has been successfully publishing her writing since the early 1960s, and, more openly and overtly than the younger writers I discuss in this book, she engages with the moral and social issues addressed by civil rights struggles and the consequent changes at each level of southern society.

In 1989 Douglas wrote the afterword to a new edition of *Black Cloud, White Cloud,* in which four of the short stories she wrote in the 1950s and 1960s are collected. In it she remembers: "The separate black and white societies of the South and the country were grinding against each other with the agonized crunch of continental plates, preparing the earthquakes and volcanic eruptions of the sixties. . . . I continued in all my later books to write about the complexities of family ties and the lives, cheek by jowl, in bed and out, in and out of the ditch, of blacks and whites."[26] The language is cataclysmic, but she is indubitably positive about the changes that have ensued. For her purposes as a southern novelist, the idea that "stories and truth pull against each other in their ancient tug of war" continues to underpin the representations of southern characters, especially in the friendships they attempt to form.[27]

In *Can't Quit You Baby* Ellen Douglas investigates the possibilities that exist for friendship between white middle-class Cornelia and black working-class Julia (or Tweet, as she is familiarly known) in a specified place, Mississippi, and at a particular historical moment, 1969, although the narrative encompasses events from around the mid-1930s to the beginning of the 1970s.[28] Cornelia employs Julia as her domestic help. This immediately fixes their relationship within a framework that is historically knowable and exacting, set as it is against the backdrop of the civil rights movement. Since the association between employer and domestic is a paradigmatic relationship, as the discussion of Ellen Gilchrist shows, a tempting conclusion to draw *before* opening this novel is that a reiteration of a much-observed relationship will be forthcoming. Prevalent amidst a plethora of fictional representations is the interracial relationship that Trudier Harris has described as specifically "handed down from slavery" and which "the majority of mistresses and maids are not inclined to alter."[29]

However, Douglas examines the many obstacles that work to prevent an easy identification between the two women. She confronts the issue of clichéd characterizations, constrained within historical moments early on, when the narrator supplies a catalog of some of the scenarios available to the writer who constructs an interracial relationship in the South of the 1960s:

> The white woman—Cornelia—is driving Julia home from work. The latter is sitting on the backseat of the car (or the front seat. For the purpose of dramatizing a point either will do).
>
> Cornelia is taking Julia to register to vote (or declining to take her, or Julia is declining to go) under the perilous circumstances of black registration in Mississippi in nine-teen sixty-four. (5)

Douglas is self-conscious about the ways in which her novel might transcend its periodization yet retain the specificities of the historized relationship it describes at the micro level. She fights against falling into a fictional timelock that might relegate the significance of interpersonal dynamics to the desire to accurately reproduce a historical encounter. Douglas's work of 1988, then, operates, as a creative critical exploration of the 1960s. Rather than record a microhistorical encounter between two women in the era of civil rights reforms, it examines the women characters and their circumstances in the manner of a historically conscious metafiction that encourages critical interrogation. It is a work of fiction that does not shirk the sociopolitical significance attached to interracial relationships.

Can't Quit You Baby is not the only contemporary southern novel that attempts to reconfigure this particular relationship via a periodization of the 1960s. In Nanci Kincaid's Crossing Blood, the Sheppard family lives next door to the Williams family in Tallahassee, Florida, and white

Sarah Sheppard employs black Melvina Williams, "the best maid in the world."[30] Sarah appears to employ Melvina as a favor to them both, in that their friendship and mutual support can be allowed to exist in the community in which they live if it takes the guise of employer and household help. They conspire, cry in unison, challenge and sustain one another, as Kincaid determines what the fundamental commonalities may be in maintaining a friendship across similar and different experiences. But she also ensures that the reader is aware that Sarah is exceptional. She is a white woman who lives out her antiracist principles.[31] Sarah and Melvina are interpreted, as are all circumstances, by Lucy Sheppard, Sarah's daughter, and her teenage perceptions exhibit a subtle blend of naïveté and astute observation, reminiscent of Ellen in *Ellen Foster*. Lucy approaches an understanding of the extent to which it is impossible for her mother and Melvina to see each other outside of the historical agencies that control their opposing social positions; the intersection of gender with race and with class or material status is controlling for both women. Theirs is an unbalanced relationship and consequently a limited one. Despite the mutuality that exists between Sarah and Melvina, ultimately they are unable to transcend the domestic framework in which their friendship is contained: that nexus where race and economics meet. Melvina still refers to Sarah as Mrs. Sheppard regardless of the personal depths that they have plumbed. Finally, the two women cannot help but look past the individual who has become friend and see each other as reflective of and accountable for the general behavior of blacks and whites around them. Lucy detects that her mother would probably pay Melvina, whatever the circumstances, "for being colored," and Sarah is referred to as "that white woman" in the last pages of the novel when she attends the funeral of Melvina's husband: she is a lone white figure whose "respects" are dismissed as misguided in the context. There is no permeability in terms of their roles. Lucy's assertion that her mother is able to enter the consciousness of any other mother, by virtue of this connection alone, and that Sarah "could go into Melvina and be a colored woman with a houseful of kids" is problematic, to say the least. Critics like bell hooks have explained how a white woman might be "successfully socialized, via racism" into assuming that no connection exists between herself and a black woman, and Sarah could be read as a woman involved in the first stage of resocializing herself out of the "myths, stereotypes, and false assumptions" that "deny her capacity to bridge gaps created by racism."[32] In *Can't Quit You Baby* Ellen Douglas pursues those very gaps in more depth, largely through her deployment of metafictional devices. She pushes Cornelia and Tweet toward a friendship Sarah and Melvina were ultimately unable to maintain.

✍♥ Specific within *Can't Quit You Baby* is the author's location in recent literary-critical thought. The characterizations are located within a feminist politics that emphasizes the intersection of gender, race, and class, and the writer exploits the kinds of metafictional literary devices that may effectively explore these connections. Douglas deliberately blurs the distinction between the implied author and the narrator's subject positions in order to construct an experimental narrative where a dramatized author works her way through the politics of responsibility that her subject matter may entail: "It's as if she has some buried connection with these lives, a connection she must explore and understand. And besides, she has the power to distort, if she chooses to exercise it" (38).[33] Douglas foregrounds awareness—on the part of the fiction maker, the storyteller, the characters, and the implied reader—of the paradigms that may trap both writers and readers when attempting to locate a relationship like Cornelia and Tweet's. Both women are southern, but their experiences are segregated. Cornelia is bound up in the paradigmatic formulation of southern womanhood that fixes her as a white woman and seeks to exclude Tweet as a black woman. Tweet's own position is mediated through an accumulation of powerful controlling images— maid, aggressor, emasculator, Sapphire, Aunt Jemima—especially via Cornelia's shocked response to some of the stories she tells. Cornelia reads Tweet through some of these images as she half-listens to stories: of a white man's sexually harassing her and of her angry response, of her shooting her husband for his affair with another woman and then resuming their marriage once the problem has been addressed. Cornelia's reaction is clouded by the images, and she assiduously prevents herself from acknowledging the intimacy between the women that such confidences bespeak. The narrator, too, admits late in the story that she is unable to fully or adequately "acknowledge or express the complexity of all those layers of circumstance and imagining—in all our lives but particularly in Tweet's" (239). Literary techniques are themselves underpinned by social constructions that cling to characterizations. An analysis of images of black womanhood, for example, might well also apply to the traditional narrative lines within which black and white relationships have been imprisoned. As Patricia Hill Collins explains, "Even when the political and economic conditions that originally generated controlling images disappear, such images prove remarkably tenacious because they not only keep Black women oppressed but are key in maintaining interlocking systems of race, class and gender oppression."[34]

The relationship the reader is introduced to in the early part of the novel incorporates a critique of Cornelia's artifice, of her blank, if polite, withdrawal from Tweet. Cornelia exists in a quiet, ordered world, exemplified in her deafness and a tendency to turn down her hearing aid to avoid participating fully in the realities of others. She is cradled securely by a solid family life. Her husband, John, loves and protects her, and they co-own and manage a bookstore. Her two children (to Cornelia "lovely, safe young people—straight backs, straight teeth, straight A's") do not usually impinge overmuch upon her quietude. Tweet also has a family, is married to Nig and mother to his two daughters from a former marriage. Tweet's world is not quiet or ordered; clutter fills her home, in contrast to the order she facilitates in Cornelia's. She fights for the survival of her marriage and locks horns most days with the various agents of her oppression. The first conversation of the novel involves the funeral of a married white man Tweet remembers harassing her years before when she worked in his diner. Whereas Tweet revisits even the most painful personal and family memories, Cornelia exhibits a kind of myopia with each member of her family, seeing her husband in terms of his role and her children as children rather than independent adults; ironically, considering her unimaginative response to Tweet's stories, she has created them as imaginary people in her own image of perfection.

Can Cornelia and Tweet's relationship be narrated and critiqued simultaneously? This is the kind of question the novel poses. Ellen Douglas sets herself the task of investigating the facets of Cornelia and Tweet's connectedness, while aiming never to privilege metafictional play over the political reality of their social positions: "Try for now to be absent minded about race and class, place and time, even about poverty and wealth, security and deprivation" (5). Even if the reader colludes in the avowed attempt, the narratorial process confounds the possibility of dismissing the lowest common denominators that ground any reading in the interlocking systems of race, class, and gender oppression.

Metafictional framebreaks are generally understood to break the illusory reality of a fictional world.[35] But Ellen Douglas has her narrator allude to the "illusion of freedom" *within* the fictional world (38). A safe, secure fictional world is never completely created in *Can't Quit You Baby*. The opening paragraphs, written in the continuous present tense, immediately crack the reader's frame of reference that expects a storytelling past. The two women are staged dramatically, posited as an idea, as subjects for fictional exploration: "The two women are sitting at right angles to each other at the kitchen table on a sunny July morning in the nineteen-sixties" (3). The narrator goes on to examine her subjects, both politically and linguistically: "Servant? Mistress? They would be uneasy with these words, and so am I. The servant might quote the Bible: And the last shall be first, Lord. Yes. As for the mistress, the sexual connotation might drift across her mind. . . . So, let's settle for housekeeper and employer. Yes, that's better" (5). How should the women be explicated? Are *housekeeper* and *employer* the more politically correct terms, the least historically marked? Is it possible to capture the nuances of their identities and their experiences, linguistically and ontologically and yet fictionally? The women are conjoined via the metaphor of the kitchen and its sociohistorical significance in women's lives: "There would have been no way in that time and place—the nineteen-sixties and seventies in Mississippi—for them to get acquainted, except across the kitchen table from each other, shelling peas, peeling apples, polishing silver. . . . In this house the white woman had to choose to sit down to set the tone of their connection" (5).[36]

In her reading of *Can't Quit You Baby* and other selected texts, Minrose C. Gwin has examined how much time she spent wandering into her own kitchen when she had designated that very time to the writing of her article, and she finally decides, through thinking grounded in both study *and* kitchen, that in the kitchens of contemporary southern women's fiction "anything can happen, anything is possible: new recipes are being formulated; life and death decisions are being made; a kind of fermentation is taking place which is transformative, radical and profoundly woman-centered."[37] Ellen Douglas attempts this kind of transformative, "woman-centered" approach here. The foundation of the relationship between the two women is the kitchen. Domestic culture serves as a vocabulary through which to apprehend complex relations between white employers and black domestic workers, as Ann Romines has suggested it may in *The Home Plot*.[38] Tweet enters Cornelia's world continually in her role as a domestic servant, a crossover that works in one direction only and involves compromises for the black woman, as Trudier Harris argues: "In moving from her home to that of the white woman, the black woman connects two racially and spatially distinct worlds in one direction."[39]

Cornelia, despite two documented visits to Tweet's home and apparently a number of others, does not cross the threshold of understanding of the acute differences in their positions on any of these occasions in the story's "past." On her bereavement call after Martin Luther King's assassination, Tweet finds it difficult to respond to Cornelia's apparent sympathy, and Cornelia cannot cross the cultural space that divides them: "She dares not reach out, dares not cross the two paces that separate them" (99). The second scene remembered by Cornelia took place a year earlier, in 1967. Cornelia replays the scene in her mind; the women are ministering to Tweet's stepfather as he dies of cancer: "She and Tweet are lifting his long emaciated body. . . . Cornelia and Tweet look at each other, businesslike, detached as two nurses might be. It seems to Cornelia that they act as one, their intimacy and mutual understanding is perfect" (202). Both scenes provide a white other's view of Tweet's home and existence: a scene "pops into [the] mind" of the narrator, who, it is pointed out, the reader will have assumed is a white woman (38), and Cornelia, the white character located in New York, far away from Mississippi, muses on an episode from her as yet unnarrated "past." Cornelia is gradually coming to recognize that she has refused to connect with Tweet, except superficially on rare occasions when there was the opportunity to reciprocate in some small way for the time and patience Tweet bestows upon Cornelia's household, over and above her "domestic" duty. Significantly, though, Cornelia feels the need to emphasize their detachment from one another in the scene that she reworks, so that any possible intimacy or mutual understanding is unequivocally understood as practical and businesslike, and therefore unemotional.

In Cornelia's kitchen race and class politics within a female frame exclude any concept of the black woman's reality in society at large and exclude any identifying experiences that are not directly related to the pragmatism of her relationship to her employer. Judith Rollins has pointed out, as a result of her research, that domestics were able to describe in precise and intimate detail "the personalities, habits, moods, and tastes of the women they had worked for," since "domestics indeed know the Other." But in contrast, the employers' descriptions were "less complex and insightful . . . because they had less need to study the nuances of their domestics."[40] This exemplifies the kind of relationship Ellen Douglas works through for the first three sections of the novel and bespeaks the distance that Cornelia justifies by a supposedly natural and polite disinclination to pursue information as to the nuances of the lifestyle of a member of a lower class.

Tweet's life experiences are incompletely understood by Cornelia, who skates over life. They can be more safely interpreted as story, as tales Tweet produces like her gifts of flowers for the white woman. Tweet's story is told in the first person before Cornelia's, which is told in the third; the narrator refrains from entering the consciousness of the black woman in the way she has access to the white woman's thoughts, but the structuring of the telling signifies a shift of emphasis *toward* a double-voiced representation of the women's lives. The shift from *Ellen Foster,* where Starletta's story is never revealed, and from *Copper Crown,* where

Allie's précis of her family history forms only a brief four-page aside in Cass's story, is considerable. On a surface level, in terms of the delineation of their characters, Tweet's story denotes her facility for confronting the facts of her life as set against Cornelia's propensity for self-delusion. Cornelia represses her own internal questions and censors the persons and events in her background that have helped shape her present—like her mother and the boy, Lewis, she so loved in her adolescence but lost, repressing her feelings for him until decades later. More interestingly, though, Tweet's narrative foregrounds the way in which the white narrator endeavors to plumb the depths of her own racism and, perhaps also, conjoins with an African American tradition of writing.

✍ On the part of the dramatized narrator, Tweet's tales represent some insight into an African American oral and literary tradition that tells and retells the story of black protest, suffering, and survival.[41] Ostensibly, the story of Tweet is created as the first story in the novel, the one the narrator intends the reader to engage with from the very first. Tweet's parents split, and she is left in the care of her grandfather, a man so elderly that he is reported to have served in the Civil War, gaining a federal pension, and who lives until 1935. Grandpa's presence and his wise perspicacity and love affect Tweet her whole life, as do his beliefs in good and evil and the supernatural as tangible forces. This black story follows and reworks a pattern recognizable from African American storytelling traditions.[42] Toni Morrison, in the essay "Rootedness: The Ancestor as Foundation," discusses distinct literary features that influence her understanding of African American literary traditions. She outlines motifs and intertextual preoccupations also present in Tweet's story: "It seems to me interesting to evaluate Black Literature on what the writer does with the presence of an ancestor. . . . there is always an elder there. And these ancestors are not just parents, they are sort of timeless people whose relationships to the characters are benevolent, instructive and protective, and they provide a certain kind of wisdom."[43] *Can't Quit You Baby* is not black literature but attempts to tell a black story incorporating some of the tenets that Morrison discusses. For Tweet, her grandfather is "my welcome table on this earth" (17), as in more complex and myriad ways is the grandfather in Ellison's *Invisible Man*. Both Tweet and her grandfather may also be read according to the following: "We are very practical people, very down-to-earth, even shrewd people. But within that practicality we also accepted what I suppose could be called superstition and magic, which is another way of knowing things. But to blend these two worlds together at the same time was enhancing, not limiting. And some of these things were 'discredited knowledge' that Black people had; discredited only because Black people were discredited therefore what they *knew* was 'discredited.'"[44]

Tweet's narration stands in the text in its own right; Douglas ensures that the reader learns much more of the racial, gendered, class circumstances of Tweet's life than one does of Starletta's in *Ellen Foster* or Allie's in *Copper Crown*. It is also a vehicle by which Cornelia may gain access to Tweet's way of knowing things. Cornelia can be privy to those elements of Tweet's life she chooses to reconfigure, but she continually backs off from the encounter, discrediting Tweet's knowledge and experience and ultimately Tweet herself. Even though Cornelia's concentration wavers, her general incredulity, and at times total disbelief, are indicated repeatedly and emphatically: "But Julia! Cornelia stepped back, folded her arms across her breasts and shook her head. *No*" (27). The reader may wonder why Tweet chooses to battle to be heard, why she should insist on shouting past Cornelia's hearing aid and her apathy, and work on with an audience who neither asks questions nor exhibits any interest and does not accept the gift of her story with an open heart or mind. Cornelia takes on a polite persona who hides behind the etiquette of *appearing* to listen, but the narrator betrays Cornelia's latent sense of class and racial superiority and her deprecation of Tweet's attempts at forging a connection between them:

Cornelia over the years has considered herself a listener. Another woman might not have had time for Tweet's gifts—for the tales of childhood, the snatches of song, the handful of ragged robins. But from the beginning Cornelia, kneading dough, fluting a piecrust, cutting carrot curls or radish rosettes, has never by a word or gesture betrayed the boredom, the condescension she sometimes feels, her rejection of the moral code that Tweet's stories sometimes imply, her doubts about the veracity of some set of outlandish events. She accepts the tales like the flowers that she sticks in a jelly glass and sets in the window by the kitchen sink and forgets. (13)

Cornelia treats Tweet's stories as she might those of a garrulous child, to be countenanced but doubted as occasionally amusing irrelevancies. As the ragged robins, Tweet's gift to Cornelia, remain in the kitchen, so Tweet's life experiences are suitable only for kitchen table talk while the lady of the house busies herself with the culinary touches that could not possibly be left to anyone else to perform. When they are finished, Cornelia leaves her housekeeper behind in the kitchen, and, going about the rest of her daily life, automatically, as she does so many things, she forgets her.[45]

It is specifically with Cornelia's deafness to Tweet and her nonseeing of Tweet's reality that the novel concerns itself. This is a similar concern to that expressed in von Herzen's *Copper Crown,* where a home is a site of intimacy on the one hand and unknowability on the other. Cass and Allie embrace each other physically and emotionally in a way that would transgress the established etiquette of Cornelia and Tweet's relationship, but in Cass's embrace is an unacknowledged reluctance to know Allie. The inability or refusal to see another's reality is a concern that again echoes particular traditions in African American writing. Ellison's *Invisible Man* elucidates the idea of a distorted lens that covers over the eyes of white Americans rather like a cataract, causing them to refract from rather than focus upon African Americans: "I am invisible understand, simply because people refuse to see me . . . When they approach me they see only my surroundings, themselves, or figments of their imagination—indeed everything and anything except me."[46] Ellen Douglas shows Cornelia to be guilty of this form of opaque nonseeing and extends the reader's comprehension of its negative effects on Tweet and on Cornelia herself through a series of metaphors around hearing and sight.[47] Just as Brother Tobitt, who does not "see" Ellison's Invisible Man, has a glass eye, so Cornelia, who does not "hear" Tweet, wears a hearing aid. Cornelia's hearing aid is a very sophisticated and sensitive device, but it does not aid a woman whose own sensitivity is restricted in range. Cornelia sees and hears Tweet at a mundane daily level of her consciousness, since Tweet is a purveyor of a service that Cornelia requires, but Cornelia acknowledges little interaction outside the quotidian cooperation of domestic duties. Much later, Cornelia comes to realize that she perceived Tweet's life as she saw Tweet's house, on the periphery of her vision, as "clutter, disorder, pierced through with sorrow and mystery" (202). She has been preserving herself from disorder, sorrow, and mystery as assiduously as she preserves her figs, shutting them tightly in jars and storing them away. She refuses to confront these elements as compounded in her own personality and instead attaches them like labels to Tweet, as she would automatically label her jars of preserves—just as the vase of Tweet's *ragged* robins is no longer noticed by her either, once it has been *tidied* to the window sill. In Cornelia's ordered world things are clear—"Right is right and wrong is wrong" (25)—but the world to which Tweet allows Cornelia access blurs many of the dichotomized "black and white" distinctions upon which Cornelia's ideology rests.

Douglas shows that Cornelia's rigid realism in discrediting Tweet's life stories precludes any real awareness of things as they may be for others, or even for herself. There is little evidence in the novel that Cornelia sees race relations as anything other than largely benign on an interpersonal level—they are in her house, after all. David Goldfield tries to tease out the nuances of this attitude in a taxonomy of southern race relations: "Appearances are important in the South, and white Southerners have a great capacity for ignoring unpleasant things. . . . But at some point it is no longer possible to pretend; the thing being avoided may make its presence known in a very decided manner, or the burden of trying to square values and culture with ignorance becomes too great to bear."[48] What begins as a particular characterization moves more usefully into a kind of psychosocial meditation on repressive behavior which echoes the warnings that the narrator interpolates into the synopses of Cornelia's attitudes and behavior. These operate to prescribe and circumscribe the reader's understanding of her character. When Cornelia, age nine, is beaten with a switch by her mother, the narratorial comment is telling: "This absurd occasion is something first to ignore and then to blot out" (40). Cornelia continues to blot out unpleasant and problematic features in her adult life, as with the problems that endure in her relationship with her mother and those that beset the volatile society as civil rights activists struggle to change the status quo: "To reveal, after all, is to admit—to reveal oneself" (47).

Having limned out this repressed and repressing character, Ellen Douglas subjects her to the shattering trauma of her husband's death and the self-absorbing guilt that ensues. Shortly before John's death, Cornelia is hurt by the discovery that he has always been fully aware of his children's lives—their mistakes, their relationships, their selves—whereas she has been oblivious, excluded from anything other than their successes. She has not faced the potential disorders, sorrows, and mysteries in her children's lives any more than in her own. Hurt and angry, she shuts down behind her hearing device and bitterly cultivates a silent self that she will not allow John to penetrate, emotionally or sexually. She sees her silence as the most potent weapon with which to punish her husband, finding it easier to see her family as conspirators against her than to examine her own responsibility. Her life has always been bound to John's, but she stealthily unpicks the emotional ties that bind them in shared endeavors, lets him float loose, and turns away. Just before his heart attack on an airplane above Birmingham, she finally disgorges the bitter gall her silence has repressed and tells the "fucking bastard" she hates him (153). Cornelia's potential for telling her feelings, even saying her anger, is undone by the tragedy of John's death and his consequent silence in the face of her accusations. Cornelia withdraws even further into a cocoon of insulated silence as a result. She is unable and unwilling to confront the meaning of her silence and instead allows it to govern her existence. She refuses to investigate the guilt that is instrumental in defining her world and eschews the need to fight the paralysis of thought and feeling that overwhelms her.

Douglas explores this issue within the experiences of both her characters, in an attempt to reinforce the varying difficulties involved in preparing the ground on which they may speak together, or be given words to say to each other. The narrator becomes a kind of troubled presence investigating her characters—troubled by not having full and unimpeded access to Tweet's experiences. Whereas Kaye Gibbons deployed a stutter in *Ellen Foster* as a means to render Starletta silent in the text, in this novel the situation is more complex. Tweet is disabled partway through the text; she is disengaged from speech at the very point that Cornelia begins to penetrate the blank walls of her own silent world. Tweet's accident, in which she is rendered cataleptic except for the silent and veiled ruminations of her conscious mind, may be indicative of the narrator's loss of Tweet partway through the text, of her voice, and of the facility to imagine the words of her black character:

> She is silent . . . she whose voice has echoed in my ears, spun its tales in my head for so long.
>
> It's as if some dark magician has cast a spell over her, over us all, has snatched away the voice with which, all these years, she's given us the gift of her life. What can I do to break the spell? (241)

In this passage the narrator implicates the reader through the repeated use of "us," a reminder, perhaps, of the innumerable times through the history of the feminist movement that white women have failed to hear black women and the loss that is entailed in this failure for both sides. Douglas, though, in tackling the story at all, refutes the debilitating silences that the Cornelias of this world enshrine, or that white storytellers uncomfortably pursue with regard to black characters. The dramatized narrator is in a precarious position. bell hooks has outlined in some detail the negative scenario of what can happen when those at the center try to appropriate the stories of those who inhabit the margins: "No need to hear your voice when I can talk about you better than you can speak about yourself. No need to hear your voice. Only tell me about your pain. I want to know about your story. And then I will tell it back to you in a new way. Tell it back to you in such a way that it has become mine, my own. Re-writing you, I write myself anew. I am still author, authority. I am still the colonizer, the speaking subject, and you are now at the center of my talk."[49]

This is difficult territory; if a white woman pays no attention to the black character, she is not acknowledging her; but when she listens and learns, she risks exploiting the black woman. The risk for the critic lies in the tendency to erect moral yardsticks with which to measure texts, characters—and authors. In Douglas's case I have already examined the extent to which Tweet may be rewritten out of the literary traditions that African American writers have initiated. It is significant that at one point the white narrator takes over Tweet's story of her grandfather by penetrating the consciousness of this character, choosing from a series of directions his story might take, and thereby breaking the illusion that his story belongs only to Tweet (49–53). Similarly, in parts 4 and 5 of the novel Tweet becomes a character in Cornelia's story rather than the teller of her own. This is a difficult balancing act, and one is reminded of Alice Walker's appreciation of Flannery O'Connor for the fact that her black characters are sketched so lightly that they remain free within the text and are never pinned down or limited. If Douglas's project is to be understood as effectively interventionist, though, it is because she is, ultimately, negotiating a space that black and white women might *jointly* inhabit. For hooks this is "a radical creative space which affirms and sustains" the subjectivities of both black and white women at a more hopeful juncture.[50]

As a writer of fiction, Ellen Douglas has no obligation to interrogate the social and cultural prisms through which black and white women's subjectivities are constructed in a southern context, but she chooses to ally her fiction with wider discussions about friendships and cooperative alliances forged in a domestic context, where, as Judith Rollins notes, "each woman encounters the other essentially alone; other family members are on the periphery, the intensity of the arrangement is between the women."[51] Cornelia and Tweet's is a dyadic relationship and is consequently transactional, in that one character's interpretation of the other affects that other's future behavior. Certainly in this relationship Tweet acts as the primary communicator, but her words, to which Cornelia nods absently for the first half of the novel, are soaked into the deep structure of Cornelia's character, to be filtered up through her consciousness in parts 4 and 5 of the novel. Wandering around New York, she casts back over her life and slowly awakens to her self—her potential and her responsibilities—and recognizes that Tweet is the closest she has to a friend.

The relationship is not transactional, however, with regard to a communal working through of the problems inherent in their distinctive positions as superordinate and subordinate. Douglas deliberately retards this feature of her investigation, for her narrator and for her reader. The gold barrette that Tweet takes from Cornelia's home acts as the catalyst for this level of inquiry in the novel. The narrative eye is superimposed with Cornelia's character-perspective when, on a visit to Tweet's home, it pans around the seemingly inconsequential clutter to focus on a single item and invest it with meaning (202). The gold barrette is one of the means by which Douglas encodes the problematic stereotypes that impinge upon an interracial friendship of the kind she describes: that black domestics will steal, for example—an idea that has its historical antecedent in slavery. Douglas reworks this stereotype as part of a southern belief system in order to examine the heightened emotions that are hidden behind a deceptively simple incident. In the reworking she seeks to confront the underlying tensions. For Tweet the eighteen-carat barrette signals her hatred for Cornelia the woman and Cornelia as representative of white women of her class; it symbolizes her hatred for all white women:

> Hated you, Tweet says. She rocks back, leans forward in her chair. You ain't got *sense* enough to know I hated you. I hate you all my life, before I ever know you. . . . Every day, every hour of my entire life from the day I'm born. Hate you when you acting like you the only woman in the world ever got sorrow when her husband die. I hate you, hate you, hate you. And I steal that gold barrette to remind me of it, in case I forget. She laughs. Sometimes I forget, she says. (254)

Focusing on the significance attached to this tiny object that Cornelia never even noticed was missing helps to unravel the layers of nonunderstanding and misunderstanding that have characterized their relationship. Tweet is able, finally, to use the barrette as the prop, in a psycho-dramatic sense, that enables her to confront Cornelia with her silence, with her refusal to acknowledge the fears and phobias that have affected their relationship historically and personally:

> Maybe your hair was caught in it? You think maybe I took your hair? Make a mojo? Fingernail clippings? Blood, too, like blood from old used Tampax, Kotex? I throwed out enough in my day. From your panties when you-when you-fff-flooded? Washed enough of them. Shit? Cleaned enough of your toilets. (254)

Their connection has been intensely intimate, but the white woman has denied its very closeness, its intimacy, at every turn.

✍ It is most particularly the issue of *ressentiment* that dominates Douglas's sixth and final section in her novel. *Ressentiment* also provides the linguistic exactitude that Judith Rollins requires to capture the burning, cumulative fury that underlies a domestic's suppressed emotions in the face of her employer: "*Ressentiment* is more than hostility; it is a long-term, seething deep-rooted negative feeling toward those whom one feels unjustly have power or advantage over one's life." [52] It is the suppression of such powerful feelings that leads to painful silence, but Douglas works through what happens when they can be repressed no longer. Tweet pounds out the anger that, until the denouement, had sparked only momentarily in Cornelia's presence. When Cornelia visits Tweet after Tweet's accident, it is as if her massaging of the black woman's enfeebled body induces a kind of peristalsis whereby Tweet's anger pulses to the surface: "Cornelia lifts her hands from Tweet's shoulders, stands still, still. The memory of the beat throbs in her body like the pulse of her blood. . . . Shit, shit, shit. Tweet pounds the chair arm. Shit, shit, shit" (247).

Various feminist critics have emphasized the political significance of speaking one's anger and addressing it in order to move forward, as I discuss in chapter 1 of this book. Eichenbaum and Orbach, in their study of women's friendships, note the importance of anger in the face of denial, betrayal, and negation. They explore what they term "merged attach-ments" between women, where one factor is that any confrontation of underlying pain or anger may be avoided in the blind and comfortable assumption that the relationship is operating satisfactorily: "preventing the discussion of difficult feelings . . . also acts as a brake on women discussing aspects of one another's lives."[53] In my reading, the attach-ment between Cornelia and Tweet has always remained *sub*merged; as the novel shows, Cornelia did not see beyond Tweet's color and her job until her visit to New York. Not until she is at a clear geographical dis-tance from Tweet or submerged in shock, as when John dies (she even leaves Tweet to do her mourning for her), does the significance of Tweet's presence in her life register in her conscious mind. Tweet was always present on the level of her *un*conscious, as the first person she wanted the airline to call after John's death, for example (155). Ulti-mately though, it is Tweet who hauls their friendship into the open, where it may be examined at close quarters and carefully contextualized, without eliding the irreducible differences between its protagonists, if it is to evolve.

Examining their relationship involves transforming silence into speech for Cornelia. But for Tweet, who has battled long and hard against being silenced, her struggle is to "change the nature and direction of [her] speech, to make a speech that compels listeners, one that is heard," in the way that bell hooks has frustratedly described: "Our speech . . . was often the soliloquy, the talking into thin air, the talking to ears that do not hear you—the talk that is simply not listened to."[54] But is it enough that Tweet and subsequently Cornelia tell each other of their hatred and hurt? Fierce feelings are framed in expletives that Tweet wrenches from her strained voice box, "Fuck you then" and "Damn you." Cornelia re-peats the recitation of hate to echo the sudden hurt realization of her own complicity in that hatred (255). It is Tweet who conclusively serves up the postscript to her many stories—"You ain't never *seen* me, *heard* me in your entire life" (255)—and whose vehement honesty of feeling provokes Cornelia, finally, into emotional engagement with both Tweet and her stories: "You can't take back what you've told me. It's here. It's mine. Mine, mine, mine. Not just yours. Listen to this [and she repeats the other's very words]: I'm afraid. Nevertheless I go. I make myself strong to listen. That's mine. Mine too" (255).

A celebratory moment? Certainly a revelatory one; there is, with the end of the novel, new hope for these two women whose lives, although apparently shared, have thus far proved determinedly separate. They have been brought together by a narrator who has strained—masking her frustration in metafictional play—to draw them together: "Can't someone else search for the end of this story? Discover where it is leading us? No. It has to be me" (250).

Can't Quit You Baby works as a story within a story—a black woman's story that helps to clarify the story of a white woman—a story told ostensibly by a black woman to a white woman but that ultimately inspirits and animates both women. At one point in the novel, Tweet becomes a visionary guide for Cornelia. She is the disembodied voice that protects Cornelia on her travels around New York, and it could be argued that it is, belatedly, at this point that Cornelia finally begins to "hear" Tweet. I would note, however, that she begins to "see" her solely in terms of another paradigmatic formula: rather than the somewhat anodyne, auxiliary presence in her home, she becomes the conjure woman or wise woman who may rejuvenate Cornelia.[55] For Cornelia, Tweet begins to embody the mystical configurations of life, death, and time, and to forge connections between different worlds. Tweet becomes mentor, savior, and guardian, and acts as a catalyst to induce Cornelia back into the reality she has forsaken since her husband's death. For Cornelia this may signal a kind of acquiescence to the bond that connects her to Tweet, but it is Tweet who coexists with Cornelia in this novel, and whose physical debilitation, the burning of her body and the aneurysm that pumps in her brain, *mirrors* Cornelia's metaphorical debilitation: "It occurred to her something had happened in her head. Synapses were not working. She visualised her brain—stacks of greyish worms doubling over and under, netted as if in a shopping bag with throbbing veins and arteries. . . . it was as if God had taken a needle and slipped it carefully into her brain" (163).

Douglas investigates the possibility for friendship between the two women by dramatizing their across-the-kitchen-table talk in the context of the traumas and the tragedies that beset them in their lives. She also makes self-conscious reference to the tropes and paradigms that beset any representation of a friendship that develops between an employer and the domestic she employs. If Cornelia falls into the trap of seeing Tweet as her guardian angel in her time of need, then Douglas ensures that Tweet's accident places Cornelia in the role of nurse and companion who endeavors to reawaken Tweet's efforts at communication. Listening to one another's stories, forcing oneself to hear these stories, helps, as Suzanne W. Jones points out, to "loosen the hold that stubborn myths and harmful stereotypes have had on the imaginations of both black and white women."[56] It is not inevitably the case: Minrose C. Gwin has begun to address the debilitating epiphanies when one reads oneself as other in another woman's story and finds it almost impossible to surmount the pain and guilt of recognition. But it is in loosening the stranglehold of myths and paradigms that Douglas succeeds in this self-reflexive novel. The self-consciousness of a narrator who is neither self-effacing nor comfortably omniscient, but who confronts stereotypes at every turn and admits to finding these confrontations difficult, helps to locate this fiction in a distinctly southern tradition, and also as a possible response to contemporary feminist inquiries. Like Gwin and Barbara Christian, Audre Lorde and Adrienne Rich, Mary Childers and bell hooks, Douglas makes an attempt to begin and to maintain dialogue between a black and a white woman. This is a narrative about the construction and communication of women's stories, of how they differ, interrelate, and ultimately are plural. Ellen Douglas has succeeded in raising pertinent problems as to how to tell black and white women's stories. Her metafictional stance provides the kind of intellectual suspicion that recognizes that stories cannot be effectively or self-consciously told by creating monologic voices or unassailably homogenous identities for one's characters. Douglas grapples with questions around representation, the allegorical nature of female identities in literature, and the dynamics of women's interaction. And, she does not succumb to easy answers.[57] Douglas's narrator leaves Cornelia and Tweet, at the novel's close, on the threshold of finally beginning to get to know each other. The song by Willie Dixon that forms the epigraph to the novel, "I Can't Quit You Baby," is sung out by Tweet as Cornelia leaves her house. Cornelia hears the words and begins to understand the sentiment.

The importance of listening to one another's stories, of interpersonal communication and dialogue, is the focal concern of the final chapter. Most specifically, Carol Dawson's *Body of Knowledge* plays out these concerns as narrative strategies, and they operate to interesting effect.

CHAPTER FIVE

The Keepers of the House

A Southern Family Saga

The phrase "keeper of the house" has amassed special significance in southern literature. In 1964 Shirley Ann Grau won a Pulitzer Prize for the novel *The Keepers of the House,* in which Abigail and Margaret, both members of the Howland family, try to keep that family's secrets. The history of the homeplace is shown to be inevitably biracial. In this novel Margaret, a black woman, lives for thirty years as Abigail's grandfather's second wife, and "living with him, she lived with us all, all the Howlands, and her life got mixed up with ours. Her face was black and ours were white, but we were together anyhow. Her life and his. And ours."[1] Margaret is a family member as well as a housekeeper, a character in whom the traditional roles black women were deemed to occupy in white southern households and a long-established fear of sexual miscegenation in southern families are seen to meet.

In this chapter my primary focus is Carol Dawson's 1994 novel *Body of Knowledge,* in which the relationship between a black family retainer and her white charge is represented as a talk-story; Victoria and Viola tell the story of the besieged Ransom family and keep their history safe. The same year *Body of Knowledge* was published, another white writer, Rebecca T. Godwin, reworked the phrase "keeper of the house" in another context when a young black woman from a coastal South Carolina community tells the story of her life as housekeeper in a brothel and of her long relationship with its white madam. In Godwin's *Keeper of the House,* Minyon Manigault and her employer, Ariadne Fleming, come to share the responsibility for Hazelhedge, but Minyon is left the sole keeper of its secrets when it closes after forty years: "I was more than just keeper of this house; I had to keep the memories, too," especially since Ariadne prefers to bury them and to forget the past.[2] Neither Margaret and Abigail nor Minyon and Addie Fleming communicate as purposefully or in as structured a fashion as Viola and Victoria in Dawson's novel. Abigail refrains from asking Margaret the intimate questions she craves answers for, about her grandfather and about the black woman's relationship with him and with their children: "All the time we'd been in the same house, and not able to talk" (221). Minyon and Addie are mutually supportive; but each retains some secrets of her own, and an overt exchange of intimate revelations is rare. Viola, on the other hand, is resolute in her determination to speak, to give up the secrets of the Ransom house and family and to have them understood by Victoria. Victoria too needs to understand Viola in very specific ways, and, consequently, the novel is quite a radical departure from the cross-racial relationships of *Ellen Foster* and *Copper Crown.*

Instead, it can be more usefully compared to Kaye Gibbons's most recent novel, *On the Occasion of My Last Afternoon,* in which Emma Garnet Tate Lowell, preparing for death in the year 1900, remembers back over the last seventy years of her life. She remembers Miss Clarice Washington, the black housekeeper with whom she shared half a century, life on the Tate plantation on the James River, and the Civil War, when she tended the sick in Raleigh, North Carolina. In a carefully researched novel Gibbons creates Seven Oaks, five miles from the Carters' Shirley plantation and across the river from John Tyler's Sherwood Forest plantation; she makes its owner, Samuel Tate, a proslavery planter who has come from nothing to push for the governorship in 1840. Carefully she patterns history and memory into a novel about a tragic southern family: Emma Garnet's brother dies horribly of syphilis; her mother is killed by the attentions of Samuel Tate's favored physician; and her husband, Doctor Quincy Lowell (son of the man "whose family witnessed Harvard's birth in 1636" and "cousin" to Amy Lowell), dies of exhaustion after treating the Civil War wounded. Throughout it all, until her death, there is Clarice, a free woman who stays with the family and who is immortalized: "She was the strongest woman I had ever known, ever would know, and I include Varina Davis, Dorothea Dix, and three generations of Lee women. She had worked for and loved all of us and been our constant guardian. . . . Her mission was not to change history but to help both white and black prevail over the circumstances of living in that place, the South, in our time."[3] Clarice supplies order in Emma Garnet's life. Clarice helps her to put to rest the bitter and twisted ghost of the father who haunts her memories, and she speaks hidden truths. She is the keeper of the white woman's soul as well as her house.

Like *On the Occasion of My Last Afternoon*, *Body of Knowledge* is an expansive novel, epic in theme and scope.[4] It shapes and reshapes the myth of southern family, as gothic, as romantic, as Faulknerian in character, and as inextricably bound up with race and region. The plot is convoluted and complex, and, as in Gibbons's novel, coincidences and catastrophes abound. Whereas this could understandably make for a loose and ramshackle structure, the whole is held together by the storytellers: Viola Lewis, the black woman and family retainer who has witnessed most of the Ransom family's history, and Victoria Grace Ransom, the last of the Ransom clan, who live on the edge of Bernice, a small town in Texas. Through their double-voiced discourse, a long and uncertain chain of events and calamities is patterned into coherence and proffered for interpretation. The self-conscious structuring of *Body of Knowledge* is foregrounded from the very beginning when Victoria sets out the epistemological interdependency that exists between herself and

Viola: "It was Viola who told me everything. But I was the one who found this, the letter from my great-grandfather that began it all" (3).

What Viola and Victoria share is the role of keeper of the Ransom house, and their voices synchronize to tell the story of the Ransom family. In this way the novel can be described as dialogic, but the black woman's voice is vital, foremost even, in the unfolding of this Texas family's history. Viola is the primary housekeeper, in the literal sense of her post as servant, and this chapter examines whether the powerful image of the mammy that shadows her representation also functions to undermine and to relegate her to an auxiliary status in the text. My reading of the novel will explore the extent to which she maintains a consistently important role in a dialogic encounter and the extent to which the balance between the black and white storytellers shifts toward Victoria.

Dawson comes from Corsicana, southeast of Dallas, and Bernice may be a version of the Texas town, but it is the surreal and gothic qualities of the literary South and the conventions of the family saga framed by a particular cross-racial relationship that matter most in the novel.[5] The oral tradition invested in by east Texas writers, notably William Goyen in stories like "Ghost and Flesh" and "Water and Dirt," would seem to influence Dawson much more than regional verisimilitude in *Body of Knowledge*. Goyen professes his interest in the "teller-listener situation" and in finding the "buried song in somebody," and it is the language of the place that permeates the timbre of Viola's voice in Dawson's novel. Goyen's description of the cadences of east Texas serves as an indication of the ways in which the region is identified through the voice of its inhabitants rather than mapped geographically in *Body of Knowledge*. Viola's voice is "rich with phrases and expressions out of the King James Bible, from the Negro imagination and the Mexican fantasy, from Deep South Evangelism, from cotton-field and cotton gin, oil field, railroad and sawmill."[6] Viola and Victoria join voices to reassess Ransom family history, but neither has the authority to reproduce events outside of the home. Wars take place, civil rights legislation comes into force, but no "official" history interrupts the steady demise of the Ransoms that preoccupies these two women throughout days lived within the walls of a

house that remains sequestered from Bernice, even when the town develops and sprawls to the edges of its grounds. Bernice is rendered central metaphorically, however, as the point at which east and west Texas
coincide, "the equivocal part of Texas . . . the heartline where everything
meets. . . . a place where it all ties up" (126–27). In this way place and
region become ancillary to story, the nexus of which is the communication between the two women in whom the history of four generations of
Ransoms meets. Nothing interrupts the imperative to tell the story of the
Ransom individuals that becomes the basis of the two women's existence.

In many ways *Body of Knowledge* is a testament to a southern gothic
tradition filled with family curses and gloomy wrongs, hidden motives
and covert relationships. But rather than an old, aristocratic family, the
Ransoms are the nouveau riche, their fortune made from ice via Garner
Ransom's first business venture with Archibald Macafee in 1908, an encounter that draws two families into orbit of one another and sparks a
feud that persists down the twentieth century. The plot knots together a
large cast of characters, and they suffer a multiplicity of dire and devastating bereavements. The Ransom matriarch, Garner's wife, Arliss, finally
dies of pneumonia after two strokes precipitated by family tragedies; her
daughter, Sarah, dies far from home from spinal meningitis;[7] her son,
William, tired to death of Ransom calamities, decapitates himself with
a chainsaw; William's eldest son, Baby Boy, dies from alcohol poisoning
in suspicious circumstances; another son, Bert, is stabbed and disem-
boweled in his own home, and no murderer is charged; and Bert's twin
brother succumbs much later to his incipient alcoholism after a raft of
problems, and he too finally wastes away. Violence and untimely deaths
proliferate in a novel that feels grotesque and verges on the burlesque.
But while some of the events border on the bizarre and the preposterous,
the reader is seduced into seeing plausibility in each and every coincidence and contrivance, since Viola's is the voice that narrates most of
these events. She knows her white folks and, to borrow Lillian Smith's
phrase, is "familiar with every bone of every skeleton in their closets."[8]

Viola's persistent and stoical narrative presence is left unquestioned
and unchecked until very far into the family's history. She is largely un-

assailable in her hold on past events and present equivocations and un-
stoppable in her determination to preserve the stories in the keeping of
Victoria, the last Ransom. Viola fixes events within a framework of her
stalwart support of the Ransom family and her unswerving belief in the
evil of Archibald's son, Grant Macafee, their nemesis. She places a grid
of her own understanding over the stories, a grid that sets Grant Macafee
as the agent of change, destruction, and mayhem of all kinds for the
Ransoms: in short, he is "a miserable hunk of hell" (195). It is strongly
implied that the Macafees are out to ruin the Ransoms, and a catalog of
disasters, twists, and turns prefigures their demise, from the time of the
First World War to the Vietnam crisis. Almost entirely insulated from
such conflicts, Ransoms keep to their three-story stone mansion on the
edge of town. Venturing outside only precipitates disaster, as in the case
of Baby Boy, who loses his life in his sixteenth year, in December 1939,
on his first drive around Bernice in his first car. The incident occurs on
the eve of a party at the Ransom place that would have helped to ease
the way of its occupants into Bernice society, but death casts a hush
over the house and draws the remaining occupants back into its shadows
and secretive silences.

Importantly, marriage does not figure in the novel despite its status as
a southern family romance. Southern white women have long been represented as upholders of the importance of home and region. As one
critic puts it, "From reproducing the family they would join hands to
reproduce the region."[9] But, as in most of the novels discussed in this
book, neither the white nor the black women protagonists in *Body of
Knowledge* reproduce biologically. Victoria is a virgin, and there is no
evidence in the text that Viola has any sexual experience at all; her experience of mothering is vicarious, since she cares only for the Ransom
children. Nor are there marital relationships that endure. William Ransom marries a woman who is left unnamed and who spends only a
month in the family home before dying in childbirth. His son, Willie
Junior, marries Annabelle, who is described as frigid by her own daughter, Victoria, and whose aversion to sex combined with only moderate
affection for her husband drives him to drink and leads her to quit the

house one day, not to return for five years. Although Willie and Annabelle establish happy marital relations on her return, their romantic bliss is cut short by Annabelle's untimely death from pneumonia after three short years of harmony. Dark secrets and difficult silences predominate, and interludes of happiness and contentment are brief.

Significant amidst the many silences that characters maintain in the novel is that which Grant Macafee and Sarah Ransom uphold until their deaths. They are irresistibly attracted to one another, and their attraction becomes a secret, frenzied passion as destructive as it is honest. Sarah, pregnant after the encounter, fears that she would be entirely subsumed by Grant were they to embark on a longer relationship or marriage, so she escapes the situation, leaving Bernice and Grant bitter and angry. Only Viola knows Sarah's mind, and, as is her wont, she keeps its contents to herself. Silence about their baby's existence precipitates a tragic chain of events: in a bid to hide his emotions, Grant quickly marries the woman that William Ransom happens to love. Grant's wife, Sophie, and William embark on a secret affair that results in Baby Boy; and Grant, all too aware that the child is not his, fakes its death in childbirth and creates the public façade of the most lavish funeral Bernice has ever seen. Sophie is forced to commandeer the help of her maid, Dandy, to contrive the child into the care of Mavis Ransom. Believing she has found the child abandoned in a church, Mavis brings up Baby Boy as her own, and William is forced to play the role of uncle. He and Viola collude in a further silence about the child's parentage, and the masquerade continues until Viola reveals the details to Victoria.

Is *Body of Knowledge* the depiction of a specific personal relationship but also another example of a text in which the black woman functions only to aid a white protagonist's coming to terms with the circumstances of her own life and context? As one works this problem through, it becomes evident that Viola is the housekeeper, metaphorically as well as literally, in her role as keeper of stories and as the conduit of memories, and Victoria is in many ways her apprentice and disciple. Victoria is, of course, the legal heir to the Ransom house, and therefore the idea of her fulfilling the role of apprentice to the family servant may appear improbable. But Victoria is as inextricably linked to the house as the older black woman, though in different ways. In fact, after Viola's death Victoria strikes up secret friendships with the books in her grandfather's library, with the plants in the conservatory, especially a *Ficus lyrata* fern she feels herself loved and courted by, and with the house itself. She is much like the housewife in the opening lines of Anne Sexton's poem:

> Some women marry houses.
> It's another kind of skin; it has a heart,
> a mouth, a liver and bowel movements.[10]

As her life is married to the history of the Ransoms, she is sealed hermetically within the house for almost the entire novel. *Body of Knowledge* embodies and even parodies black and white women's traditional positions as keepers and caretakers of the house. Through Viola, though, Victoria derives the means to liberate herself from the house as well as to care for it; she learns where she fits into the Ransom dynasty and genealogy. She is thus able to transcribe the body of information that she inherits so that an oral history finally becomes a manuscript, a tangible and material document that is a separate entity, discrete from Victoria herself. She reads the document aloud to a small audience at the novel's close. It resonates with significant personal detail for each of them, and, once shared beyond its two compilers, it can finally be laid to rest.

✍♥ In order to come to terms with the interracial relationship that is at the heart of this novel, it is essential to consider how Viola and Victoria communicate and how communication is affected by their respective roles. There are significant structural contradictions between the two narrators and between the two books of the novel. Viola re-creates the past as a serial for her listener in the manner of nineteenth-century serializations of "big baggy monsters," to apply Henry James's expression for the huge sprawling novels of Dickens and Eliot or, in the American context, Melville's *Moby Dick* and Harriet Beecher Stowe's *Uncle Tom's Cabin*. The latter two are, in fact, echoed intertextually in Dawson's novel, as are a number of other texts—Burton's *The Anatomy of Melancholy*,

Dickens's *Bleak House,* the works of Heidegger, Husserl, and Hegel—so that the processes of fiction making, storytelling, and epistemological and ontological strategies for interpreting stories are brought to the reader's attention. Viola reels out the episodes, looping back and forth from the distant past to more recent events: "She would unwind a reference from her spool, and start clacking away like a spinning jenny" (285). Between them she and Victoria tease incidents into a semblance of chronology and a shape that coheres into an apparent explication of events, as is indicated by the chapter titles. In book 1 chapters follow early novelistic conventions in managing the plot. The chapter headings point to an episodic patterning, with each new chapter bringing a new situation: "Where Sarah Went," "What Sarah Did Next," "How Mavis Took the Helm," "How Willie and Bert Were Born." This is Viola's book, and the structuring reveals the way in which plot and character intermesh in Viola. As Peter Brooks argues, plot itself has been molded by nineteenth-century narrative traditions that "in history, philosophy, and a host of other fields as well as literature, conceived certain kinds of knowledge and truth to be inherently narrative, understandable (and expoundable) only by way of sequence, in a temporal unfolding." [11] The constitutive units of plot are restricted by Viola's teleological perspective, whereas the chapter titles for book 2 are much more abstract and open, since it is Victoria's subjectivity that dominates: "My Condition," "Abandoned," "Valedictory," "Panic."

Male power relations may structure the plot, but the text of this and other family interactions is replotted and restructured by the narrators' patterning of events. History is therefore understood as an imaginative space, a domestic space even, shared by Viola and Victoria, who remain separated from world events during their lifetimes and between whom family stories may be recycled, reimagined, and reconstituted. Their philosophies combine in a domestic perspective: events exist as dialogue and are made available to the reader in the space or intersection between speaker and listener. Dialogues or discursive relationships are, as Robert Stam has argued, microhistorical encounters,[12] which are inevitably political, and the domestic relationship that frames the two women's dialogue is an ancient and powerful dyad upon which much of southern history and tradition depends.

In Viola and Victoria are combined two narrative styles and intentions; the reader could be seduced, by a desire for linear coherency, into skipping over the uncertainties in the narrative, but through Victoria in book 2 Dawson exploits the desire for mysteries to be solved, misunderstandings resolved, and truths detected. In fact, Victoria consumes the plot that is book 1; she swallows it literally as well as metaphorically, until she weighs six hundred pounds and is a baggy monster of a text herself.[13] She is swollen with stories, and she consumes the past in the sense that Sartre has described the past as "the ever-growing totality of the in-itself which we are."[14] As Victoria grows in size—and the process may be equally usefully compared with Michel de Certeau's description of history as cannibalistic, since for Victoria history is lived corporeally—she grows in existential understanding of ontology and temporality until she comes to interpret a historical fact as "a pushing-off place toward freedom" (176). Consequently, such a shift involves her in reassessing the facts, the equivocations, the ambiguities and misprisions, the lacunae in Viola's chronicle.

Viola is privy to Sarah Ransom's reasons for running away from the family home, her plots and pretences; and the news of her death, and the grief that she is forced to hide from other family members, seals her irrevocably to them. What Viola knows, what she has hidden, and what she suffers commit her more forcefully to her role as the family's secret repository of knowledge than her duties in the home ever could. This is what fuels her obsession to relieve the burden of her knowledge by filling Victoria to the very brim with the detail of it all, as Victoria comes to realize:

> Sometimes when I think back to that moment [when Viola heard of Sarah's death], I see Viola's life, with its solitude, marching straight from the peak of the terrible news to the present day in a straight line that no other events might ever divert again. There was no way for her. Her home had vaporized, long before. Her old friends, her family members in Bernice, saw her as a

defector, even in the midst of their knowing she had no other place to go. Her promise to Sarah rendered her into a fixed position of loyalty from which she could not swerve, no matter what might tempt her elsewhere. And after Sarah's death, the promise seemed to Viola more cast iron than ever. So if her choices later ground down on me in a way no child on earth deserves, then it is not so surprising that she resolved to take that path. In her soul, I think she too longed to be free. (91–92)

This passage is key to any understanding of the relationship that dominates the novel. White householders have traditionally given their cast-off items to the black workers in their homes, to garner superficial moral power or as a palliative for meager wages. Here the black family retainer casts her stories for the white girl, who catches their content because she is weighed down by the burden that has been left to her to carry.

Bakhtin's contention that language is always half someone else's has special significance in a reading of the women's cotextual relationship.[15] Victoria does not confide her interpretation of the meaning of Viola's life to Viola herself. She cannot. Words cannot be formulated into a pattern that will succinctly or adequately express or define Viola's centrality to the lives of all the Ransoms.[16] Viola herself alerts Victoria to the aphoristic and aphasic nature of speech in this context. She remembers indignantly how Victoria's grandfather William once tried to express his gratitude: "'It's just that, well, you know, you've done a lot for us in the past few years. . . . You could have—I feel like we've perhaps been selfish, taken you for granted, enclosed you—.' His eyes slipped away from her frown. 'It's just that you've done an awful lot for us, Viola. For me. Shoot, you've been central to my life ever since I could remember. My rudder.' He smiled apologetically" (214). Rather than the rudder which endows her with agency, Viola has been the family's safe deposit box, and she has been filled not with valuables but with deeds and decisions that they prefer not to reexamine once they have been safely filed away. But Viola, the keeper of the house's secrets along with the house itself, cannot but pore over deeds done, and their moral consequences.

This book, dryly acerbic as it can be at times, is also quite principled and ethical in its focus and conclusions, as is the work of Lillian Smith, whose ideas influence my reading. In his discussion of Smith, "From Therapy to Morality," Richard H. King describes memory as "the vehicle of therapeutic healing and the restorer of authentic morality," which involves remembering, repeating, and working through and over the past.[17] In many ways, Viola's moral concerns turn on this idea of a therapeutic reconciliation with self, and she projects this desire onto Victoria. Instead of proving immediately therapeutic, however, Viola's talk-story becomes an extended form of repression, since she deposits her memories in Victoria as if she too is a living family vault. She omits to consider how the child might heal herself once the weight of family tragedy has overwhelmed her. Viola has been overwhelmed, and the force and weight of her weariness has communicated itself to her charge, almost in some form of terrible osmosis, as in the sorrow over Baby Boy's death:

"Ah," I whispered, even as the sting of Baby Boy's death went numb with the deadness of her tone. I had ached as she ached; I had felt that death through her. That was its meaning to me.

And now she was meaning: It is all fruitless, all dream. There is no meaning.

Or so I thought she was saying.

Then she looked at me.

I saw the eyes, their tiredness, their disgust, which overrode whatever she had gained from telling me the story: love, a reliving, an entertainment for a lonely child, a sense of fealty. The disgust accused the house, the lawn, and me, of a breakdown of nerve, a failure of strength and moral certitude, that subsumed all history. (289)

By book 2, Victoria is brought into clearer focus, and she is left alone to reconstitute the family saga of the Ransoms and the Macafees after Viola's death. A by-product of the transaction between Viola the storyteller and Victoria the storer and interpreter of the knowledge is an explication of their interrelationship. Victoria the child, badgering Viola with questions, coexists with the older, more mature Victoria, who reviews the knowledge she has gleaned in the way that the older

Miranda interprets the child in Katherine Anne Porter's Miranda stories. The narrator is a dual figure whose progress through life unites her past and present in the desire for story. The contents of Viola's storehouse of knowledge are inherited by Victoria. In her keeping they are sifted and scrutinized until it becomes apparent, little by little, that some of the family history that Viola imparted was inaccurate, since hers was a negotiated reading of events. As she pored over them, she touched them with her own hurt and her own fears—which subsumed all history.

Despite its twists and turns, Dawson structures the novel so that Viola is either present during or a hidden witness to the key and pivotal conversations and episodes in the plot, and in this way Dawson ensures an internal consistency in Viola's rendition of events. As Victoria comes to realize as she listens to Viola's stories and ruminates on the remaking of events as history, "nothing is ever really left to chance; the circumlocutions are too tight, coincidence too reliable" (114). Like Nellie Dean in *Wuthering Heights*, Viola construes each episode *as* event and so intercedes on her listener's understanding of what she describes. There are numerous examples of this, but to consider one in detail: Viola contrives to listen to a private conversation between Grant and Sarah on the evening that they meet in the Ransom house. As Victoria reports, "At some point during the later hours, Grant Macafee approached [Sarah] and sat down. Viola, on whose report I rely, was roaming to and fro among the guests, with a tray of punch cups. She saw him speak, earnestly and with an austere frown, and she stepped behind the row of chairs in order to hear better" (19). Viola always places herself in the background as an eavesdropper, the natural place for a family servant and a place that no white family member could occupy unobtrusively. She is in the shadows, standing away from an important conversation at a dinner and hidden on her knees polishing in one room, close enough to hear what is going on in the next on another occasion. On the occasion of Sarah and Grant's conversation, as on all others, Viola judges what she sees or hears. She adjudges Grant Macafee so dizzy with longing for Sarah that it is like a sickness, and, although Sarah escapes him very abruptly mid-conversation, she feels she has witnessed the beginning of an encounter doomed to wreak havoc on more lives than theirs. She incorporates the hindsight of years of watching havoc work itself out when she recounts these incidents for Victoria, her words testifying to what she believes are the long-term effects as well as her memory of the incident itself.

Oral history is constructed as memory, as testimony, and oral historians have emphasized the interaction of the interviewing process. Victoria gradually interviews Viola in an informal and unstructured way, encouraging her to repeat episodes for clarity, for sheer enjoyment, or for their special significance in her own life. She examines Viola's storytelling style and scrutinizes the context for each memory. This form of interaction as a collaboration between speaker and listener, teller and interpreter, helps to clarify the strengths and weaknesses of oral storytelling as a form in which to chronicle past lives, and as a typically southern method of articulating a problematic historical past. So when Richard Gray calls southern writing a "literature of memory" and observes that "problems, deriving from the interaction between event and dream, or history and myth" are characteristic of modern southern writing, his argument can prove to be just as helpful in elucidating the structure and methodology of recent texts—like *Body of Knowledge* or Lee Smith's *Oral History*—as it has proved successful in interpreting the works of canonical writers like Faulkner, Warren, and Welty.[18] Viola is somewhat reminiscent of Granny Younger in *Oral History,* herself an old woman whose memories combine with the ideas of a young woman to shape events into an ongoing coherent pattern. Oral history is a collaboration between teller and listener whereby history is always in construction. So it is as subject to misreadings and misunderstandings as it is to edifying and illuminating insights.

Susan Tucker, in *Telling Memories Among Southern Women,* deploys episodes and instances from southern fiction to enhance the oral histories of the black family servants and white employers that she retrieves from the women she interviews. She notes the processes of selection and editing that typify the southern stories she is told. Two effects of memory that she becomes particularly aware of are those of revision and reconciliation. It is these features of the storytelling process that change the past as it is mediated in the memories and descriptions of the story-tellers.[19] The past is part of a continuing process of reinvention, reinter-pretation, and revision, but the issue of reconciliation is one Tucker be-lieves applies specifically to the intertwined histories of black and white women. Arguably, such women, who lived through segregation while bound into very intimate daily interactions across racial and economic divisions, survive the internecine entanglements of race and gender in power relationships by reconciling themselves to the bad as well as the good. It is in this kind of process that Dawson ensures both the narrators are engaged.

✍ A relationship that has become paradigmatic and stereotypical therefore forms the basis of Carol Dawson's fiction of a Texas family, but it is creatively reworked. Viola is Victoria's mammy, and she has been mammy to three generations of Ransom children. Victoria is her last child. The mutuality present in their relationship can be distinguished historically, but the dialogue in which they participate signals a kind of apprenticeship in communication, across race, across the generations, and between women, that continues to have significant resonance in contemporary feminist debates.

In *Of Woman Born*, Adrienne Rich suggests that this particular cross-racial relationship remains "so little explored" and "so unexpressed," but it "still charges the relationships of black and white women": "We have been mothers and daughters to each other; and although in the last few years, black and white feminists have been moving toward a still-difficult sisterhood, there is little yet known, unearthed, of the time when we were mothers and daughters."[20] But Rich proved wary of expressing her own feelings when she edited the above reference to black mother sur-rogates and their white daughters in the second edition of *Of Woman Born*. She feared, she said, the "tendency to be too personal" and the impossibility of adequately excavating or imagining the feelings black nurses may or may not have had for their white charges.[21] The sensitivity of the subject matter marks this relationship out as one of what Lillian

Smith enumerates as the "ghost relationships" that haunt the mind of the South and, consequently, the imaginations of those who write about the region.[22]

Smith described the relationship between a young white child and his or her mammy as "the ambivalent and tragic relationship" of southern childhood.[23] She describes the love she felt for her own nurse, Aunt Chloe, in *Killers of the Dream*. White southern society expected her to feel love but also expected her to outgrow it as a childish thing. She says, "I learned to cheapen with tears and sentimental talk of 'my old mammy' one of the profound relationships of my life."[24] For Smith the tragic feelings are the child's and the exact nature of the black woman's feelings about the relationship are, understandably, left unexplored and unexpressed, though she does attempt to examine what has clearly been an exploitative relationship.

The characterization of Viola can evade much of what was expected of the mammy, but the mammy image informs an understanding of her character, nevertheless. Despite Rich's and Smith's observations, the mammy is one of the "four most frequent" female southern types and the success of *Gone with the Wind,* in which she is not named outside of her slave role, helped to seal her image in twentieth-century popular culture as tightly as her history binds her to the nineteenth-century slave South.[25] The mammy figure moderated into the Aunt Jemima stereotype, so carefully examined in its literary encodings by Diane Roberts.[26] This black woman's sexuality has been downplayed to the extent that her ample bosom was intended solely as a comfort to the children in her care, and she frequently remained unmarried, her "family" loyalty unswayed by romantic or sexual liaisons. Typically she has emerged a transcendent figure in the way in which Faulkner's Dilsey is understood to transcend the tragedies of the Compson family and to endure after their demise, and after the fashion of Julia Peterkin's black women survivors in her Pulitzer Prize–winning *Scarlet Sister Mary*.[27] The tendency toward apotheosis that this character type brings out in writers and in critics is striking. She is deployed symbolically, as an abstract carrier of moral values and southern history and heritage, whether the context is sentimental nostalgia for the Old South and its codes and mores or a more radical reclamation of her worth. Forbearance and endurance are inextricable from stereotypes of the good black, since, as James Baldwin has pointed out, they are historically the qualities that codified the only acceptable means of survival for blacks in America.[28] The family servant was the very best and most reliable of the images of blacks constructed under slavery and segregation. The black woman of many mass cultural images is circumscribed by the needs of the white family that employs her, and so her life, largely unmediated by external or community forces, becomes inextricable from the lives of those she cares for. In literature she can be extricated unproblematically from any familial contingencies in order to serve as the omnipresent devoted servant, or even friend, to the white protagonist.

It is very difficult to shake the mythification of the mammy/nurse figure.[29] The representation of Viola in *Body of Knowledge* is as a sensible and sensitive protagonist rather than a minor character with a "flat surface" or a "dark-skinned vacancy," as black servants in white homes can so easily be codified.[30] One character's description of Viola as "the old style mammy" is immediately called into question, but it relies on another stereotypical assumption; that the black woman could be "one of the family."[31] Studies of black women working in white homes tend to argue that a familial connection was never really possible, but they also tend to concentrate on black women who travel to work in white homes on a daily basis and fail to address those live-in housekeepers who have no family or home of their own.[32] Viola is an orphan and is given over to the Ransoms by what remains of her extended family, who cannot afford to keep her. She takes up the post of nanny and housekeeper at the age of eleven. The black live-in housekeeper, traditionally backgrounded, is given center stage in *Body of Knowledge;* she is a speaking presence for more than three quarters of a five-hundred-page novel, a crucial figure on almost every page, even after death has silenced her. But even a particularized representation remains disquieted by the potency and endurance of the mammy stereotype, as reviewers of the novel demonstrate in the vocabulary they deploy when assessing Viola: they hesitate over whether she may be "authentic" or "realistic" and fall into the clichés.[33]

In a paradigmatic literary text about the relationship, Carson Mc-Cullers's *The Member of the Wedding,* Frankie Adams, the twelve-year-old protagonist, spends most of her time hanging around the kitchen with the black housekeeper-cook, Berenice. Typically, Berenice is surrogate mother to the motherless Frankie, as Calpurnia in Harper Lee's *To Kill a Mockingbird* is to Scout. She serves to intensify the reader's understanding of the young protagonist. In the majority of literary depictions, the black woman's function has been to shadow the white child. Berenice's life—her four marriages and her life in service—is bound up in the representation of Frankie's development in *The Member of the Wedding.* Consequently, her purpose is complete once the young girl embarks on a new phase in her life and once her youthful fears are allayed. However, in recent fictions there have emerged quite complex and interrogative variations on the theme. Lyn Lauber imagines a relationship between a young white woman and an older black woman in *21 Sugar Street* but excludes from her representation all facets of the prototypical reliance of the white girl on the black woman. Loretta, a high school student, meets Annie Biggs when she begins a relationship with Annie's son and sits at her table asking endless questions of Annie, whose stories she loves. As with Viola and Victoria's relationship, theirs is based on a deep affinity for story and talk and a deep-seated connection that Loretta describes as "family." But their relationship has none of the complications of the tie of responsibility. Their friendship springs from mutual feelings across race and across a generation, an idea pursued from a very different angle in *Clover,* by Dori Sanders. Clover and her white stepmother work through Adrienne Rich's biracial mother-daughter metaphor via a reversal of the maternal cross-racial connection.

Viola is not the ideal of the self-effacing mammy; her emotions, carefully hidden from some, spill over and affect others deeply. Diane Roberts has argued that the mammy "absolves whites of guilt." Although this is clearly the case across a range of representations, revised characters like Viola and Clarice in *On the Occasion of My Last Afternoon* may, contradictorily, impress the issue of guilt on whites. Viola, a family retainer in the twentieth century rather than a mammy in the nineteenth, finds little to praise in the actions of those who employ her and at times expresses her opinions to this effect, at least to William Ransom and to Victoria, both of whom are profoundly affected by her words. Gloria Naylor posits the idea that the mammy "existed without a history or a future" but Carol Dawson's mammy figure is the most powerful historical source in this novel, and it is on the foundations she builds into Victoria's understanding of "family" that the small community can rest at its close.[34]

It is impossible to appropriate Viola's voice and to also understand what she has to say. Victoria, who hangs on her every word, must pursue the meaning of Viola's life as painstakingly as she pursues meaning in her own. Thus Dawson has Victoria point out just before Viola's death that Viola has actually been telling her own life as she told the lives of those in her care. Viola draws her last breath in the midst of a story about herself, an anecdote perhaps rather than a story but the only reminiscence in which not a single Ransom features. She has gone to Bernice on behalf of her employers, but on the way one of the members of a New Orleans jazz band booked to play singles her out for special attention: "What you doing tonight, with you fine proud legs?" (161). Viola is flattered as a woman, rather than as somebody's nurse or somebody's housekeeper; she is appreciated for herself. Sadly, this is a lone incident, but its inclusion alerts the reader to how insignificant Viola's own feelings, desires, and cares actually are in the novel; the single occasion on which a nameless man appreciates her as a woman provides an opportunity for self-exploration through another on her own terms. The opportunity is lost as soon as Viola turns her attention back to Ransom business, and a glance at the man's figure receding into the distance cuts sharply to a conversation with Dandy, her alter ego and the servant in the Macafee home. The content of their conversation is the content of their characters: self-abnegation in an overriding concern for the white individuals for whom they work but for whom they are also seen to care. Later, their allegiance to their respective white families is precisely what severs the connection between Viola and Dandy. They each choose white "kin" over their own "kind" and over any possibility for sisterhood with each other. Maintaining the white dynasties at the center of their existence leaves them no time for families of their own—or for friendships. In this way Carol Dawson would seem to subordinate Viola to the greater story of the Ransom dynasty. There is, however, a careful context for the level of subordination: Viola's privacy remains intact. Although the reader feels that she knows the character type well, Viola remains something of an enigma to the Ransoms and to the reader, and she leaves behind an enigmatic legacy. This is not enough to rescue her from what is an unromantic, somewhat lonely life; but Viola has pragmatic as well as personal requirements, and she finds some of them met by the Ransoms.

While the machinations within the white Ransom and Macafee families are pursued in their minutiae in Victoria's reconstruction of family history, the family connections and kinship of the blacks in the novel remain largely unclarified. Viola has invested her life in the white family, and she keeps their secrets as closely as she guards the memories of her own family. When Uncle Shine accuses her of accepting her role—"You believe they're *your* family, you so particular to them all" (115)—she neither replies nor defends herself. Dawson is aware of the implications, and so Viola's mammydom, exemplified in her willingness to place the well-being of the family over her own, is overlaid by dignity and a certain perverse lonely martyrdom in the role, as in the case of Paula Fox's depiction of Luisa in *A Servant's Tale,* where the protagonist even discovers a kind of liberation through her service role. Bessie and Ezra are the cook and yardman, Ransom servants of long standing, but Dawson allows neither to conform to stereotype. It becomes clear after Ezra's death that Bessie's primary allegiance has actually been to Viola, whose presence in the house is clearly of cardinal importance and with whom she has shared so many years. She has no compunction about leaving the moment that Viola is no longer present in the Ransom house; her job done, she leaves it with a flippant but caustic reminder, "It's just my work" (397).

Bessie might have cooked for Ransoms for fifty years, but she was never interested in their lives: "Fed enough Ransom stomachs now to keep me till the Judgment" (397). It is only Viola of the black characters who acts as the conscience of the novel, concerned with the emotional and psychological well-being of those around her. Characters, black and white, even those who do not exhibit any *overt* affection toward her, like Bessie and Mavis, are becalmed and made secure in her rightness on a number of occasions, convinced that she knows best. Lillian Smith, again, succeeds in apprehending the significance of the role of a black woman like Viola in a white household and consequently the significance of her presence in big, sprawling family sagas in southern literature: "Her knowledge alone, of how to grow children was too precious a thing to throw away lightly," and "her value extended far beyond child rearing." [35] What the black woman knows—the children she cares for better than their biological mother or the skeletons in the family closet—has long been a key feature in writers' understanding of this family servant. But Dawson explores the consequences that being marooned in "her isolation of private knowledge" (97) have on Viola.

℘ Victoria is an allegorical figure of her own and Viola's making. She is the family vault where Viola, as well as the white Ransoms, is finally buried. She is a prison house of language, imprisoned in the house and in the meanings that Viola's words create within her. Her self-consciousness about her size is compounded by her obsessive need to interpret what has been told to her, since it has been her lot to be gorged with words along with food and to become trapped as well as fascinated by their meanings. She is the living embodiment of generations of inaction and lassitude, epitomized in her grandfather, who locked himself away with philosophy and history books in which history always preceded the twentieth century and allowed him to avoid the ramifications of Ransom history that followed the first joint Ransom-Macafee business venture, though they persisted in his fears. Such concerns have only ever been intimated to Viola, and she in turn interprets them for Victoria until Victoria becomes the site of memories that have been repressed. Viola fills Victoria's body with stories, explicating the aphoristic silences of

Victoria's grandfather. But it is Victoria who must finally produce the text of the Ransoms by learning to read her own body. Hers is an abstract textual body that is not described biologically at any point; her body functions entirely as a textual metaphor. In fact, at one point she compares herself to Moby Dick, the archetypal American allegory of the quest for meaning, describing herself as the "Great White Whale" on whom Ahab heaped his fears and his desires for revenge and renewal. She is doomed to pursue the meaning of her family history if she is to have any success in interpreting her own life as "the end result in a pattern of habits" (175).

If Viola carries the stories, Victoria is given an interlocutory role. She must reconstitute the "facts" of the history—of which she is one—from the stories she has heard and in so doing free herself from the pain and self-disgust that she feels. In fact, the two narrators are distinguished from each other through the emphasis on reportage over interpretation or interpretation over reportage. Viola is the narrator as eyewitness— "There's nothing I don't see like it was a picture painting, setting on my mind's eye" (192)—whose mind's eye is clouded by deep tiredness and a thin film of disgust at times. Victoria is the narrator as interpreter and restorer, seeker of the way through the stories, exemplifying in Barthesian terms the hermeneutic code once Viola has primed her through the code of action. Both are narrator-participants in the stories but Victoria creatively interprets the information she has at her disposal and imaginatively reconstructs the moments about which she has the least knowledge. Hers is the more phenomenological inquiry into the past and its relation to her own subjectivity. Victoria's creativity is notable in the scene where she narrates her father's experience at the ball at which Annabelle asks him to marry her. This fact is preceded by a description of Willie Junior's state of mind. He is suffering a malaise reminiscent of Quentin Compson's in *The Sound and the Fury*. Unhappy at college— in Texas rather than at Harvard, where Compson, and indeed Willie's father, William Ransom, were students—he contemplates the gloom that will be his future in the Ransom house, which maintains its heavy Pyncheon-like curse and overshadows his life. His daughter, as the chief agent of the story, allows herself an omniscient peek into his emotional state in a scene where she was not born and her storytelling avatar was not present. Viola has given no indication that she has any interest in or knowledge of the workings of educational establishments or the etiquette of student balls. The imagined element within the "history" becomes clear. Victoria has gleaned ideas and information from the books in her grandfather's library as well as from Viola's palimpsested stories. Frequently she alludes to texts and sometimes draws analogies with them, as in the case of *Bleak House,* where the tale of nineteenth-century trials and errors reminds her of Viola's "rehashing" of twentieth-century examples (287). But Viola's stories are her lifeblood and they supersede the books, clippings, and all other sources she consults.

Victoria has long been a mirror of Viola's understanding and values; in her has been reflected the older woman's assumptions wrapped up as facts. Her reliability is called into question only after Victoria herself is left to sift the information contained in the stories she imbibed in order to organize them into a written form. She demonstrates the construct-edness of meaning and at this stage orders and patterns the chaos of Ransom lives into her own design. She becomes self-authorizing, as the stories Viola inscribes on her body are combined with other texts, like her great-aunt Mavis's scrapbook and her mother's news clippings. Inter-textually these are palimpsests, as is Victoria herself—the living Ransom text—and she must learn to read herself in order to write herself out of the hold that the burden of history has had on her person. It is impos-sible for her to comprehend the full historical and personal import of her family's saga without the figure of the black woman who raised her and who proved to be the only constant figure in her life; Viola forms the axis of investigation. In coming to terms with her past, Victoria comes to terms with her self, a self fed and nurtured by a black woman. At this point she begins to write, and when Victoria begins to purge herself of her thoughts and of the stories that have filled her since childhood, her body begins to shrink. The fat that has impeded her falls away as her confidence in her own language and her ability to tell her history increases.

So the double-voiced narration of Victoria and Viola is structured as a set of apparently binary oppositions between the experiences of the two women: white and black, young and old, servant and served, family member and "family" member; but whereas in the usual structuralist formation the first is privileged over the second, the apparent antithesis is deconstructed in a narrative that privileges the dual perspective in a nonhierarchical way. The genealogy of fathers and sons that is so pervasive in Faulkner's South is relegated to background so that the women's version of events may be brought to the fore. Faulkner's multiple narrators are reduced, and a double interpretative framework operates: the stories Viola tells to Victoria are mediated into Victoria's first-person narration, and episodes Viola recalls are reimagined and presented as contemporaneous with Victoria's own experiences, with her own observations often included in parenthesis. In this way past and present are gradually intertwined in a novel where past events are seen to inform the novel's present at every turn, until they are finally resolved. Faulkner does not allow the past to be integrated into the narrative present in a way that resolves the paradoxical and chimerical, as well as historically verifiable, realities of a family's past. For Faulkner the paradoxes are the crux of southern history itself, whereas Dawson would clear them away to provide a happy and hopeful ending, choosing reconciliation over the recurring southern nightmare that Rosa rages against even to the final lines of *Absalom, Absalom!*.

Insofar as it follows Faulknerian themes, *Body of Knowledge* relies most heavily on *Absalom, Absalom!*, in which Quentin Compson is summoned by Rosa Coldfield, who needs to "tell about the South," about the Coldfields and the Sutpens and the house on Sutpen's Hundred. Viola, like Rosa before her, recounts the history from the standpoint of an eyewitness; William Ransom, rather like Mr. Compson before him, asks questions but expects no clear answers, and Mr. Compson's fatalistic idea that history is "a horrible and bloody mischancing of human affairs" would not seem out of character if uttered by Dawson's William Ransom.[36] Quentin listens to Rosa without knowing why he has been chosen as the recipient of her memories, as Victoria began unsure of her own position vis-à-vis Viola; and like Quentin she becomes detective-narrator, pursuer of the clues, the silences, and the absences in Viola's text, following the same story over and over as it is told and retold. *Absalom, Absalom!* epitomizes the qualities of southern storytelling that continue to interest Dawson: the obsession to pick over the past; circular oral narrations in which repetitions and revisions of the past occur; people, whether white or black, haunted by southern family history and legend. These themes are present, despite Fred Hobson's assessment that young writers no longer invest in "traditional" Faulknerian themes. Quentin Compson, as he appears in *Absalom, Absalom!,* is the figure who corresponds most nearly to what Dawson wishes to achieve through Victoria and her narrative function. Faulkner describes Quentin's body as the inevitable family vault: "He was not a being, an entity, he was a commonwealth. He was a barracks filled with stubborn backward-looking ghosts" (12). The military image and the ever-present Civil War is set aside for a domestic emphasis in Victoria's case, but the southern maxim that "*maybe nothing ever happens once and is finished*" (210), redolent throughout Faulkner, Wolfe, and much southern writing—epitomized in Allen Tate's famous statement that southern literature is a "literature conscious of the past in the present"[37]—is again reinscribed by Carol Dawson, this time on a woman's body.

⚜ Victoria is a body of language and a signifier of history at its most aleatory. Victoria exists as a cipher of the Ransom dynasty and its accumulated sorrows, in a wry and grotesque twist away from Faulknerian pastiche into postsouthern parody.[38] She is a text empty of sensuality until, without Viola's memories to fill her days, she suddenly feels the freakishness of her situation and cries that her body craves caresses. Onto a fern in the plant-filled conservatory, where she spends day after day in a reinforced concrete seat, she projects the heat of her desires and imagines them returned in waves of sensuous heat in some autoerotic and surreal travesty of love. In this she finds little release, however. Her body craves expression beyond that of her own making. Her desires echo those of ladies throughout twentieth-century southern literature—Dabney Fairchild, Scarlett O'Hara, and Blanche DuBois, as well as Faulkner's women characters—despite the fact that Victoria's body is a grotesque parody of their slim frames. The cult of southern white womanhood created the image of the southern lady on a pedestal elevated above the common passions and sexual desires projected onto black women.

But Victoria in her bulk is nothing like other southern daughters. She is also bookish and tends to involve herself only in studied, philosophical conversation with one other, while the ideal lady was a socialite, mistress of small talk and eminently at ease with guests of all kinds. Victoria is a recluse. She risks going the way of other twisted female characters disabled in their desires, physically as well as psychologically and metaphorically, like Cather's Sapphira Colbert, Victoria's own hunchbacked great-aunt Mavis in *Body of Knowledge,* and the four generations of emotionally crippled southern ladies that Dawson delineates in her first novel, *The Waking Spell.*[39] Mavis could only skirt the sanctified social space occupied by the "true" southern lady, and she hurls herself off the top of the statue of a prominent southern male icon of Bernice society. Her act is symbolic, and through it the reader recognizes how the lives of Ransom women, before Victoria, were also curtailed by their bodies and by the patriarchal expectations that trapped them into believing in themselves as symbols of white ladyhood. Arliss, the arch Ransom socialite, has her activities cut short when she is literally paralyzed and made socially inept and inarticulate by a stroke. The soirées for which she is famed stop, and the Ransoms' social circle dissipates, since poor hunchbacked Mavis is considered a poor social secretary and no southern belle. By the time Annabelle, Victoria's mother, makes the house her home, she finds it stifling in its stuffiness, and her influence in a town where she is unknown is limited. Annabelle, as her name indicates, is a belle, but she is without an audience to appreciate her charms. When she returns to the Ransom house after an unsuccessful foray into the wider world, she too returns to become a recluse. Her face has been disfigured by rosea, a fact she wishes to keep secret and does by wearing a veil at all times. The belle is transformed into a Hawthornian gothic grotesque who comes to prefer the gloom of the old house, as have all of the women in the family she has married into.

It is Victoria, however, who must dominate any discussion of the physical body. Her size is explained as the result of a medical condition; a dangerous bout of the measles in early childhood resulted in glandular problems. But her condition is as much mythical as medical; her size is as allegorical as Moby Dick's whiteness. It is made clear that she cannot control her weight but neither can she control her eating. In *Killers of the Dream* Lillian Smith describes how she refused to eat as she adjusted to a younger sibling of whom she was jealous. She was left to the care of her nurse, Aunt Chloe, who persuaded her to resume eating by chewing a little food first, before putting it into the mouth of young Lillian, who promptly ate it up. The intimacy of this gesture as a solution to a problem of a lack of emotional sustenance aids an examination of Victoria's digestion of Viola's stories along with her food. The stories are as real to her as the spoon with which she eats (158). In a largely dysfunctional family, Victoria cannot gain her fill of emotional sustenance. She craves the attention she receives as recipient of Viola's memories as she craves food itself. Viola is willing to give her both, weaning her through the loneliness of her childhood in this fashion:

> "You listen to me, child, it's the stomach from where we get the juice of human love. Most people think it's the heart, but it ain't. . . ."
>
> She turned to me. "That's why I'm glad my lamb here is so nice and round. It means you bursting with good juice."
>
> "I am?" I stared at her longingly. (15)

Unlike Mammy in *Gone with the Wind,* Viola does not try to fit her charge into the mold of southern lady but leaves her "lamb" to grow as she will. Mitchell's mammy is clear that a lady should not be overly concerned with food or with sensual appetite of any kind ("You kin allus tell a lady by dat she eat lak a bird"[40]), but Viola stands in direct opposition to Victoria's mother, who seeks to erase her physicality by removing it from her sight. Tests upon tests at clinics throughout the South and as far away as New York have no effect on Victoria's prodigious frame, and at the point when her mother "gave up the battle," the stories begin. At seven Victoria is sent into seclusion, seclusion being the kitchen or what Goffman would call the "back region" of society instead of the "front region" her mother inhabits.[41] Victoria is left to Viola's society and to eat all meals, except for more formal dinners, in the kitchen. It remains this way until her mother leaves. Before Victoria's illness commenced, her mother let her see her jewelry, the gems that traditionally would become her own inheritance, but Annabelle sells them in order to escape her family, thus breaking her own matrilineal connection with Victoria. She leaves her daughter without a word or a look and with only food, Viola, and her tales to comfort her.

As she grows into a teenager and a young lady, Victoria continually gorges herself, her eating resembling a disorder symptomatic of what might be termed a psychocultural illness, since she is gradually filled to bursting with the bitter gall of her family's guilty secrets, as well as the juice of human love. Viola's love is tinged with the bitterness she feels, and this too cannot help but communicate itself and contribute to the distortion of Victoria psychologically as well as physically. Slowly but surely, she is disabled by her size; as a teenager she discovers to her chagrin that it takes her a good twenty-five minutes to climb the stairs to the second floor and her bedroom. She has to have an industrial elevator constructed in order to bear her bulk to the upper floors, and she hides out while the engineers take two weeks over its construction, preferring that they carry no description of her lumbering bulk away to Bernice. Members of the family who haven't seen her for years, like her uncle Bert, and even her own mother after her five-year sojourn outside of the Ransom stronghold, gasp in shock at her approach, and her father winces on each occasion that she refers to her "condition." Victoria Grace, as she is ironically named, is a graceless and hulking spectacle of southern womanhood, vitiated ancestrally by her family's congenital inaction and ineffectuality. Viola always looks upon her clear-sightedly and openly, however, and, in fact, something they share is the fact that neither conforms to the physical characteristics expected of their "types." If Victoria is as unlikely a representative of a young southern belle as could be imagined, Viola does not have the full and ample figure of the mammy or nurse but is "a thin, small woman" (47), attractive enough to catch the eye of the New Orleans band member passing through town and, as Dandy observes in begrudging fashion, "Miss Viola Lewis, proud and proper, fanciest colored woman Bernice ever seen" (314).

Whereas the body of the mammy has been traditionally read as grotesque and the body of the white woman as classical, her person ethereal rather than physical,[42] Dawson turns the tables. Viola remains credible where Victoria becomes surreal and mythical. The mythical dimensions of the mammy are reworked but then displaced, leaving Viola relatively free from her role and leaving care and custody of the Ransom family history, if not the Ransoms themselves, to Victoria. Dawson walks a fine line. She does not entirely extricate Viola from the tradition of literary mammies, but she establishes her primary significance over that of the white characters, who, in their almost pathological concerns about the intricacies of their own lives, fail to prepare the youngest Ransom for life in the present or hope in the future.

As the attention from family members declines after her recovery from measles visits upon her an unseemly dependency on food, Victoria comes to understand the nature of dependency—her own on Viola and Viola's on her, and the family's on Viola. She comes to recognize that Viola is the only sustaining living presence within a tragically dysfunctional family. The enmeshing of the two characters and their dual concerns is transcribed into the very structuring of the novel as it interlaces past with present, black with white, and old with young. It is difficult, in fact, to disentangle the two narrators from their narration and to decipher the exact nature of their relationship and reciprocation, even though this is integral to the narrative and to the meanings that the reader pursues. An understanding of the significance of Victoria Grace's body and size and of the nature of her relationship with her nurse is homologous to the structuring of the novel itself.

Viola's service role has mutated into a Frankenstein-style relationship to her grotesque prodigy. Victoria is Viola's creation, her invention, and her memorial: "She had made me what I was: a repository of all the events left behind her and relived, an archive of her own acts and feelings" (290). If Viola weighs Victoria down with the moral weight of it all, she also sheds her concerns in a way that begins to reverse the tradition of the black woman as keeper of secrets. Viola chooses to tell about the lives of those she knows but chooses not to impart the details of her own inner life. Whether this is as a result of the suppression of that inner life in service or whether she maintains her own privacy despite her desire to talk is a crucial ambiguity that the novel leaves unexplained. Viola is not Dilsey, told and retold by the Compson men and the Faulknerian narrator, who, as Diane Roberts has carefully argued, is "valued not for what she might reveal of herself but what she suppresses of herself in giving to the Compsons."[43] To adopt part of Roberts's argument, though, Viola's sacrifices do not prevent the decline of the Ransoms, as Dilsey could not have prevented the decline of the Compsons, but where the portrayals are rendered significantly different is in the hope that is engendered in Victoria, the last Ransom woman, a hope that is altogether denied Caddie Compson in *The Sound and the Fury*. Victoria's hope in the future and in her own ability to grapple with the past rather than succumb to its forces is instilled in her by Viola rather than any member of her family. Viola's anger and sorrow militates against the past and stirs Victoria into knowledge. Viola is the most powerful presence in the novel. Victoria's physical body dominates any understanding of the novel's title, but Viola's consciousness pervades the work and creates the body of knowledge it contains. Viola is, however, buried in the Ransom plot along with the white family members who together constitute the Ransom past, and it is Victoria who in her youth and hope will constitute a future.

Viola and Victoria's is a biracial story, bivocal, shared, with mutually dependent discourses carrying the stories of southern individuals into the wider realm of southern social meaning. Forms of narration, shifts, and encodings of subjectivity bespeak a fascination with the power of language and of words themselves, with shifting and ambivalent meanings and interpretations, and with language as a locus of difference and the nexus where gender, race, and history meet. Viola is the agent of episode and event, but Victoria is the agent of meaning. Ultimately, Viola cannot disengage from the past; she lives there and so is unable or unwilling to engage in a quest for meaning that might lead to change for herself. Victoria is pursuing meaning outward while Viola continues to press her memories onto Victoria, but she becomes progressively more reflective, ruminating inwardly after William's death. Viola, with more urgency as she declines in health, sets time aside each day to bequeath her thoughts to Victoria, and she expects much of the girl. Most of all she bequeaths her the weighty questions of why it all happened and what there is to be done with the information she has preserved so carefully as Victoria's alternative inheritance.

It is clear that Viola controls the extent and the nature of the exchange, controlling the release of memories, their accretion and accumulation. She set up the process by which she would fill the child with her family stories and would leave her with a question of her own to contemplate and to answer. However, Viola leads Victoria toward meanings and conclusions that she discovers are not always exact or reliable; not everything was as unimpugnable a "truth" as Victoria first supposed. Viola creates misapprehensions and misreadings that Victoria must clear away in order to ensure her own survival outside and beyond her family history. Victoria the fact finder and solver of mysteries fails to read a photograph of her tragic ancestors with an exacting eye but reads it with the tacit assumption that the only actor upon the image—the photographer—must be Grant Macafee. This is a clear indication that Viola's version of events has influenced her reading and understanding, as by extension it has the reader's. Victoria overreads the image as Viola has overread the chain of tragedies that struck the Ransoms. She overreads her father's shooting, sure that Grant is behind the "accident" in which her father loses his arm, only to discover much later that it was indeed an accident and that Grant Macafee was not present. The whole town misreads the "funeral" of the "Macafee baby," who is neither dead nor buried, nor in fact a Macafee. The reader has followed suit for most of the novel and is reliant, in the final analysis, upon Victoria to alter the lens of interpretation in order to approach an ending that may privilege reconciliation over recrimination. In her prescience, however, Viola left Victoria with questions that might spur her into such an action: she frees herself of the past, though she is determined by it, through her decision to recognize the extent to which her sense of self has relied upon her apprehension (and misapprehension) of past events, and she is finally willing to act upon this realization. For Victoria, the need for story is a need for recovery and, finally, for release. On the final page of the novel, Victoria is contemplating burning the manuscript she has written about the Ransoms, and the signal the fire will create will signify the beginning of a wider life for the Ransom representative of the present generation than that experienced by previous family members.

The symbolism of creating a new beginning out of a historical past works similarly to the "ending" of Faulkner's *Absalom, Absalom!* and to the ending Godwin plays out for Minyon Manigault in *Keeper of the House* when she burns the book in which the history and accounts of the Hazelhedge brothel have been assiduously inscribed and follows this by burning the house itself, since the story of it still remains, "long as I choose." Victoria chooses to reestablish a community in the Ransom house. Randall, Grant Macafee's young cousin and heir, blinded first by the older man's hatred of the Ransoms and later literally losing his sight fighting in Vietnam, enters the old Ransom house looking for friendship and reconciliation. Nyla, brought mysteriously to the house by Victoria's grandfather, is the only remaining servant, and the reader, far earlier than Victoria, realizes that she is Sarah and Grant's child, quietly rescued from an institution by her uncle. These three casualties of the Ransom-Macafee saga are finally united in the knowledge of the parts they were forced to play in the saga's unraveling. They are united through Viola and Victoria's story, and its relation to their own memories, in what turns out to be a composite southern narrative. Interestingly, Randall was previously unable to apprehend Viola's significance in the story of the two families: "Your maid. . . . She had nothing to do with you, not really" (448). But the novel closes with a scene in which reconciliation, comradeship, and forgiveness are combined with the body of knowledge that Viola provided. There is even the possibility of romance in Victoria and Randall's future together; they walk in the gardens and make plans to turn the gloomy Ransom house into a communal home. A "family" is created out of the debris of lost lives, illness, and injury in a southern garden. Finally, old secrets, pacts, and puzzles signify no more than the components of a long and complicatedly plotted story, a story that a black woman told to a white girl to entertain her through a lonely childhood.

The Trouble with Friendship

Toward "Happily Ever After"?

Carol Dawson's *Body of Knowledge* closes with its protagonist, Victoria, coming to terms with her family's past and hopeful about her future. But the novels I have discussed in this book are fraught with contradictions in terms of the primary relationships they create. Dawson leaves us with an open-ended text, a feature described by Richard Gray. In fact, Gray employs the phrase that is the title of Dawson's novel in a discussion of Faulkner and the problems of coming to a final understanding of a text: "Like any body of knowledge that referred to something possessed of its own identity, with its own self-authenticating existence, it could never be assumed to be complete."[1] However, the promise of, or potential for, sisterhood or complete community at the end of each book involves a slipping off of many of the contradictory features of the friendship in order to locate a pair of women or a group of people for whom working to understand, or even beginning to resolve, conflicts has prefaced the larger project of community. Happy harmonious fictional endings are a particular problem when one's politics are conceived as critique and opposition and when ideas of social transformation are inevitably framed within dominant discourses. The question is, How enabling are such endings?

It is worth remembering that there have been many, if problematic, visions of interracial social harmony in American novels by white and black writers. One thinks immediately of Melville and Stowe, writers so radically different but in whose work interracial and interethnic community is a significant feature. On the *Pequod*, through Ishmael and Queequeg and Ahab and Fedallah, Melville constructs a multicultural vision of America, albeit one presided over by a monomaniacal white man in pursuit of the apocalyptic whiteness of the whale. When in *Uncle Tom's Cabin* George, Eliza, and Henry, divided by slavery, are reunited around the table of an idealized white family in a Quaker settlement, the communion is a dreamlike sequence, seen as it is through Eliza's eyes when she awakens from sleep. But it is followed by George Harris looking forward to a new start in Liberia for his reconstituted wider "family" of friends and relatives.[2] Louisa M. Alcott's *Work: A Story of Experience* closes with a female community. The white protagonist, Christie, joins hands with her mother, daughter, sister-in-law, a fugitive slave named Hepsey, and two other white women of contrasting class backgrounds: "a loving league of sisters, old and young, black and white, rich and poor, each ready to do her part to hasten the coming of a happy end."[3] This vision of a happy end occurs at the end of the Civil War as a recuperative reinvestment in the future. Reconstituting community in the aftermath of devastating violence and loss has become an archetype, and one in which contemporary writing retains an interest. In *Copper Crown* a new community has its beginnings after the First World War and in the aftermath of racist violence at home, and in *Body of Knowledge* Victoria and Randall make amends to each other following the war in Vietnam. Wider national or international conflicts work allegorically and interactively with representations of harmonious race relations in a number of novels by contemporary southern writers.

In Margaret Walker's *Jubilee,* Vyry makes a speech about the need for interracial interconnectedness: "We both needs each other. White folks needs what black folks got just as much as black folks need what White folks is got, and we's all got to stay here mongst each other and git along, that's what."[4] Echoes of the spirituality and humanitarianism of this former slave can be detected in the atmosphere von Herzen tries to create in her novel. Vyry is a symbol of hope in harmonious reconciliation, "a living sign and mark of all the best any human being could hope to become . . . with her obvious capacity for love, redemptive and forgiving love."[5] *Jubilee* is one of the relatively few twentieth-century novels set against the horrors of the period of Reconstruction, however, and in it Walker refrains from imagining the coming together of black and white as a happy ending, articulating instead the possibility of such a community. Like Margaret Walker, many contemporary writers continue to stretch toward imagining the conditions in which interracial attachments might form the basis of community. They do so by imagining specific friendships that act as models for socially transformative communities, within the confines of the novel at least. One of the problems they face relates to whether the community they imagine remains like the one Leslie Fiedler describes in the fiction of earlier decades, that of an "ideal community of buddies isolated from the world": "As the old myth sinks deeper and deeper into the national mind, intertwined with nostalgic memories of books that we have read as children, like our fathers before us and theirs before them, it comes to seem truer than the reality of headlines."[6]

Writers like von Herzen and Carol Dawson retain elements of the fantasy of a happy ending in communities that are cut off from society, existing on its borders in garden wildernesses or old family homes that are no longer so prominent among the dominant images of the American South. They retain elements of the dream of a close-knit "family" of friends that Ellen Douglas disdains to imagine. In *Can't Quit You Baby,* Douglas refuses to dilute the focus she gives to an already entangled primary relationship by inducting the women into a wider circle, or by allowing the women to fully or successfully negotiate the rocky terrain of their belatedly acknowledged close friendship. Leaving her protagonists on the slippery threshold of an uncertain future, Douglas fights shy of the seductive happy ending that, Fiedler argues, "however qualified, is more and more desperately insisted upon in the face of the contradictions between the relationships we dream and the relationships we live."[7]

Utopian visions at the end of texts continually disappoint some readers and critics; Valerie Smith is disappointed by the ending of *The Color Purple,* which she believes "undermines the complexity of narration and characterization that has gone before"; she prefers the more ambivalent endings of Alice Walker's short stories.[8] It is certainly true to say that the difficulties that have been engaged with via a single interracial friendship in some of the novels I discuss are shelved in favor of an emphasis on broader coalitions in the closing sequence. Happy endings are seductive, and writers can be affected or seduced into ending a novel, or for that matter a theoretical text, on a positive note in which the utopian is combined with a nod in the direction of the inclusive agendas of the new social movements. I began this book with a look at the close relationship between contemporary theoretical positions and contemporary fictions and pointed to the significance of democratically charged social agendas. One only has to look at the chapter headings of the conclusions or epilogues to recent feminist studies (including my own in parody) for exemplification. Texts stretch beyond the confines of their theses: words like *toward* and *beyond* figure prominently, as do *democracy* and *coalition.* Despite recent assertions of postfeminism and of a poststructuralist flattening out of fragmented subjectivities, the rhetoric of the movements of the 1960s—as well as more recent reconceptualizations of community, and civic communitarianism and republicanism in the 1980s—remains strong.[9] Jane Gallop worries whether, in fact, "difference is being dissolved through wishful fantasy" and asks, "Can the happy ending represent a usable model?" The writers discussed in *Advancing Sisterhood?* forgo answering her question, preferring to leave their characters at a hopeful juncture but declining to test the model itself.[10]

Nancie Carraway closes her study *Segregated Sisterhood* with a panegyric to community via multiculturalism, having moved her biracial model of contemporary feminist theory on in the direction of a polyethnic feminist politics: "Above all, a crossover dream demonstrates our inherent commitment to and appreciation for many social densities beyond those to which our specific skin, culture and history consigns us. This is the emancipatory gift of multicultural feminist politics. And we may look to a future whose daily enactment involves that most erotic attribute of politics, what Alice Walker has called the 'machete of freedom'. Talk. Endless talk."[11] The language is uplifting, and the sentiments are those of so many contemporary white feminist critics who close their books with chapters entitled "Imagining Democracy" or "Visions and Revisions."[12] Ideas of community, theorized or fictionalized, have prompted vigorous debate, and the same terms and descriptors are reprised to express opposing views. In their "Conversation About Race and Class," Mary Childers and bell hooks take their friendship as the basis of a cross-race dialogue in an attempt to combine theory and praxis, in the belief that "the issues on which we focus may be necessary preliminaries to concerted, mass political activity."[13] Iris Marion Young disagrees with such a premise. Recognizing this position as an "understandable dream," she decries its success in comparable terms: "The vision of small, face-to-face, decentralized units that this ideal promotes . . . is an unrealistic vision for transformative politics in mass urban society."[14] In fact, both essays chart different trajectories toward similar conclusions, a politics of difference that might reach beyond the academy and beyond ideals of community, but Young's thesis is important for having pointed up the pitfalls of the ideal of sisterhood as it may be translated into practice. She alerts us to the fact that "community" is intrinsically homogenous and homogenizing, as I explored in my reading of *Copper Crown,* and that community in the southern states is likely to form oppositionally across racial and ethnic lines, or flounder when the desired commonality is not immediately forthcoming.[15] Patricia Williams also addresses some of these concerns and concludes: "One reason discussing race is so difficult in the United States is that moving past the divide of 'black/white' requires juggling so many other factors: color has long been a powerful tool of class, religion, history, most ethnicity, gender and sexual orientation, disembodied institutional power, and so on."[16]

In *Ellen Foster,* Kaye Gibbons tussles with some of these factors. But ultimately the learned and projected otherness of the black child confounds the white protagonist's first efforts to understand where and how the friendship may be supported and endorsed in her locale. Writers continue to create stories around racial crossovers and anxieties, and the challenge is, as Williams says, "how to envision a racially integrated world that will represent . . . the fluid hybridity of races, culture, and much much more."[17] In the United States ethnicity has always been considered fluid, where racial identity has not.[18] Contemporary writers have continued to explore and expose the divide of "black/white" in southern settings and are beginning to deploy images of a biracial community as a foundation upon which more diverse communities may be imagined.[19]

In the case of fiction, Jay Clayton notes the shift, highly detectable for those of us who read and teach contemporary American writing, in novels by white women writers from those which emphasized individualism and the coming to consciousness of self, personally and sociopolitically, in the 1970s, to novels where family and community feature in the 1980s: "The issue of women's connections was supplementing that of women's liberation."[20] Moving past black and white to envision communal harmony based in models of friendship is an arduous and precipitous road to follow, even in fiction of the 1990s, when utopian desires can be momentarily and symbolically realized. The novels I have discussed are flawed as well as illuminating examples of some of the steps being taken on that road at the end of the twentieth century.

☞ The ideas of the critics Audre Lorde, Adrienne Rich, Minnie Bruce Pratt, Barbara and Beverly Smith, Charlotte Bunch, Dorothy Allison, and many others inform significant aspects of my discussion in this book. Only *Copper Crown,* of the texts I discuss in detail, imagines an erotic attachment between its protagonists, but interracial love between women has proved important and difficult terrain. In 1974 the black

Kentucky writer Ann Allen Shockley published *Loving Her,* which I believe to be the first novel to explore an interracial lesbian relationship in detail, to a mixed critical reception.[21] Renay and Terry, her black and white lovers, are beset with tragedies and prejudice, but Shockley ensures that their relationship survives. Following this flawed but iconoclastic romance novel, she continues to pursue the subject of cross-racial love and dialogue in more closely historicized and interrogative short stories. She is joined by other black writers like Becky Birtha and, later, Jewelle Gomez in imagining what she calls the "uncommon affinity" of black and white women who bond romantically. Shockley's uncommon affinity derives primarily from her stories of interracial love born out of mistress/maid relationships in the South. For example, in her short story "Women in a Southern Time," Shockley situates Miss Tish and her young maid, Eulah May, against a backdrop of America's involvement in the Second World War and Tish's developing lesbian identity. She has her paired women "secreted in the monastic seclusion" of daily domestic ritual after the deaths of Tish's husband and her white lesbian lover. What is most significant in Shockley's elaboration of this coexistence is that Eulah May shelves her own ambitions to train as a nurse in order to care for her mistress and that finally Miss Tish encourages Eulah May into sharing her bed as well, in a pointed expression of the potential power and intimacy of this particular relationship. "Smothered" beneath the sheets with her mistress, Eulah May determines never to leave her. "Women in a Southern Time" explores a relationship between two women who are bound together in what Shockley terms "an uncommon affinity of servant and mistress, black and white, whose roles had become distorted in this southern time," and by preceding this story with one entitled "The Mistress and the Slave Girl," the predication of the one relationship upon the other is made overt.[22]

The past that white writers inherit and risk reinscribing involves the history of white privilege that is predicated on the inferior status of black women. This potential snare, which contributes to making the affinity of woman loving across racial lines uncommon, is ingeniously demonstrated in Alice Walker's story "A Letter of the Times" via a friendship that becomes strained.[23] In a letter to her white friend Lucy, Susan Marie explains that she wishes to maintain their friendship despite Lucy's having chosen Scarlett O'Hara as the "feminist" she most admires and in whose image she has molded herself for a fancy dress ball to raise funds for women's causes. Susan Marie endeavors to explain to Lucy what it feels like to be "captured and enslaved" by stereotypes of servitude. She tries to convince her that if she celebrates heroines whose power exists as a direct result of the "other" women they oppress—even if they *are* rebels and survivors like Scarlett—she reorchestrates the ideology of a relationship that, if it continues to endure in the minds of white and black women, will compromise any hopes for an interracial sisterhood. Two factors are interesting here for their *not* having been directly addressed in the story: one is that the reader has no idea how the black woman "dressed up" for the fancy dress ball—she mentions Harriet Tubman and Sojourner Truth, but there is little possibility of reproducing the images of these particular women, who were summarily ignored as feminists until relatively recently, without "dressing down," as it were, and caricaturing them. There is no black southern belle ruched in lace (or even good-quality curtain material) for her to re-create as a visual icon. The second is that Susan Marie never bemoans needing to explicate issues of woman-on-woman oppression for her white woman friend. The inevitable divergence between white and black southern women's inherited histories and the consequent tensions inherent in cross-racial relationships is never openly articulated in Walker's "letter" but exists as a deeper layer of meaning fretted across its lines. It seems to me that white women writers have been apprehensive of this deeper layer of meaning, and, consequently, there are few examples of novels in which they describe interracial love affairs. Those that exist tend to read like women's studies pamphlets or politically correct excavations of race and racism when, as Adrienne Rich has opined:

When my dreams showed signs
of becoming
politically correct

no unruly images
escaping beyond borders
. . . .
then I began to wonder

The lesbian feminist writer Dorothy Allison also criticizes "politically correct parables" and asserts that "no amount of political analysis will force people to believe in an idea they cannot imagine."[24]

A radical lesbian white writer, Cris South, in *Clenched Fists, Burning Crosses: A Novel of Resistance,* does take on the Ku Klux Klan and white race hatred in her story of Jessie and her black friend Laura and Laura's loving relationship with a white woman, Moon. Cris South tackles a heterosexual marriage that is abusive, a hostel for battered wives, a radical antiracist newspaper, and women loving women in friendship and romantically. In the end, however, she has placed too many issues on the agenda, too many for the novel to carry and succeed in retaining its sense of story. But *Clenched Fists* is a brave book and a rare one. As in other recent lesbian novels that focus on interracial bonding, South tries to allow her black and white characters to face each other's anger and to overcome its debilitating obfuscation of what their relationship might become, "a heretical and generative idea," as Audre Lorde has described it, that challenges the immutability of racism,[25] and one with which Ellen Douglas and Lane von Herzen also attempt to engage.

In Rita Mae Brown's early work, in the friendships she creates between Molly and Holly in *The Rubyfruit Jungle* and between Adele and Carole in *In Her Day,* her tendency was to create black women characters but to reveal only later and slowly that they are black, once sisterhood with the white woman protagonist had been established in the novel. Cris South and Carol Ann Douglas, in *To the Cleveland Station,* paint their characters with bolder strokes, and Douglas's novel is a love story, the only novel I have discovered by a white writer that focuses entirely on an interracial friendship that becomes a love affair. The white protagonist, Brenda, is an incredibly self-conscious character in a self-reflexive fiction in which Carol Ann Douglas creates the impression that her protagonist is telling the story of the love affair with hindsight and acute uneasiness but is driven by the impetus to tell it completely and openly.

For Benjamin DeMott the tendency to tell stories openly has given way to a "friendship orthodoxy" in which racial problems are airbrushed out of popular cultural representations. For DeMott the shaping influence is the "goodwill" of individual white Americans, oddly and ironically recalling Martin Luther King Jr.'s call to people of goodwill to stem mass resistance to civil rights reforms. But DeMott is quite specific in his critique: "The crux to friendship orthodoxy—key to both its decency and to its wrongheadedness—is faith in black-white mutuality and essential sameness."[26] He draws evidence from movies, TV, and social criticism but very few from literature, and none from novels that explore relationships between women. Elements of DeMott's social criticism trouble my own ideas; there are certainly utopian hopes and desires for sisterhood underpinning some of the fictions I discuss. But there is little denial of the history that DeMott contends is swept away in the "self-congratulatory epic[s] of amity" he cites.[27] Each of the writers I discuss in detail departs from convention in ways that problematize their representations of interracial friendship, even when the structuring of their fictions undermines the "friendship plot." The white writers I have selected involve themselves in a degree of risk to penetrate their subject. They dispute the territory on which paradigmatic formulations of southern friendship have been traditionally played out, and the results are novels that show representations of friendship to be in the process of change and development out of the stereotypes that constrain them. Whichever road writers follow and explore in the twenty-first century, the signposts I've constructed are a means of charting possible paths through the immensely rich terrain of contemporary southern writing, while trying not to lose sight of the importance of contradictions by being seduced into ideals of interracial sisterhood in a search for a happy ending.

Notes

Introduction. Setting the Parameters

1. "Bestsellers," *Guardian*, July 24, 1999.

2. Bebe Moore Campbell, "Your Books Ain't like Mine," *Philadelphia Tribune*, September 19, 1995. See Campbell, *Brothers and Sisters*.

3. Marable, "The Rhetoric of Racial Harmony," in *Black Leadership*, 149.

4. See *Jailbirds* (dir. Burt Brinkerhoff, 1990) and Joe E. Lansdale's *Mujo Mojo* (1994) and *The Two-Bear Mambo* (1995), for example.

5. Warren, *Segregation*, 66.

6. John Hope Franklin, quoted in Applebome, *Dixie Rising*, 339. See also Kirby, *Media-Made Dixie*.

7. See, for example, Barbara Vobejda, "Turn Back, Blacks Moving to the South—Economy, Racial Mood Cited for Dramatic Shift," *Washington Post*, January 29, 1998. My thanks to Suzanne W. Jones for providing me with this article.

8. See Alice Walker, *In Love and Trouble* (1973; London: Virago, 1984), and *You Can't Keep a Good Woman Down*; Shockley, *The Black and White of It*; Golden and Shreve, eds., *Skin Deep*, 4.

9. Williams, *Dessa Rose*, 233.

10. Michie, *Sororophobia*. Carla Kaplan also discusses this propensity and worries about what feminist critics do with those texts that "fail to fit the new paradigm and its collaborative, sisterly, dialogic ethics," in her incisive critique "Recuperative Reading and the Silent Heroine of Feminist Criticism," 168–94.

11. Joseph values what she believes is a particularly strong history of friendship in black communities: "women gathering together in beauty parlors; women meeting in the kitchen over a cup of coffee, or soup; women talking on the stoops; and women congregating at church meetings," in *Common Differences,* ed. Joseph and Lewis, 194. Joseph and Lewis examine friendship as one of the fronts on which the battle for feminist collaboration may be fought. Lugones in collaboration with Rosezelle, "Sisterhood and Friendship as Feminist Models," 135–45.

12. For example, Evans in *Personal Politics,* 88.

13. Marita Golden, in *Broken Silences,* ed. Jordan, 94.

14. Friedman, *What Are Friends For?,* 199–202.

15. Burke [Olive Tilford Dargan], *Call Home the Heart,* 383–84.

16. See Shipler, *A Country of Strangers,* who in interviewing blacks and whites across the nation describes himself as struck by the ease with which blacks discuss race and the problems whites have in formulating their views on the subject. Roediger, *Black on White.*

17. hooks, "Moving into and Beyond Feminism," in *Outlaw Culture,* 216–18. For a more detailed reading of *Yearning,* see my "Critical Interrogations of Self and Culture," 138–49; and King, Monteith, and Yousaf, "Interview with bell hooks," 1–16 in the same issue.

18. DeMott, *The Trouble with Friendship.*

19. Sanders, *Clover,* 117.

20. Snead, *Figures of Division,* x.

21. Gates Jr., *Black Literature and Literary Theory,* 343. Gates has recently begun to review novels by white writers. His comments on Joyce Carol Oates's *Because It Is Bitter and Because It Is My Heart* have been described by the author as "probably the most intelligent the novel has received." Oates views Gates's decision to review texts by white writers as "exciting and controversial." See Shirley Jordan 152.

22. Bakhtin, *The Dialogic Imagination,* 421.

23. Gwin, *Black and White Women of the Old South;* Roberts, *The Myth of Aunt Jemima.* Roberts's final chapter, "Twentieth-Century Women on Race," considers Willa Cather and Lillian Smith, among others, with the most recent writer discussed being Margaret Mitchell. Gwin comes so far forward as to consider Margaret Walker's *Jubilee.* This area of contemporary southern fiction remains to be explored in detail and depth, although Linda Tate, *A Southern Weave of Women,* begins the process.

24. Roberts, *Faulkner and Southern Womanhood,* 219.

25. Douglas's essays "Faulkner in Time" and "Faulkner's Women" are anthologized in *"A Cosmos of My Own,"* ed. Fowler and Abadie. Susan V. Donaldson compares her *Black Cloud, White Cloud* to Faulkner's *Go Down, Moses,* arguing that the women who exist on the periphery in Faulkner's stories are recentered in Douglas's. See "Ellen Douglas's *Black Cloud, White Cloud* and the Fragmentation of Narrative," 51–64.

26. Brown, "Beyond New Forks," in *Tongues of Flame,* 152. In this story Brown unravels a relationship between a white woman narrator and a black woman servant of long standing (145–62).

27. See Tate, *Southern Weave.* Tate's intention is to be inclusive and celebratory, and this is an important first step in surveying contemporary southern women's fiction.

28. Christian, "The Race for Theory," 43; Warren, *Black and White Strangers,* 139.

29. Urgo, *Novel Frames,* xvii. Urgo splits his book into three separate sections, "The Racial Self," "The Sexual Self," and "The Historical Self," and consequently doesn't consistently address the ways in which his categories overlap in characters and texts.

30. Porter, "Women's Interracial Friendships and Visions of Community in *Meridian, The Salt Eaters, Civil Wars,* and *Dessa Rose,*" 251–67.

31. Canfield, "A Conversation with Shirley Ann Grau," 42.

32. See Nancy Porter; Jones, "Dismantling Stereotypes," 140–57; Schultz, "Out of the Woods and into the World," 67–85; Gwin, "Sweeping the Kitchen," 54–62.

33. Hobson, *The Southern Writer in the Postmodern World.*

34. Hobson 9.

35. Kreyling, *Inventing Southern Literature,* 127.

36. Ellen Douglas, "I Have Found It," *Southern Quarterly* 33, no. 4 (summer 1995): 48.

37. King, "Politics and the Fictional Representation," 162–78.

38. Thadious M. Davis addresses the problem of definition head on in "Southern Writers," 10–16. Davis concludes that place of birth is not necessarily important but that a sense of the South, as the backdrop for formative experiences, is. King and Taylor's *Dixie Debates* addresses the problems of definition in a contemporary southern context.

39. The issue of terminology is a fraught one. I shall use *black* and *white* to

characterize the writers and many of the characters discussed. Jesse Jackson has deployed the term *Euro-Americans* to distinguish between white cultural heritage and that of African Americans. See Shohat and Stam, *Unthinking Eurocentricism,* 22. Manning Marable quotes Jackson as saying, "Black tells you about skin color and what side of town you live on. . . . African-American evokes a discussion of the world." See *Race, Reform, and Rebellion,* 229. Robert Hughes, on the other hand, in a broadside against "political correctness," professes that "by the time that whites get guilty enough to call themselves 'European-Americans' it will be time to junk the whole lingo of nervous divisionism; everyone—black, yellow, red, and white—can revert to being plain 'Americans' again, as well they might." His phrase "nervous divisionism" captures one of the effects that a constantly changing nomenclature can exacerbate, but he does not specify what he means by reverting to the term *American* for all, since this has never been an unproblematic signifier. See *Culture of Complaint,* 24. I describe the literature of the South as biracial: this is not to say that there have not been extensive studies made of the relations among a variety of social and racial groups in the South. For example, David Goldfield's work on Jews in the South, including *Black, White, and Southern,* and the burgeoning study of Native Americans, Latinos, and Vietnamese Americans in the South. See Suzanne W. Jones and Sharon Monteith, eds., "South to a New Place," special issue, *Critical Survey* 12, no. 1 (2000). Ronald Takaki, in *Iron Cages,* uses a Marxian analysis to relate white racism to a number of America's ethnic groups rather than solely African Americans as in this study. See also Boelhower, *Through a Glass Darkly;* and Sollors, *Beyond Ethnicity* for readings of America and American literature as polyethnic.

40. Ellen Glasgow, in her opening speech to the Southern Writers' Conference of 1931, as reproduced in *Friendship and Sympathy,* ed. Magee, 6.

41. Noble, "The Future of Southern Writing," 587.

42. Linda Tate also comments on the interrelation of unrelated individuals who come together as "family." However, Tate prefers to emphasize the fluidity of southern black kinship structures as the basis for this coming together rather than ideas of alternatives to family in a radical or utopian democracy or an interracial South (33–42).

43. Taylor, *Scarlett's Women,* 121.

44. Culler, "Story and Discourse in the Analysis of Narrative," in *The Pursuit of Signs,* 186.

45. Fraser and Lacey, *The Politics of Community.*

46. Marable, *Race, Reform, and Rebellion,* 197.

47. Omi and Winant, *Racial Formation in the United States from the 1960s to the 1980s,* xiii.

48. See, for example, Dyer, "White," 47–48.

49. Ellison, "That Same Pain, That Same Pleaure: An Interview," in *Shadow and Act,* 13.

50. Ellison, "Change the Joke and Slip the Yoke," in *Shadow and Act,* 57; Eagleton, *Marxism and Literary Criticism,* 90.

51. Williamson, in the chapter "Community," in *William Faulkner and Southern History,* 403.

52. Jordan, "Where Is the Rage?" in *Technical Difficulties,* 146.

53. Marable, "Malcolm X and the Crisis in Black America," 192.

54. DeMott 190.

55. Cawelti, "The Concept of Formula in the Study of Popular Literature," 381–90. Janice Radway also considers the extent to which popular fiction functions as a conservator of social values: "Each form's particular conservatism also appears to be a response to specific material changes posing a threat to the social structure's legitimating belief system. . . . social relations can therefore apparently serve as evidence of germinating change in cultural attitudes and beliefs." See "The Utopian Impulse in Popular Literature," 161. Although Radway is cautious in her statement here, her ideas have been taken up with more force by a number of critics, including Tom Moylan, Terry Eagleton, and Radway herself in her later text *Reading the Romance,* where the imaginative oppositions to dominant ideologies that the texts encode are the subject of tighter definitions.

56. Clayton, *The Pleasures of Babel,* 10.

57. Rorty, *Contingency, Irony, and Solidarity,* xvi.

58. Virginia Woolf, "The Eccentrics," *Athenaeum* 25 (April 1919), quoted by Jane Marcus, "Invisible Mending," 394.

59. Clayton 30–31.

60. For discussions of this kind, see hooks, *Sisters of the Yam;* Raymond, *A Passion for Friends;* and the way that healing and recovery are worked through in novels like Gayl Jones's *Corregidora* (1976) and Toni Cade Bambara's *The Salt Eaters* (1980).

61. Jefferson Humphries registers a shift from the "Rubin-generation" to the post-Rubin generation, who are more likely to employ theory and to refute a more organic approach to the South that sees its fictions as reflecting that

South. See Humphries, ed., *Southern Literature and Literary Theory;* Kreyling; and Donnalee Frega, who has summarized the differences in critical expectations over two generations of southern critics in "Questioning History and Revision," 9–21.

62. Pratt, "Identity: Skin Blood Heart," 16.

63. Butler, "Still Southern after All These Years," 34.

64. Lucinda H. Mackethan overstates commonality in *Daughters of Time.* The emphasis of her thesis is "the points where the gender interests of white and black women intersect to create similar expressions of growth into voice," that is to say, harmonious voices. But she goes on to connect the women metaphorically through the single image of a caged bird, in order to conflate the autobiographies and fictions of black and white southern women as a "lifegiving, freedom-singing story" (9–13). Nor does she note that the anomalous phrase "women and blacks" disrupts the very commonality she wishes to pursue.

65. Butler 38–40.

One. Advancing Sisterhood?

1. Eichenbaum and Orbach, *Between Women,* 26.

2. Anne Goodwyn Jones discusses friendship as one of the four stages of Augusta Jane Evans's "fictional quest" in *Beulah* (1859), a quest to join in community in the South which she examines and critiques: "Only the virtual absence of blacks from the novel, one suspects, prevents the completion of the southern equation." See *Tomorrow Is Another Day,* 84. See also Taylor, *Gender, Race, and Region in the Writings of Grace King, Ruth McEnery Stuart, and Kate Chopin.* Taylor observes that "the diversity of Southern white and black women's experience is as yet only sketchily documented" and adjudges that their "inability or refusal to confront [racism] created critical problems and severely limited [the] achievement" of the writers she discusses (x, 156).

3. De Beauvoir, *The Second Sex,* esp. 555–68 and 608–17.

4. Hannah Arendt as quoted and discussed by King, *Civil Rights and the Idea of Freedom,* 136. See Arendt, *The Human Condition.*

5. Rubin, *Just Friends,* 4–5.

6. Rubin 175.

7. Terri Apter, Ruthellen Josselson, and Jaimie Baron, *Best Friends: The Pleasures and Perils of Girls' and Women's Friendships* (New York: Crown, 1998).

8. Shreve, *Women Together, Women Alone,* 237. *Women Together* is that rare thing, a fiction and a study. It combines passages of creative writing, in which seven women who belonged to the same CR group in the early 1970s stage a reunion in 1987, with framing passages in which Shreve assesses CR, and interviews many more women whose ideas augment those of her characters. Its hybridity makes it a pertinent example of the interface between fiction and theory. Of the seven characters Shreve explores, one is a black woman.

9. Annette Kolodny, "The Integrity of Memory: Creating a New Literary History of the United States," quoted in Showalter, *Sister's Choice,* 168.

10. Marable, *Race, Reform, and Rebellion,* 197.

11. O'Connor, *Friendships between Women,* 43. The index lists page numbers for age and class as separate topics of inquiry, as is the case for employment and heterosexuality and marital status, but not for race and culture. This problem is compounded by Suzanna Rose's foreword, in which she asserts that O'Connor examines friendships "from every angle" in a "comprehensive analysis" (ix). O'Connor is not, of course, alone in raising but not pursuing the issue of differences across women's lives. For Eichenbaum and Orbach they are "particulars": "We have not attempted to discuss the particulars of class, race and sexual orientation as they create divisions between women." But they write in the hope that they "are writing for all women" and the book will be read as "an inclusive account" of friendship ("Authors' Note").

12. O'Connor 184–91.

13. Adrienne Rich, "Disloyal to Civilisation," in *On Lies, Secrets, and Silence,* 281. Stephen Small's *Racialised Barriers* is a good example of a text that combines cogent analysis of both nations and the ways in which race and racism shaped realities in the 1980s.

14. Joseph and Lewis.

15. Carby, "White Woman Listen!," 212–35.

16. Gloria Steinem, "Networking," in *Outrageous Acts and Everyday Rebellions,* 197–205.

17. Audre Lorde's open letter to Mary Daly is a well-known and oft-quoted example of a black feminist responding directly and constructively to a white feminist's work. See Lorde, *Sister Outsider,* 66–71. For Abel and Gardiner, see Abel, "(E)Merging Identities," and Gardiner, "Response to Abel," 413–42, which is followed by Abel's short reply to Gardiner.

18. Lorde 123.

19. Magee, *Friendship and Sympathy;* Thadious Davis, "Women's Art and Authorship in the Southern Region," 33.

20. See Scharf and Jensen, *Decades of Discontent.*

21. Lewis R. Gordon makes a similar point when he asserts that "in the United States, *racism* means *anti black racism.* All other groups are assessed and ultimately discriminated against or favored in terms of the extent to which they carry residues of whiteness or blackness" ("Race and Racism: A Symposium," *Social Text* 42 (1995): 41).

22. Raymond 229.

23. Raymond 191.

24. Exemplification is difficult, since the context always creates particular emphases, but Nan Bowman Albinski, in a study that covers almost the whole of the twentieth century, opens the path through her thesis this way: "Although life was not uniform for all women in both countries—for class and race must also be considered—exclusion and discrimination transcended other distinctions, affecting them equally as women." See *Women's Utopias in British and American Fiction,* 1.

25. Raymond 9.

26. Anne Phillips, *Engendering Democracy,* 32.

27. Lorde 116–19.

28. Downing, *Psyche's Sisters.* Downing's focus is the sororal attachment of biological sisters. She expresses disappointment in the general feminist concentration on motherhood and mother-daughter bonds. In a loose psychologically-based exploration, she celebrates female siblings but, naturally enough, pays little attention to those women who are sisterless.

29. Childress, *Like One of the Family.* Audre Lorde considers similar anomalies in the context of academic feminism: "How do you deal with the fact that the women who clean your houses and tend to your children while you attend conferences on feminist theory are, for the most part, poor women and women of color?" in "The Master's Tools Will Never Dismantle the Master's House" (1979), in Lorde 112. Anita Shreve devotes a section of her *Women Together, Women Alone* to this same issue, raised by the only black woman in a group of seven, who is herself the employer of a Hispanic childminder.

30. Bunch, "Making Common Cause," 149–57.

31. Fox-Genovese, *Within the Plantation Household,* and *Feminism Without Illusions.* See also Genovese, *Roll, Jordan, Roll.*

32. See, for example, Steven M. Stowe, "Writing Sickness: A Southern Woman's Diary of Cares," in *Haunted Bodies,* ed. Jones and Donaldson, 257–84.

33. Anne Phillips 3.

34. King and Taylor 5. Their reference to "barbarism" alludes to Walter Benjamin's axiom that "every document of civilization is necessarily a document of barbarism."

35. For example, Michelle Erica Green notes how utopian fiction releases or represses the differences between people that give rise to conflict. Green, "'There Goes the Neighborhood,'" 166–89. She deploys the work of the African American writer Octavia Butler to demonstrate an insistence on difference. I consider Lane von Herzen's *Copper Crown* and the ways that it releases and raises issues of difference in Chapter 3.

36. Nicholas D. Smith, preface, *Women and Utopia: Critical Interpretations,* ed. Barr and Smith, 1.

37. Moylan, *Demand the Impossible,* 1.

38. Moylan 18.

39. Elam, *Feminism and Deconstruction,* 1.

40. Zagarell, "Narratives of Community," 498–527. I have examined Zagarell's definition elsewhere, most particularly for the way in which it fails "to encompass novels where the women characters are mutually implicated rather than openly affiliated and where the novel is in dialogue with the idea of community, rather than descriptive of a particular society." See my "On the Streets and in the Tower Blocks," 26–36.

41. Todd, *Women's Friendships in Literature;* and Auerbach, *Communities of Women.*

42. Fiedler, *Love and Death in the American Novel,* 12, 92.

43. F. O. Matthiessen, *American Renaissance: Art and Expression in the Age of Emerson and Whitman* (New York: Oxford University Press, 1941), 443.

44. Nina Baym, "American Dramas of Beset Manhood," in *New Feminist Criticism,* ed. Showalter, 74–75.

45. See Dargis, "Roads to Freedom," 14–19. For a discussion of some of the controversy that divided feminists, see Botcherby, "Thelma and Louise Go Shooting," n.p.

46. Abel, "(E)Merging Identities," 416 n. 5.

47. Gardiner 437.

48. Abel, Christian, and Moglen, eds., *Female Subjects in Black and White.* Jean

Walton's essay is representative of the level of engagement that the crosscurrents among feminism, psychoanalysis, and African American studies promote, as she revisits Joan Rivere and Melanie Klein in order to explore and expose their constructions of female subjectivity as white. The traditional occlusion of black women as analysts or analysands is investigated as psychoanalytical feminism is placed under scrutiny most successfully in essays by Hortense Spillers and Judith Butler in the collection.

49. In his journals Charles W. Chesnutt discusses the difficulties of cross-racial friendships under segregation: "I hear colored speak of their 'white friends.' I have no white friends. I could not degrade the sacred name of 'Friendship' by associating it with any man who feels himself too good to sit at a table with me, or to sleep at the same hotel. True friendship can only exist between men who have something in common, between equals in something, if not in everything; and where there is respect as well as admiration." Brodhead, ed., *The Journals of Charles W. Chesnutt,* 172. Chesnutt's claims for friendship are understandably high, though he makes distinctions as to status and class, intraracially as well as interracially.

50. Alice Walker, in Magee 180.

51. Gwin, "A Theory of Black Women's Texts and White Women's Readings," 21–31; and Barbara Christian, "Response to 'Black Women's Texts,'" 32–36.

52. Gwin, "Theory," 23.

53. Gitlin, *Twilight of Common Dreams,* 208–9.

54. Charles Fister, "Not Just Whistlin' Dixie: Music, Functional Silence, and the Arbitrary Semiotics of Oppression in Ellen Douglas's *Can't Quit You Baby,*" *Southern Quarterly* 33, no. 4 (summer 1995): 116.

55. Ward, "'Lifting As We Climb,'" 199–217; Kubitschek, "A Personal Preface," in *Claiming the Heritage;* Rich, *What Is Found There,* 181.

56. Ralph Ellison speaks on this subject in *Shadow and Act* and *Going to the Territory* (New York: Vintage International, 1995). Morrison, "Unspeakable Things Unspoken," 1–34, and *Playing in the Dark.* For a more detailed discussion of Morrison's position, see my "Writing for Re-Vision," 173–80.

57. Warren, *Black and White Strangers;* and Doyle, *Bordering on the Body.*

58. Morrison, "Recitatif," 422–36.

59. Abel, "Black Writing, White Reading," 470–98.

60. Davis, *1959,* 79. See Sherley Anne Williams's views of representations of white women in *Give Birth to Brightness,* 218–34.

61. Smith, *Killers of the Dream,* 20.

62. W. J. Cash, *The Mind of the South,* 84; Seidel, "White Anxiety," in *The Southern Belle in the American Novel,* 135–46; Williams, *Give Birth to Brightness,* 223.

63. David Richards, *Masks of Difference: Cultural Representations in Literature, Art, and Anthroplogy* (Cambridge: Cambridge University Press, 1994), 1–8.

Two. Between Girls

1. This chapter is a longer version of Monteith, "Between Girls," *Journal of American Studies.* I would like to acknowledge Cambridge University Press for permission to reprint parts of the article here.

2. Ellison, *Shadow and Act,* 4–6. David J. Garrow cites Martin Luther King Jr. describing an incident that happened to him at the age of six, when his best friend, a white boy, was prevented by his father from playing with him: "For the first time I was made aware of the existence of a race problem." *Bearing the Cross,* 33.

3. For example, Toni Morrison's "Recitatif" is set in a children's home. In Cynthia Voight's *Dicey's Song,* a novel for young adults, Dicey, when forced to live away from her mother and to attend a new school, finds friendship with Mina; and Jacqueline Woodson's *I Hadn't Meant to Tell You This* describes Lena and Marie being drawn to each other because they have both lost their mothers. In Belva Plain's *Crescent City,* a slave girl and a European immigrant new to the South make friends.

4. Jacobs, *Incidents in the Life of a Slave Girl, Written by Herself,* 29.

5. Jacobs 29.

6. Even as recently as 1995, Harvey J. Graff asserted that images of children are "typically binary," resting on similar Manichean oppositions: "good-bad, ours-theirs, male-female, white-black, past-present." See *Conflicting Paths,* 17.

7. Olsen, "O Yes," 48–71.

8. Frankenberg, "Growing Up White," 24–25.

9. Lynn Z. Bloom, "Coming of Age in the Segregated South: Autobiographies of Twentieth-Century Childhoods, Black and White," in *Home Ground,* ed. Berry, 113.

10. Examples include *Corinna, Corinna* (dir. Jessie Nelson, 1994), set in the 1950s, which examines cross-racial relationships predominantly through the

white child/black nurse formulation; *The Long Walk Home* (dir. Richard Pearce, 1990), in which the white mistress/black domestic relationship features in Alabama in the 1950s; and *Driving Miss Daisy* (dir. Bruce Beresford, 1989), in which a "friendship" between an elderly Jewish lady and her elderly black chauffeur is played out in Atlanta over twenty-five years.

11. Kincaid, *Crossing Blood*; Allison, *Bastard Out of Carolina.*

12. Fowler, *Before Women Had Wings,* 228.

13. Gibbons, *Ellen Foster,* 22. Subsequent references will be included parenthetically in the text. Most reviewers have assumed the novel takes place in rural Nash County, North Carolina, the area in which Gibbons herself grew up, but particulars of place are not specified in the monologue.

14. Fowler, *Before Women Had Wings,* 73.

15. Allison, *Bastard Out of Carolina,* 86.

16. Kaye Gibbons has written of how words like *nigger* and *white trash* can "burn a hole in [a] child's mind," and Allison tells how in her own childhood "we were taught to be proud that we were not Black, and ashamed that we were poor": "The lies went to the bone, and digging them out has been the work of a lifetime." See Gibbons, in *Broken Silences,* ed. Jordan, 77; Allison, *Skin,* 225. See also Allison, *Trash.*

17. Smith, "Children and Color," in *The Winner Names the Age,* ed. Cliff, 30.

18. Joel Kovel would appear to support Smith's ideas: "If we are to study the existence in culture of a fantasy creation such as racism, it is to the infantile roots of mental experience that we must first turn." See *White Racism,* 251.

19. Smith, *Killers of the Dream,* 29. Smith's mining of her memories is echoed by McLaurin, *Separate Pasts,* in his description of spitting after putting in his mouth a football pump that had been in the mouth of his black friend Bobo. At this point in his narrative McLaurin becomes aware of his acculturated belief that he and Bobo belonged to "two fundamentally different worlds and that society demanded that we each stay in the world designated for us," despite years of shared play (27–41).

20. In *The Temple of My Familiar,* Alice Walker creates a situation where Fanny, a black woman who grew up in Georgia, repressed the memory of her white playmate Tanya. It is only through therapy that she regains this memory, which she had suppressed after the shock of being hit by Tanya's grandmother for kissing her little white granddaughter.

21. See Frankenberg, *The Social Construction of Whiteness.* Tangentially, white interviewees remembered that black childhood friends were "'tracked' into vo-

cational and remedial classes in high school," and they lost contact with them after this point (79).

22. Shreve, *A Country of Strangers,* 66. Subsequent references will be included parenthetically in the text.

23. Katherine C. Hodgin, in *Contemporary Fiction Writers of the South,* ed. Flora and Bain, 411.

24. Walker, *Meridian,* 105.

25. Gray, *Writing the South,* 234.

26. Belsey, *Critical Practice,* 73; my italics.

27. Mason, "Kaye Gibbons [1960–]," 161.

28. Abel, "(E)Merging Identities," 423.

29. Kaye Gibbons, in Shirley M. Jordan 78.

30. Mikhail Bakhtin, as quoted in Todorov, *Mikhail Bakhtin,* 95–96.

31. Todorov 107.

32. Stam, *Subversive Pleasures,* 232.

33. Morrison, *Playing in the Dark,* 52.

34. Kaye Gibbons, in Shirley M. Jordan 78.

35. Clayton, *The Pleasures of Babel,* 140. Clayton considers *Ellen Foster* only in passing, but, in an otherwise illuminating and important study, he misreads the example on which he bases his argument. He has it that Ellen *visits* Mavis and her family and so begins to articulate what a family may be, whereas in the text Ellen is only *spying* on the black families who live on the edge of her grand-mother's plantation. Her assessment of a family unit is a projection of her own desires.

36. A popular writer of historical romances, Plain sees the dramatic potential of New Orleans in the period from the 1830s to the Civil War. She goes South and reinscribes motifs that owe much to *Gone with the Wind* in a romantic and sentimental story. The black child, Fanny, is an adjunct to the white child, Miriam, and a foil for her, little else.

37. Toni Morrison, in an interview with Nellie McKay, as quoted in Furman, *Toni Morrison's Fiction,* 42.

Three. Envisioning Sisterhood

1. Daphne Patai believes that utopian fiction can provide a vision for the future and a reminder that feminist projects are themselves visionary: "Femi-nism today, is the most utopian project around. That is, it demands the most

radical and truly revolutionary transformation of society." "Beyond Defensiveness," 149–69.

2. Moers, *Literary Women*, 257–63; Kolodny, *The Land before Her;* and Westling, *The Green Breast of the New World*, 52. See also Westling's *Sacred Groves and Ravaged Gardens*.

3. I would like to acknowledge my graduate student, Rosalind Poppleton-Pritchard, whose keen interest in ecocriticism consistently broadens my own. See Buell, *The Environmental Imagination;* Garrad and Murphy, eds., *Ecofeminist Literary Criticism*.

4. See Simpson, *The Dispossessed Garden*.

5. Fowler, *Before Women Had Wings*, 128.

6. Fowler, *Before Women Had Wings*, 97.

7. Herzen, *Copper Crown*. Subsequent references will be included parenthetically in the text.

8. James W. Lee, "The Old South in Texas Literature," in *The Texas Literary Tradition*, ed. Graham, Lee, and Pilkington, 46–47.

9. Fowler, *River of Hidden Dreams*, 234.

10 See Westling, *Green Breast*, 78.

11. Harrison, *Female Pastoral*, 133.

12. Carpenter and Kolmar, *Haunting the House of Fiction*, 10.

13. As Lynette Carpenter, in her study of Ellen Glasgow, argues: "The ghost stories value sympathy, compassion, and sensitivity, and portray these qualities as a primary source of bonds between women." Carpenter and Kolmar 120.

14. Ude, "Forging an American Style," 50–64. Ude traces the development he detects via Faulkner, arguing that what he contends are the "six common elements of Magical Realism" are present in Faulkner's work. Significantly, for a reading of this novel, he notes: "Nature, once the wilderness, has become a place of peace, safety, and harmony, where intuition, perhaps guided and corrected by reason, is a human's most important sense. And civilization has become the untamed, savage, logical but not rational, dark side of life" (60). This helps to explicate the kind of relationship von Herzen imagines between Copper Crown and the restaurant the women set up in the wilderness in the "Heart of the World" section of the novel.

15. Goyen, Author's Preface to *The Collected Stories of William Goyen*, xi.

16. Richard Chase, *The American Novel and Its Tradition* (Baltimore: Johns Hopkins University Press, 1993), 13.

17. Judith Kegan Gardiner expresses the idea that female friendships are usually written to be "exemplary of their times and nations," in "Response to Abel," 437. The novel incorporates, for example, what has come to be called the "Red Summer of 1919," a particularly evil spate of lynchings, race riots, and burnings in which blacks and their homes were destroyed across North and South. In this period, as Manning Marable has argued, "for all practical purposes, the black American was proscribed by the state from any meaningful political and social activity for two generations. Behind this powerful proscription, as always, was the use of force." *Race, Reform, and Rebellion*, 11. But one has to look elsewhere for historical detail. For the sheer number of lynchings in the post-Reconstruction period, see Williamson, *A Rage for Order*, 180–223.

18. The phrase is Diane Roberts's, describing the climate of the 1930s in *Faulkner and Southern Womanhood*, 151.

19. Davis, *Women, Race, and Class*, 160.

20. Susan Willis describes the southern plantation as the "defining instance of agrarian production in America," citing the slave, not the yeoman farmer, in her socioeconomic reading. See *Specifying*, 4. Harrison makes a similar point, but she conflates black and white rather too easily (poor whites with all blacks, black and white farmers). This is understandable to the extent that her thesis invokes the conclusions of Glasgow's *Vein of Iron*, Cather's *Sapphira and the Slave Girl*, and Walker's *The Color Purple* as envisaging farm communities where "shared labor eliminates class, race, and gender hierarchy" (14).

21. Eudora Welty's *Delta Wedding* is set on a Mississippi plantation in 1923. See Gray, *Writing the South*, for a discussion of how violence is codified in the novel. He argues that the black characters who occupy the margins always figure in the episodes where violence is an undercurrent and that "what the black characters do is remind us of a secret, subterranean, and slightly frightening dimension of experience that the patriarchal order tends to minimise, ignore, or strenuously exclude" (241). The exact opposite is the case in *Copper Crown*, since the patriarchal order is the site and the center of violence.

22. Westling, *Green Breast*, 64.

23. Levy, *Fiction of the Homeplace*, 3.

24. This is the vision that characterizes the end of a recent Hollywood film also set in Texas. In *Places of the Heart* (dir. Robert Benton, 1984) living and dead, black and white, male and female, young and old, finally sit together in a Christian church in Waxahachie, Texas, on a Sunday morning in 1935. The

camera pans around their faces, good and bad sitting together, as the sun streams over them and they take communion together—and this despite the oft-quoted idea that the most segregated hour in America was eleven o'clock on a Sunday morning. See, for example, Williamson, *Rage for Order,* 173.

25. The etymological derivation of the word *culture* is, of course, the Latin *cultura,* from *colere,* with the primary meaning "to cultivate, till."

26. Mackethan notes a similar facility across texts in *Daughters of Time.*

27. This would indicate another potential reading of *Copper Crown* as a novel about relationships between mothers and daughters, a theme I choose not to pursue here but one which Lane von Herzen takes up more openly in her second novel, *The Unfastened Heart.*

28. Michael Sandel, as cited by Clayton, "Feminism and the Politics of Community," in *The Pleasures of Babel,* 133.

29. Janice Raymond describes the "essential tension of feminism" as that of "near and far sightedness." *A Passion for Friends,* 207.

30. Elizabeth Fox-Genovese, "The Personal Is Not Political Enough," quoted in Thornton-Dill, "Race, Class, and Gender," 132.

31. Bammer, *Partial Visions,* 161.

32. For discussions and definitions of feminist utopias through the centuries, see, for example, Jones and Goodwin, eds., *Feminism, Utopia, and Narrative;* and Donawerth and Kolmerten, *Utopian and Science Fiction by Women.*

33. The phrase "ideal polity" is Bammer's (13). Alice Walker's definition of *womanism,* outlined in the introduction to *In Search of Our Mothers' Gardens,* remains underexplored. For a short appreciation of womanism rather than the critical engagement promised in the title, see Sherley Anne Williams, "Some Implications of Womanist Theory," in *Reading Black, Reading Feminist,* ed. Gates, 68–75.

34. Bammer 3.

35. Linda Tate (125) points out that in *The Color Purple* Alice Walker makes the point that blacks are morally "the rightful owners" of the land when Celie returns to the homeplace she inherits at the end of the novel. Episodes like these in contemporary fictions work to symbolically represent a moral and somewhat utopian recodification of southern ancestry and accountability, rather than operating as a historicized representation of verifiable southern realities.

36. Alcoff, "The Problem of Speaking for Others," 285–309.

37. Evelyn Brooks-Higginbotham, "The Problem of Race in Women's History," in *Coming to Terms: Feminism, Theory, Politics,* ed. Weed, 132.

38. See Hall, *Revolt against Chivalry*. As Brooks-Higginbotham explains: "Lynching, rationalized by the white South as its defense of womanhood, served more to maintain racial etiquette and the socio-economic status quo. It was used to enforce labor contracts and crop lien laws" (182). The threat of mob violence like that which von Herzen describes in her fiction kept the black community in submission. Ida B. Wells and Jessie Daniel Ames did much to expose this propensity. For detailed discussions of interracial rape in the South, see Davis, "Rape, Racism, and the Myth of the Black Rapist," in *Women, Race, and Class*, 172–201; Paula Giddings, *When and Where I Enter*, esp. 206–10.

39. Lillian Smith, as quoted by Giddings 207–8.

40. See Harris, *Exorcising Blackness*, esp. "The Ultimate Taboo: White Women as Initiators of the Lynching Ritual," 24–28.

41. The character of Maggie is reminiscent of Ellen Glasgow's washerwoman, Memoria, in *The Sheltered Life*. But as Diane Roberts has demonstrated, however revisionist Glasgow may be in representing white female sexuality, she tends to reinscribe traditional representations of black women. See Roberts, *Myth of Aunt Jemima*, 166.

42. Sedgwick, *Between Men*, 10.

43. In this context I disagree with Avril Horner and Sue Zlosnik, who find such symbolism subversive and argue that metaphor "can be used to challenge the fixity of dominant discourse." See *Landscape of Desire*, 5. In this novel the wall that Mondrow constructs around the women and their restaurant operates metaphorically as well as physically, but it undermines the community they form, maintaining its separateness.

44. Raymond 191.

45. Mark Snyder, quoted by Jones, "Dismantling Stereotypes," 142.

46. Lillian Smith, in *The Winner Names the Age*, ed. Cliff, 84.

47. Walker, *Down from the Mountaintop*, 30.

48. Audre Lorde, "Age, Race, Class, and Sex," in *Sister Outsider*, 116.

49. Abel, "Emerging Identities," 427.

50. Toni Morrison, *Sula*.

Four. Across the Kitchen Table

1. Noble, *Beautiful Also Are the Souls of Our Black Sisters*, 76; Turner, *Ceramic Uncles and Celluloid Mammies*, 55.

2. I would like to thank Diane Roberts for the reference to Sara Haardt and for invaluable discussion on this topic.

3. Ann Petry, *The Street,* 308.

4. Barbara Woods's "The Final Supper" (1970), in *Ten Times Black,* ed. Julian Mayfield (New York: Bantam, 1972), 100–111. The collection is dedicated to "Sister Angela Davis, Brother Ruchell Magee and Brother Hirap Brown, Freedom Fighters."

5. See Harris, *From Mammies to Militants,* 34, 156–60; Turner 57.

6. Walker, *The Color Purple,* 38.

7. Whoopi Goldberg starred as a Caribbean exoticized domestic who comes to work for a wealthy white Baltimore family as recently as 1988. See also the CBS twenty-two-part series *I'll Fly Away,* with a domestic at its center.

8. Johnson, *The Shadow Knows,* 3–4.

9. Grau, *Nine Women,* 208.

10. Humphreys, *Dreams of Sleep,* 24–26.

11. Tyler, *A Slipping-Down Life,* 38. See also Alice Hall Petry, "Bright Books of Life: The Black Norm in Anne Tyler's Novels," in *Southern Quarterly* 22, no. 1 (fall 1992). Petry celebrates what she understands as Tyler's "humanity" and her choice to "go against the grain, not only to depict blacks more positively than American society has been wont to do, but more importantly, to empower them to articulate her most salient themes." However, in my reading, her title phrase "the black norm" indicates the difficulties she too has in quantifying Tyler's position.

12. Tyler, *The Clock Winder,* 27, 189.

13. Gilchrist, *Victory over Japan,* 207–77.

14. Harris, *From Mammies to Militants,* 23.

15. Gilchrist, *The Annunciation,* 79, 106.

16. Gilchrist, *Net of Jewels,* 347.

17. Gibbons, *A Virtuous Woman,* 128.

18. Gibbons, *A Virtuous Woman,* 71.

19. See Berlant, "National Brands? National Body," 119.

20. Gibbons, *A Virtuous Woman,* 72.

21. Smith, *Strange Fruit,* 219.

22. Smith, *Strange Fruit,* 254.

23. Smith, *Strange Fruit,* 290.

24. Gilchrist, *Net of Jewels,* 308–9.

25. Ellen Douglas, "I Have Found It," *Southern Quarterly* 33, no. 4 (summer 1995): 11.

26. Douglas, afterword, *Black Cloud, White Cloud,* 230–31. In this book she explores interracial relationships across the stories. In "Hold On" her protagonist, Anna, meets Estella, who used to work for her family: "The two women looked at each other with the shy pleasure of old friends long separated who have not yet fallen into the easy ways of their friendship" (165). If the description of their reunion promises a comfortable reprise of past attachments, Douglas places the women in a life-and-death situation and pushes their "quiet, sensible friendship" to desperate limits when they find themselves struggling in a lake. Anna pulls Estella down beneath the dangerous waters as Estella tries to cradle her in her drowning. Anna pulls away and Estella is saved only when a third person intervenes. Their friendship does not entirely pass the test that Douglas sets.

27. Douglas, *Black Cloud,* 233.

28. Douglas, *Can't Quit You Baby.* Subsequent references will be included parenthetically in the text. The discussion of Douglas is a revised version of "Across the Kitchen Table," 19–34. I acknowledge the journal for allowing me to reproduce parts of that article here.

29. Harris, *From Mammies to Militants,* 21. Richard Wright, among others, warned as long ago as 1945 that "to explain the Negro race in terms of your maid is the most dangerous fallacy of all." See Kenneth Kinnaman and Michael Fabre, eds., *Conversations with Richard Wright* (Jackson: University Press of Mississippi, 1993), 66.

30. Subsequent references to Kincaid's *Crossing Blood* will be included parenthetically in the text.

31. For a detailed discussion of this idea, see my essay "'The 1960s Echo On': Images of Martin Luther King as Deployed by White Writers of Contemporary Fiction," in *Beyond Martin Luther King: Media and Culture, Race, and Resistance in the Civil Rights and Black Power Eras,* ed. Brian Ward (Gainesville: University of Florida Press, 2000).

32. hooks, *Ain't I a Woman,* 157.

33. Some critics have demonstrated their difficulties with the novel by simplistically equating the narrator with Ellen Douglas the author. This may be as a result of Douglas's dedicating the novel to the memory of Mathelde Griffin, who worked in her home for many years. Betty Tardieu, interviewing Douglas,

implies that Douglas inserts her "own voice" into fictions, and Douglas explains that her intention is that in one corner of the text there is the "fictional writer," or implied author as I have described, but not Ellen Douglas. See Tardieu, "Interview with Ellen Douglas," *Southern Quarterly* 33, no. 4 (summer 1995): 24–25. Others, while celebrating the novel, delimit any critical appreciation of it: "Douglas raises issues about storytelling itself. But, although *Baby* contains elements of what literary critics call 'metafiction,' it is hardly an academic novel." Panthea Reid Broughton and Susan Millar Williams leave it there, without explanation of what "hardly academic" may mean in their assessment. See "Ellen Douglas," in *Southern Women Writers,* ed. Inge, 65. The novel is not academic in its sense of the esoteric, but I feel that there is an undisclosed value judgment here in the blanket uncritical assessment of the style of the novel.

34. Collins, *Black Feminist Thought,* 68. K. Sue Jewell also examines images of African American womanhood in *From Mammy to Miss America and Beyond.*

35. See, for example, Goffman, *Frame Analysis;* and Patricia Waugh's work, esp. "The Analysis of Frames," in *Metafiction,* 28–34.

36. Harris, *From Mammies to Militants;* and Rollins, *Between Women.* Both emphasize this feature of a very specific relationship. Harris attests that "the kitchen is the one room in the house where the white woman can give up her spatial ownership without compromising herself" (15).

37. Gwin, "Sweeping the Kitchen," 54–55. This is a much more positive view of the dynamics of interracial friendships within the kitchen than that propounded by Elizabeth Schultz in "Out of the Woods," 67–85. Schultz sees literary kitchens as secure places, with an atmosphere epitomized by the raft in *Huckleberry Finn.* For Schultz, the kitchen is a place where a friendship that would be otherwise doomed in another context may flourish. The kitchen has also been seen as a site of ideological struggle, however; it is the place where Barbara and Beverly Smith choose to site their "Across the Kitchen Table: A Sister-to-Sister Dialogue" on feminism, white cultural identity, and lesbian separatism. See Moraga and Anzaldua, eds., *This Bridge Called My Back,* 113–27. Paule Marshall in her autobiographical essay "The Making of a Writer: From the Poets in the Kitchen" sees the kitchen as a "wordshop," a creative space where women gather to express themselves, in *Merle and Other Stories,* 3–12.

38. Romines, *The Home Plot,* 225.

39. Harris, *From Mammies to Militants,* 14.

40. Rollins 213. bell hooks agrees: "For years, black domestic servants work-

ing in white homes, acting as informants, brought knowledge back to segregated communities—details, facts, observations, and psychoanalytic readings of the white Other." See "Representations of Whiteness in the Black Imagination," in *Black Looks,* 165.

41. See Jones, *Liberating Voices;* and Walker, *Down from the Mountaintop,* for discussions of protest fiction, together with my review of both texts, "Liberating Voices, Telling Stories," 62–77.

42. All identifying terminology—black, African American—is bound up with historical and political connotations and misunderstandings. In this instance I take Manning Marable's definition: "Blackness, or African-American identity, is much more than race. It is also the traditions, rituals, values, and belief systems of African-American people. It is our culture, history, music, art, and literature. Blackness is our sense of ethnic consciousness and pride in our heritage of resistance against racism. This African-American identity is not something our oppressors forced upon us. It is a cultural and ethnic awareness we have collectively constructed for ourselves over hundreds of years." Marable, "Race, Identity, and Political Culture," 295. I would supplement Marable's celebratory words, though, with Carole Boyce Davies's observations that blackness can be "powerful" or "beautiful" in a world of cloying, annihilating whiteness and that in racially defined contexts blackness may be tactically asserted. *Black Women, Writing, and Identity,* 6. If this seems to define *black* in relation to *white,* then it also serves to clarify the narrator's interrogation of Tweet's black story in my context.

43. Toni Morrison, "Rootedness: The Ancestor as Foundation," in *Black Women Writers,* ed. Evans, 343. Naturally enough, this is not uniformly the case in a long and complex literary tradition. In *Invisible Man* the narrator tangles with his ancestor; in Zora Neale Hurston's *Their Eyes Were Watching God* and in Ann Petry's *The Street,* two texts in which grandmothers figure, neither ancestor equips the protagonists, Janie and Lutie, with the ideological tools they need to help them negotiate the postslavery South or the urban jungle of Harlem. They fail to acknowledge that, as times change, so do women's expectations of themselves, of others, and of society.

44. Morrison, "Rootedness," 342.

45. More starkly, Alice Walker makes the point in *The Color Purple* via Celie, who has adjudged that white people "never listened to colored, period. If they do they only listen long enough to be able to tell you what to do" (166).

46. Ellison, *Invisible Man,* 7.

47. In *Can't Quit You Baby,* Tweet's blind grandfather "sees pretty good" (24), which alludes metaphorically to his astute perceptiveness about people, despite his failed physical sight. Cornelia, on the other hand, exhibits "a gracious smile, the blind smile of a deaf woman" (39) to indicate the layer of insulated politeness that creates a wall between herself and others. Cornelia is variously described as a dancer and a waterskier, to indicate the way in which she glides superficially over the surface of life (39, 66, 127).

48. Goldfield, *Black, White, and Southern,* xiv.

49. hooks, "Choosing the Margin as a Space of Radical Openness," in *Yearning,* 152.

50. hooks, *Yearning,* 153.

51. Rollins 92.

52. Rollins 227.

53. Eichenbaum and Orbach, *Between Women,* 166.

54. hooks, *Talking Back,* 6.

55. Marjorie Pryse, in her introduction to *Conjuring,* has indicated ways in which images of the conjure woman have been subverted and celebrated by African American women writers. One might read Tweet here against an African American literary tradition or detect elements of the cliché. Jan Shoemaker has none of my reservations and reads the mystic healer storyteller as a very positive characterization, in "Ellen Douglas," 83–98.

56. Jones, "Dismantling Stereotypes," 149.

57. In her postscript to *Decolonising Feminisms,* Laura E. Donaldson quotes Maria Lugone's declaration of the importance of building bridges between women: "It is time to form deep coalitions by becoming listeners and speakers of each other's voices without looking for simple but complex unity, or, maybe better expressed, by looking for solidarity in multiplicity. We have to become self-critical as we learn enough about each other to become critical of each other" (137). Her words echo Ellen Douglas's.

Five. The Keepers of the House

1. Grau, *The Keepers of the House,* 78. Subsequent references in the text.

2. Godwin, *Keeper of the House,* 273. Subsequent references will be included in the text. Minyon Manigault's moral caretaking and her connection to a brothel

are combined in a way that is reminiscent of Nancy Mannigoe's role and her relationship with Temple Drake in *Requiem for a Nun*. Mannigoe is, of course, a corruption of Manigault, but Minyon is spared Nancy's fate in Faulkner's novel and maintains an unambiguous moral profile.

3. Gibbons, *On the Occasion of My Last Afternoon*, 232.

4. Dawson, *Body of Knowledge*. Subsequent references will be included parenthetically in the text.

5. In this sense, Dawson, like von Herzen, can be read in the tradition of William Goyen and William Humphrey, Texas writers whose works combine these elements. William Humphrey writes family sagas: of the Hunnicutt family, the Ordways, and the Renshaws. The last family appears in a novel entitled *Proud Flesh,* which, like William Goyen's "Ghost and Flesh," serves to connect Dawson even more noticeably to her regional literary predecessors by the titles of the novels. All three writers display a predilection for the grotesque in their stories of family histories and tragic and murky pasts. See James W. Lee, "The Old South in Texas Literature," in *Texas Literary Tradition*, ed. Graham, Lee, and Pilkington, 46–57. Tom Pilkington's review, "A Twisted Family Feud," situates Dawson's novel in relation to the literature of east Texas, and the work of William Goyen most specifically, and emphasizes the "quintessentially southern" quality of the literature of east Texas over mimetic representation of place and region: "Apparently there is something in the murky air and brown, sluggish waters of East Texas that cultivates the gothic and surreal." *World and I* 10, no. 1 (1995): 330.

6. Goyen, Author's Preface, *Collected Stories,* x.

7. Although one reviewer, Tom Pilkington, has it that she was murdered! Perhaps this is an indication of how complicated a family saga *Body of Knowledge* really is. Its overall feeling of a family destined for disaster owes not a little to a nineteenth-century tradition of novels in which young women who try to escape the terms of their existence under patriarchy frequently meet early deaths as a means of authorial moral judgment.

8. Smith, *Killers of the Dream*, 125.

9. See Hale, "'Some Women Have Never Been Reconstructed,'" 173–201, for a discussion of how white women in Georgia acted as carriers of history but often had very different ideological programs.

10. Anne Sexton, "Housewife," quoted in Heilbrun, *Writing a Woman's Life,* 113.

11. Brooks, *Reading for the Plot,* xi–xii.

12. Stam, *Subversive Pleasures,* 8.

13. There is a hidden tradition of literary fat ladies that Patricia Parker goes some way toward uncovering, from Milton to Shakespeare, and Jonson to Joyce. Parker concentrates predominantly on early modern writing, however, and makes only fleeting mention of twentieth-century texts. The purposes of her inquiry are very different from my own. See *Literary Fat Ladies.*

14. Sartre, *Being and Nothingness,* 238.

15. Todorov, esp. the chapter "Theory of Utterance," 41–59. Mikhail Bakhtin discusses this idea in "Discourse in the Novel," in *The Dialogic Imagination,* 293.

16. Lillian Smith asserts that the place of the black nurse within white family life involved "tangled contradictions": "She always knew her 'place' but neither she nor her employers could have defined it" (*Killers of the Dream,* 124).

17. King, *A Southern Renaissance,* 173. King's analysis of memory is specifi-cally Freudian, as he makes clear in his opening chapter.

18. Gray, *The Literature of Memory,* 79.

19. Tucker, *Telling Memories among Southern Women,* 4.

20. Rich, *Of Woman Born,* 254.

21. In fact, Rich says in the introduction to the tenth anniversary edition of *Of Woman Born* that she "tried to blur that relationship into the mother-daughter relationship" and believes that she was "gliding over the concrete system within which Black women have had to nurture the oppressor's children" (n.p.).

22. Smith, *Killers of the Dream,* 131.

23. Smith, *Killers of the Dream,* 124. However, Smith explores the white boy's relationship with his mammy in more detail than she does the white girl's.

24. Smith, *Killers of the Dream,* 19.

25. Taylor, *Scarlett's Women,* employs Victoria O'Donnell's typology, since *Gone with the Wind* is prototypical of many subsequent fictions (88, 161–67). She argues that *Gone with the Wind,* book and film, "sealed [the mammy's] fate in racial myth" (171).

26. Diane Roberts, bell hooks, and K. Sue Jewell each argue that cultural images like the mammy/aunt/retainer persist, even after they have been modi-fied and ameliorated out of their original formulas. Much of the original for-mulation was dependent on physical characteristics. Roberts, *The Myth of Aunt Jemima;* hooks, "Continued Devaluation of Black Womanhod," in *Ain't I A Woman,* 51–86; Jewell, *From Mammy to Miss America.* Jewell discusses the arti-facts that persist in contemporary American popular culture despite the fact that

black women have strongly objected to images of the mammy and Aunt Jemima. Turner has argued that the representation of Aunt Chloe in *Uncle Tom's Cabin* "set the standard for future fictional [and filmic] representations of mammy figures." See *Ceramic Uncles,* 46. June Jordan describes an incident in a shop in New York where she spotted a decorative magnet of an "absolutely leprous Aunt Jemima" and felt "a homicidal rush." She bought it, paying well over the odds, to remove it. See Jordan, "No Chocolates for Breakfast," in *Technical Difficulties,* 126–27. Helen Taylor also provides the example of the huge, monumental sign for a restaurant just outside of Natchez, Mississippi, that is created as a mammy: "In order to eat, you enter a door in her voluminous skirts and order your hominy grits and black-eyed peas within her warm, welcoming body" (*Scarlett's Women,* 168). In this example the stereotype of the huge mammy figure takes on new and even more grotesque meaning.

27. Faulkner's black and white characters still act as a standard against which contemporary characterizations of cross-racial relations in the South are often measured. In idiosyncratic style, Doris Betts recently pointed out: "In the K-Mart checkout line, Dilsey's descendants and those from the Compson and Sartoris clans are all wearing jeans." See "Daughters, Southerners, and Daisy," in *Female Tradition,* ed. Manning, 267.

28. Baldwin, *Notes of a Native Son,* 22.

29. It is impossible to carry the sum of a character like Viola's in a single word. Lillian Smith sees the label as "a semantic trick," intended to brush aside the power and impact of the person and of this interracial relationship by calling one of its participants "nurse" (*Killers of the Dream,* 124). Like Smith, James Snead has described the images of the mammy and the domestic servant as configurations that "hover over almost every mass cultural depiction of blacks like unquiet ghosts." Snead, *White Screens, Black Images,* 127.

30. Fox, *A Servant's Tale,* 145.

31. The phrase "like one of the family" is analyzed by Wendy Luttrell, via interviews with domestics, as a phrase that "reveals as it disguises the race and gender relations which conspired to suppress black women's knowledge and worth" (23). With this in mind, it can be seen that Dawson deploys the stereotype to especially pertinent effect here, since it is the black character's knowledge that drives the story. "'Becoming Somebody,'" 17–35.

32. See Harris, *From Mammies to Militants;* Mae, *Thursdays and Every Other Sunday Off;* and Carraway, *Segregated Sisterhood.*

33. Robert Draper, in a review that fails to explore the significance of Viola.

Despite his assertion that she is "perhaps the novel's most fully realized character," he has trouble avoiding the shorthand of the stereotype when he declares: "Far from being a simple-minded, stoop-shouldered mammy, Viola is a regal and thoughtful presence." "The Demise of a Dynasty," 3.

34. Gloria Naylor, quoted by Taylor, *Scarlett's Women*, 171.

35. Taylor, *Scarlett's Women*, 125.

36. Faulkner, *Absalom, Absalom!*, 80. Subsequent references will be included parenthetically in the text.

37. Allen Tate, quoted by Gray, *Writing the South*, 179.

38. See Kreyling's "Parody and Postsouthernness," in *Inventing Southern Literature*, 148–66.

39. Dawson, *The Waking Spell*. This debut novel explores the ways in which women keep silent, often simmering with rage, in the face of abuse, mental breakdown, and a whole raft of family problems.

40. Mitchell, *Gone with the Wind*, 78.

41. Goffman, "Regions and Region Behaviour," in *The Presentation of Self in Everyday Life*, 109–40.

42. See Bakhtin, "The Grotesque Image of the Body," 301–67; Roberts, *Myth of Aunt Jemima*, 2–4. Florence King satirizes the idea of the sylphlike southern lady when she has elderly women remember their wedding days:

"I only weighed ninety pounds."

"My husband could span my waist."

"I could hardly stand up."

"The wind could have blown me away."

"The doctor said he never saw anybody so narrow."

Southern Ladies and Gentlemen, 94.

43. Roberts, *Faulkner and Southern Womanhood*, 62.

Conclusion. The Trouble with Friendship

1. Gray, *Writing the South*, 167.

2. However, Stowe's ideal is militated against when one remembers that in the 1850s the American Colonization Society upped the ante in its efforts to "repatriate" northern blacks in Africa, and Liberia, the state founded by and for former slaves, in particular. See, for example Banks, "*Uncle Tom's Cabin* and Antebellum Black Response," 210–27.

3. Alcott, *Work,* 442.

4. Walker, *Jubilee,* 480.

5. Walker 486.

6. Fiedler, *Love and Death,* 389. The reality of recent headlines, however, also includes "Flames Forge a New Unity," in which John Carlin reports that the burning of black southern churches over 1995 and 1996 failed to cause a racial split in southern states. *Independent on Sunday,* June 23, 1996, 13.

7. Fiedler, *Love and Death,* 388.

8. Smith, "Split Affinities," 279. In contrast, Alison Light provides a reading of *The Color Purple* that appreciates the novel precisely for its "passionate hopefulness" and utopianism. Alison Light, "Fear of the Happy Ending: *The Color Purple,* Reading, and Racism" in *Plotting Change: Contemporary Women's Fiction,* ed. Linda Anderson (London: Edward Arnold, 1990), 85–96.

9. Robert Booth Fowler opens his study of American ideas of community with the words "The 1960s echo on." Fowler, *The Dance with Community,* 1. Pat Watters reissued his 1971 memoir on the civil rights movement in 1993 and describes the decade as producing "a shimmering vision of what life between the races might be, and more than that, what life in America for all people might be." *Down to Now,* 20.

10. Gallop, *Around 1981,* 163.

11. Carraway, "Toward a Multicultural Feminist Politics of Solidarity," in *Segregated Sisterhood,* 203.

12. "Imagining Democracy," in *The Color of Gender: Reimaging Democracy,* by Eisenstein; "Visions and Revisions," in *Controversy and Coalition,* by Ferree and Hess.

13. Childers and hooks, "A Conversation about Race and Class," 60. Elsewhere, hooks emphasizes the importance of leaving the "private spaces—in our houses, where we talk about what we share, the cultures we come from and ways they intersect" to "name our solidarities *publicly* with one another." See hooks, "Moving into and Beyond Feminism," in *Outlaw Culture,* 226.

14. Young, "The Ideal of Community and the Politics of Difference," 300.

15. Young 311–12.

16. Williams, *Rooster's Egg,* 188.

17. Williams 189.

18. See, for example, Webster, *Racialization of America;* and Haney-Lopez, *White by Law.*

19. See, for example, Cao's recent novel *Monkey Bridge,* about a Vietnamese American's experiences in Falls Church, Virginia; and Suzanne W. Jones and Sharon Monteith, eds., "South to a New Place," special issue, *Critical Survey* 12, no. 1 (2000).

20. Jay Clayton, "Feminism and the Politics of Community," in *The Pleasures of Babel,* 130–31.

21. Shockley, *Loving Her.* Frank Lamont Phillips wrote an intensely pejorative review: "What bothers me most about *Loving Her* is its racial angle. Has anyone besides this reviewer noticed how many white lovers populate the Black imagination? [He refrains from providing examples.] This bullshit should not be encouraged." *Black World* 89–90. Alice Walker's more sympathetic review appeared in *Ms.,* April 1975, 120, 124. Walker bases her opinion too much in her own observations of people, professing to know many black people but not many lesbians on whom she might base the novel's success or failure. Beverly Smith values the novel as a breakthrough in the representation of lesbian lives but notes that its protagonists fall into a traditional and disappointing pattern whereby the black woman takes responsibility for all domestic work in the home, leaving the white woman free to work and to develop her leisure time. Beverly Smith, Review of *Loving Her,* 16. I would like to acknowledge my former student Siobhan England, who provided me with some of the reviews noted above.

22. Shockley, *Black and White.* See also Birtha, *Lovers' Choice,* esp. the stories "Ice Castle," "The Gray Whelk Shell," and "Her Ex-Lover"; and Jewelle Gomez's highly original and adventurous novel of interracial lesbian vampires, *The Gilda Stories.*

23. Alice Walker, "A Letter of the Times; or, Should Sado-Masochism Be Saved?" in *You Can't,* 118–23.

24. Adrienne Rich, "When My Dreams Show Signs," from "North American Time," in *Adrienne Rich's Poetry and Prose,* ed. Gelpi and Gelpi, 114; Allison, *Skin,* 165, 199.

25. Lorde, "The Uses of Anger: Women Responding to Racism," in *Sister Outsider,* 129.

26. DeMott 133.

27. DeMott 180.

Select Bibliography

Abel, Elizabeth. "(E)Merging Identities: The Dynamics of Female Friendship in Contemporary Fiction by Women." *Signs: Journal of Women in Culture and Society* 6, no. 3 (1981): 413–35.

———. "Black Writing, White Reading: Race and the Politics of Feminist Interpretation." *Critical Inquiry* 19 (spring 1993): 470–98.

Abel, Elizabeth, and Emily K. Abel, eds. *The Signs Reader: Women, Gender, and Scholarship.* Chicago: University of Chicago Press, 1983.

Abel, Elizabeth, Barbara Christian, and Helen Moglen, eds. *Female Subjects in Black and White: Race, Psychoanalysis, Feminism.* Berkeley and Los Angeles: University of California Press, 1997.

Abel, Elizabeth, Marianne Hirsch, and Elizabeth Langland, eds. *The Voyage In: Fictions of Female Development.* Hanover, N.H.: University Press of New England, 1983.

Adams, Alice. *Listening to Billie.* 1975. New York: Alfred A. Knopf, 1978.

Albinski, Nan Bowman. *Women's Utopias in British and American Fiction.* London: Routledge, 1988.

Alcoff, Linda. "Cultural Feminism Versus Post-Structuralism: The Identity Crisis in Feminist Theory." *Signs: Journal of Women in Culture and Society* 13, no. 3 (1988): 405–36.

———. "The Problem of Speaking for Others." Weisser and Fleischner 285–309.

Alcott, Louisa May. *Work: A Story of Experience.* 1873. New York: Schocken, 1977.

Allison, Dorothy. *Bastard Out of Carolina.* 1992. London: Flamingo, 1993.

———. *Skin: Talking About Sex, Class, and Literature.* London: Pandora, 1995.

———. *Trash.* London: Flamingo, 1995.

Ammons, Elizabeth. "Stowe's Dream of the Mother-Savior: *Uncle Tom's Cabin* and American Women Writers Before the 1920s." Sundquist 155–95.

———. *Conflicting Stories: American Women Writers at the Turn of the Century.* New York: Oxford University Press, 1991.

Andrews, William L. "Inter(racial)textuality in Nineteenth-Century Southern Narrative." Clayton and Rothstein 298–317.

Applebome, Peter. *Dixie Rising: How the South Is Shaping American Values, Politics, and Culture.* New York: Random House, 1996.

Archer, Chalmers, Jr. *Growing Up Black in Rural Mississippi: Memories of a Family, Heritage of a Place.* New York: Walker, 1992.

Arendt, Hannah. *The Human Condition.* Cambridge: Cambridge University Press, 1958.

Asher, Carol, Louise DeSalvo, and Sara Ruddick, eds. *Between Women: Biographers, Novelists, Critics, Teachers, and Artists Write about Their Work on Women.* New York: Routledge, 1993.

Ashley, Bob. *The Study of Popular Fiction: A Source Book.* London: Pinter, 1989.

Auerbach, Nina. *Communities of Women: An Idea in Fiction.* Cambridge: Harvard University Press, 1978.

Awkward, Michael. *Negotiating Difference: Race, Gender, and the Politics of Reading.* Chicago: University of Chicago Press, 1995.

Bakhtin, Mikhail. *The Dialogic Imagination.* Translated by Caryl Emerson and Michael Holquist. Austin: University of Texas Press, 1981.

———. "The Grotesque Image of the Body." In *Rabelais and His World,* trans. Helene Iswolsky, 301–67. Bloomington: Indiana University Press, 1984.

Baldwin, James. *Notes of a Native Son.* 1955. London: Penguin, 1995.

Bammer, Angelika. *Partial Visions: Feminism and Utopianism in the 1970s.* London: Routledge, 1991.

Banks, Marva. "*Uncle Tom's Cabin* and Antebellum Black Response." Machor 210–27.

Bannerji, Himanji. *Thinking Through: Essays on Feminism, Marxism, and Anti-Racism.* Toronto: Women's Press, 1995.

Barr, Marleen, and Nicholas D. Smith, eds. *Women and Utopia: Critical Interpretations.* New York: University Press of America, 1983.

Bauer, Dale. *Feminist Dialogics: A Theory of Failed Community.* Albany: State University of New York Press, 1988.

Baym, Nina. *Women's Fiction: A Guide to Novels by and about Women in America, 1820–1870.* Ithaca, N.Y.: Cornell University Press, 1978.

Beidler, Philip D. *What We Were Reading in the '60s: Scriptures for a Generation.* Athens: University of Georgia Press, 1994.

Belsey, Catherine. *Critical Practice.* London: Methuen, 1980.

Berlant, Lauren. "National Brands? National Body: Imitation of Life." In *Comparative American Identities: Race, Sex, and Nationality in the Modern Text,* edited by Hortense J. Spillers. New York: Routledge, 1991.

Berry, J. Bill, ed. *Home Ground: Southern Autobiography.* Columbia: University of Missouri Press, 1991.

Berry, Venise T., and Carmen L. Manning Miller, eds. *Mediated Messages and African-American Culture: Contemporary Issues.* London: Sage, 1996.

Birtha, Becky. *Lovers' Choice.* 1987. London: Women's Press, 1988.

Boelhower, William. *Through a Glass Darkly: Ethnic Semiosis in American Literature.* New York: Oxford University Press, 1984.

Botcherby, Sue. "Thelma and Louise Go Shooting." *Trouble and Strife* 22 (winter 1991): n.p.

Brady, Maureen. *Folly.* 1983. New York: Feminist Press at CUNY, 1994.

Brodhead, Richard. *The Journals of Charles W. Chesnutt.* Durham, N.C.: Duke University Press, 1993.

Brooks, Peter. *Reading for the Plot.* New York: Knopf, 1984.

Brown, Mary Ward. *Tongues of Flame.* Tuscaloosa: University of Alabama Press, 1993.

Brown, Rita Mae. *Rubyfruit Jungle.* 1973. London: Penguin, 1994.

———. *In Her Day.* 1976. New York: Bantam, 1988.

Brown, Rosellen. *Civil Wars.* 1984. New York: Dell, 1994.

Buell, Lawrence. *The Environmental Imagination: Thoreau, Nature Writing, and the Formation of American Culture.* Cambridge: Harvard University Press, 1995.

Bulkin, Elly, Minnie Bruce Pratt, and Barbara Smith. *Yours in Struggle: Three Feminist Perspectives on Anti-Semitism and Racism.* Ithaca, N.Y.: Firebrand, 1988.

Bunch, Charlotte. "Making Common Cause: Diversity and Coalitions." 1985. In *Passionate Politics: Feminist Theory in Action, Essays 1968–1986,* 149–57. New York: St. Martin's Press, 1987.

Burke, Fielding [Olive Tilford Dargan]. 1932. *Call Home the Heart: A Novel of the Thirties.* New York: Feminist Press, 1983.

Butler, Jack. "Still Southern after All These Years." Humphries and Lowe 33–40.

Cade Bambara, Toni. *The Salt Eaters.* 1980. London: Women's Press, 1982.

Campbell, Bebe Moore. "Friendship in Black and White: Beyond the 'Some of My Best Friends Are . . . ' Syndrome." *Ms.,* August 1983, 44–46, 95.

———. *Brothers and Sisters.* 1994. New York: Berkeley, 1995.

Canfield, John. "A Conversation with Shirley Ann Grau." *Southern Quarterly* 25, no. 2 (winter 1987): 39–52.

Cao, Lan. *Monkey Bridge.* New York: Vintage, 1996.

Carby, Hazel. "White Woman Listen! Black Feminism and the Boundaries of Sisterhood." In *The Empire Strikes Back: Race and Racism in '70s Britain,* 212–35. London: Hutchinson, 1982.

Carpenter, Lynette, and Wendy Kolmar. *Haunting the House of Fiction.* Knoxville: University of Tennessee Press, 1991.

Carraway, Nancie. *Segregated Sisterhood: Racism and the Politics of American Feminism.* Knoxville: University of Tennessee Press, 1991.

Cash, W. J. *The Mind of the South.* 1941. London: Vintage, 1969.

Cather, Willa. *Sapphira and the Slave Girl.* 1940. London: Virago, 1986.

Cawelti, John G. "The Concept of Formula in the Study of Popular Literature." *Journal of Popular Literature* 3 (1969): 381–90.

Chappell, David L. *Inside Agitators: White Southerners in the Civil Rights Movement.* Baltimore: Johns Hopkins University Press, 1994.

Childers, Mary, and bell hooks. "A Conversation about Race and Class." Hirsch and Keller 60–83.

Childress, Alice. *Like One of the Family.* 1956. Boston: Beacon Press, 1986.

Christian, Barbara. "Response to 'Black Women's Texts.'" *NWSA Journal* 1, no. 1 (1988): 32–36.

———. "The Race for Theory." JanMohamed and Lloyd 37–49.

Clayton, Jay. *The Pleasures of Babel: Contemporary American Literature and Theory.* New York: Oxford University Press, 1993.

Clayton, Jay, and Eric Rothstein. *Influence and Intertextuality in Literary History.* Madison: University of Wisconsin Press, 1991.

Cliff, Michelle. *Free Enterprise.* 1993. London: Viking, 1994.

———, ed. *The Winner Names the Age: A Collection of Writings by Lillian Smith.* New York: W. W. Norton, 1978.

Clinton, Catherine, ed. *Half Sisters of History: Southern Women and the American Past*. Durham, N.C.: Duke University Press, 1994.

Coiner, Constance. *Better Red: The Writing and Resistance of Tillie Olsen and Meridel Le Sueur*. New York: Oxford University Press, 1995.

Collins, Patricia Hill. *Black Feminist Thought: Knowledge, Consciousness, and the Politics of Empowerment*. London: Routledge, 1991.

Cook, Martha. "Old Ways and New Ways." Rubin et al. 527–34.

Culler, Jonathan. *The Pursuit of Signs: Semiotics, Literature, Deconstruction*. Ithaca, N.Y.: Cornell University Press, 1981.

Dargis, Manohla. "Roads to Freedom." *Sight and Sound,* July 1991, 14–19.

Davies, Carole Boyce. *Black Women, Writing, and Identity: Migrations of the Subject*. London: Routledge, 1994.

Davis, Angela. *An Autobiography*. 1983. London: Women's Press, 1990.

———. *Women, Race and Class*. 1981. London: Women's Press, 1982.

Davis, Thadious M. "Southern Writers: Notes toward a Definition of Terms." *Southern Quarterly* 19, no. 2 (winter 1981): 10–16.

———. "Women's Art and Authorship in the Southern Region: Connections." Manning 15–37.

Davis, Thulani. *1959*. London: Hamish Hamilton, 1992.

Dawson, Carol. *The Waking Spell*. Chapel Hill, N.C.: Algonquin, 1992.

———. *Body of Knowledge*. London: Viking Penguin, 1994.

De Beauvoir, Simone. *The Second Sex*. 1949. London: Penguin, 1979.

De Lauretis, Teresa. *Alice Doesn't: Feminism, Semiotics, Cinema*. London: Macmillan, 1984.

———. "Eccentric Subjects: Feminist Theory and Historical Consciousness." *Feminist Studies* 16, no. 1 (spring 1990): 115–50.

———, ed. *Feminist Studies: Critical Studies*. Bloomington: Indiana University Press, 1986.

DeMott, Benjamin. *The Trouble with Friendship: Why Americans Can't Think Straight about Race*. 1995. New Haven: Yale University Press, 1998.

Dent, Gina, ed. *Black Popular Culture: A Project by Michele Wallace*. Seattle: Bay Press, 1992.

Dexter, Pete. *Paris Trout*. 1988. London: Fontana, 1989.

Dixson, Barbara. "Family Celebration: Portrayals of the Family in Fiction Published in the 1980s by Southern Women." *Southern Quarterly* 26, no. 3 (spring 1988): 5–14.

Donaldson, Laura E. *Decolonising Feminisms: Race, Gender, and Empire-Building.* London: Routledge, 1993.

Donaldson, Susan V. "Ellen Douglas's *Black Cloud, White Cloud* and the Fragmentation of Narrative." *Southern Quarterly* 33, no. 4 (summer 1995): 51–64.

Donawerth, Jane L., and Carol Kolmerten, eds. *Utopian and Science Fiction by Women: Worlds of Difference.* Syracuse, N.Y.: Syracuse University Press, 1993.

Douglas, Carol Anne. *To the Cleveland Station.* Tallahassee, Fla.: Naiad Press, 1982.

Douglas, Ellen. *Black Cloud, White Cloud.* 1963. Jackson: University Press of Mississippi, 1989.

———. *A Lifetime Burning.* 1982. Baton Rouge: Louisiana State University Press, 1995.

———. *Can't Quit You Baby.* 1988. London: Virago Press, 1990.

Downing, Christine. *Psyche's Sisters: Reimaging the Meaning of Sisterhood.* San Francisco: Harper and Row, 1988.

Doyle, Laura. *Bordering on the Body: The Racial Matrix of Modern Fiction and Culture.* New York: Oxford University Press, 1994.

Draper, Robert. "The Demise of a Dynasty: *Body of Knowledge*." *Los Angeles Times,* September 11, 1994, 3.

Du Bois, W. E. B. *The Souls of Black Folk.* 1903. New York: Dover, 1994.

Dyer, Richard. "White." *Screen* 29, no. 4 (autumn 1988): 44–64.

———. *The Matter of Images: Essays on Representation.* London: Routledge, 1993.

Eagleton, Terry. *Marxism and Literary Criticism.* London: Methuen, 1976.

Eichenbaum, Luise, and Susie Orbach. *Between Women: Love, Envy, and Competition in Women's Friendships.* New York: Viking Penguin, 1988.

Eisenstein, Zillah R. *The Color of Gender: Reimaging Democracy.* Berkeley and Los Angeles: University of California Press, 1994.

Elam, Diane. *Feminism and Deconstruction: Ms. en Abyme.* London: Routledge, 1994.

Elliott, Emory, Cathy N. Davidson, and Patrick O'Donnell, eds. *The Columbia History of the American Novel.* New York: Columbia University Press, 1991.

Ellison, Ralph. *Invisible Man.* 1952. London: Penguin, 1965.

———. *Shadow and Act.* 1964. New York: Random House, 1994.

Estes-Hicks, Onita. "The Way We Were: Precious Memories of the Black Segregated South." *African American Review* 27, no. 1 (spring 1993): 9–18.

Evans, Mari, ed. *Black Women Writers: Arguments and Interviews.* 1984. London: Pluto Press, 1985.

Evans, Sara. *Personal Politics: The Roots of Women's Liberation in the Civil Rights Movement and the New Left*. New York: Vintage, 1980.

Faulkner, William. *Sanctuary*. 1931. London: Penguin, 1980.

———. *Absalom, Absalom!* 1936. New York: Vintage, 1990.

———. *Requiem for a Nun*. 1953. London: Penguin, 1967.

Ferree, Myra Marx, and Beth B. Hess. *Controversy and Coalition: The New Feminist Movement*. Boston: Twayne, 1985.

Fiedler, Leslie A. *Love and Death in the American Novel*. 1960. London: Penguin, 1984.

———. *The Inadvertent Epic: From "Uncle Tom's Cabin" to "Roots."* Toronto: CBC Merchandising–Canadian Broadcasting Corporation, 1979.

Flora, Joseph F., and Robert Bain. *Contemporary Fiction Writers of the South: A Bio-Bibliographical Sourcebook*. Westport, Conn.: Greenwood Press, 1993.

Fowler, Connie May. *Sugar Cage*. New York: Bantam Press, 1992.

———. *River of Hidden Dreams*. 1994. London: Black Swan, 1995.

———. *Before Women Had Wings*. 1996. New York: Fawcett Columbine, 1997.

Fowler, Doreen, and Ann Abadie, eds. *"A Cosmos of My Own": Faulkner and Yoknapatawpha*. Jackson: University Press of Mississippi, 1981.

Fowler, Robert Booth. *The Dance with Community: The Contemporary Debate in American Political Thought*. Laurence: University Press of Kansas, 1991.

Fox, Paula. *A Servant's Tale*. London: Virago, 1984.

Fox-Genovese, Elizabeth. *Within the Plantation Household: Black and White Women of the Old South*. Chapel Hill: University of North Carolina Press, 1988.

———. "Social Order and the Female Self: The Conservatism of Southern Women in Comparative Perspective." Gispen 49–62.

———. *Feminism without Illusions: A Critique of Individualism*. Chapel Hill: University of North Carolina Press, 1991.

———. "Difference, Diversity, and Divisions in an Agenda for the Women's Movement." Young and Dickerson 232–48.

Frankenberg, Ruth. *The Social Construction of Whiteness: White Women, Race Matters*. London: Routledge, 1993.

———. "Growing Up White: Racism and the Social Geography of Childhood." *Feminist Review* 45 (autumn 1993): 23–42.

Frankenberg, Ruth, and Lata Mani. "Crosscurrents, Crosstalk: Race, Postcoloniality and the Politics of Location." *Cultural Studies* 7, no. 2 (May 1993): 292–310.

Franklin, John Hope. *The Color Line: Legacy for the Twenty-First Century.* Columbia: University of Missouri Press, 1993.

Fraser, Elizabeth, and Nichola Lacey. *The Politics of Community: A Feminist Critique of the Liberal-Communitarian Debate.* Hemel Hempstead, England: Harvester, 1994.

Frega, Donnalee. "Questioning History and Revision: Contemporary Southern Literature and the Canon." *Southern Quarterly* 34, no. 2 (winter 1996): 9–21.

Friedman, Marilyn. *What Are Friends For? Feminist Perspectives on Personal Relationships and Moral Theory.* Ithaca, N.Y.: Cornell University Press, 1993.

Furman, Jan. *Toni Morrison's Fiction.* Columbia: University of South Carolina Press, 1996.

Gallop, Jane. *Around 1981: Academic Feminist Literary Theory.* London: Routledge, 1992.

Gardiner, Judith Kegan. "Response to Abel." *Signs: Journal of Women in Culture and Society* 6, no. 3 (1981): 435–41.

Garrad, Greta, and Patrick Murphy, eds. *Ecofeminist Literary Criticism: Theory, Interpretation, Pedagogy.* Champaign: University of Illinois Press, 1998.

Garrow, David J. *Bearing the Cross.* New York: Vintage, 1986.

Gates, Henry Louis, Jr. *Black Literature and Literary Theory.* London: Methuen, 1984.

———. *Loose Canons: Notes on the Culture Wars.* New York: Oxford Universty Press, 1992.

———. *Colored People: A Memoir.* New York: Viking, 1995.

———, ed. *Reading Black, Reading Feminist: A Critical Anthology.* New York: Meridian, 1990.

Gelpi, Barbara Charlesworth, and Albert Gelpi. *Adrienne Rich's Poetry and Prose.* New York: W. W. Norton, 1993.

Genovese, Eugene. *Roll, Jordan, Roll: The World the Slaves Made.* 1974. New York: Vintage, 1976.

Gibbons, Kaye. *Ellen Foster.* 1987. London: Jonathan Cape, 1988.

———. *A Virtuous Woman.* London: Jonathan Cape, 1989.

———. *On the Occasion of My Last Afternoon.* 1998. London: Virago, 1999.

Giddings, Paula. *When and Where I Enter: The Impact of Black Women on Race and Sex in America.* New York: Bantam, 1988.

Gilchrist, Ellen. *The Annunciation.* London: Faber and Faber, 1984.

———. *Victory over Japan.* London: Faber and Faber, 1985.

—————. *Net of Jewels*. 1992. London: Faber and Faber, 1994.

Gispen, Kees, ed. *What Made the South Different?* Jackson: University Press of Mississippi, 1990.

Gitlin, Todd. *Twilight of Common Dreams: Why America Is Wracked by the Culture Wars*. New York: Henry Holt, 1995.

Glasgow, Ellen. *Virginia*. 1913. London: Virago, 1988.

—————. *Barren Ground*. 1925. London: Virago, 1986.

Godwin, Gail. *A Mother and Two Daughters*. 1982. London: Pan, 1983.

Godwin, Rebecca T. *Keeper of the House*. 1994. New York: St. Martin's Press, 1995.

Goffman, Erving. *The Presentation of Self in Everyday Life*. London: Penguin, 1959.

—————. *Frame Analysis*. London: Penguin, 1974.

Golden, Marita, and Susan Richards Shreve, eds. *Skin Deep: Black Women and White Women Write about Race*. New York: Doubleday, 1995.

Goldfield, David R. *Black, White, and Southern: Race Relations and Southern Culture, 1940 to the Present*. Baton Rouge: Louisiana State University Press, 1990.

Gomez, Jewelle. *The Gilda Stories*. Ithaca, N.Y.: Firebrand, 1991.

Goyen, William. *The Collected Stories of William Goyen*. New York: Doubleday, 1975.

Graff, Harvey J. *Conflicting Paths: Growing Up in America*. Cambridge: Harvard University Press, 1995.

Graham, Don, James W. Lee, and William T. Pilkington, eds. *The Texas Tradition: Fiction, Folklore, History*. Austin: University of Texas Press, 1983.

Grau, Shirley Ann. *The Keepers of the House*. London: Longmans, 1964.

—————. *Nine Women*. Boston: John Curley, 1985.

—————. "Introduction." Majorie Kinnan Rawlings's *Cross Creek*. Magee 193–202.

Gray, Richard. *The Literature of Memory: Modern Writers of the American South*. London: Edward Arnold, 1977.

—————. *Writing the South: Ideas of an American Region*. Cambridge: Cambridge University Press, 1986.

Green, Michelle Erica. "'There Goes the Neighborhood': Octavia Butler's Demand for Diversity in Utopias." Donawerth and Kolmerten 166–89.

Guerrero, Ed. *Framing Blackness: The African-American Image in Film*. Philadelphia: Temple University Press, 1993.

Gwin, Minrose C. *Black and White Women of the Old South: The Peculiar Sisterhood in American Literature.* Knoxville: University of Tennessee Press, 1985.

———. "A Theory of Black Women's Texts and White Women's Readings; or, . . . The Necessity of Being Other." *NWSA Journal* 1, no. 1 (1988): 21–31.

———. *The Feminine and Faulkner: Reading (Beyond) Sexual Difference.* Knoxville: University of Tennessee Press, 1990.

———. "Sweeping the Kitchen: Revelation and Revolution in Contemporary Southern Women's Writing." *Southern Quarterly* 30, no. 2–3 (winter–spring 1992): 54–62.

Hale, Grace Elizabeth. "'Some Women Have Never Been Reconstructed': Mildred Lewis Rutherford, Lucy M. Stanton, and the Racial Politics of White Southern Womanhood, 1900–1930." Inscoe 173–201.

Hall, Jacquelyn Dowd. *Revolt against Chivalry: Jessie Daniel Ames and the Women's Campaign against Lynching.* New York: Columbia University Press, 1979.

Haney-Lopez, Ian. *White by Law: The Legal Construction of Race.* New York: New York University Press, 1996.

Haraway, Donna. "A Manifesto for Cyborgs: Science, Technology, and Socialist Feminism in the 1980s." Nicholson 190–233.

Harris, Eddy L. *The South of Haunted Dreams: A Ride through Slavery's Old Back Yard.* New York: Simon and Schuster, 1993.

Harris, Trudier. *From Mammies to Militants.* Philadelphia: Temple University Press, 1982.

———. *Exorcising Blackness: Historical and Literary Lynching and Burning Rituals.* Bloomington: Indiana University Press, 1984.

Harrison, Elizabeth Jane. *Female Pastoral: Women Writers Re-Visioning the American South.* Knoxville: University of Tennessee Press, 1991.

Hedges, Elaine, and Shelley Fisher Fishkin, eds. *Listening to Silences : New Essays in Feminist Criticism.* New York: Oxford University Press, 1994.

Hedin, Raymond. "Probable Readers, Possible Stories: The Limits of Nineteenth-Century Black Narratives." Machor 180–205.

Heilbrun, Carolyn. *Writing a Woman's Life.* London: Women's Press, 1989.

Herzen, Lane von. *Copper Crown.* 1991. New York: Plume, 1991.

———. *The Unfastened Heart.* 1994. New York: Plume, 1995.

Hess, John, Chuck Kleinhaus, and Julia Lesage. "After Cosby/After the L.A. Rebellion: The Politics of Transnational Culture in the Post Cold War Era." *Jump Cut* 37 (July 1992): 2–5, 43.

Hill, Anita Faye, and Emma Coleman Jordan, eds. *Race, Gender, and Power in America*. New York: Oxford University Press, 1996.

Hirsch, Marianne, and Evelyn Fox Keller, eds. *Conflicts in Feminism*. New York: Routledge, 1990.

Hobson, Fred. *The Southern Writer in the Postmodern World*. Mercer University Lamar Memorial Lectures 33. Athens: University of Georgia Press, 1991.

hooks, bell. *Ain't I a Woman: Black Women and Feminism*. 1981. London: Pluto Press, 1982.

———. *Talking Back: Thinking Feminist, Thinking Black*. 1989. London: Turn-around Press, 1990.

———. *Yearning: Race, Gender, and Cultural Politics*. 1990. London: Turnaround Press, 1991.

———. *Black Looks: Race and Representation*. London: Turnaround Press, 1992.

———. *Sisters of the Yam: Black Women and Self-Recovery*. London: Turnaround Press, 1993.

———. *Outlaw Culture*. New York: Routledge, 1994.

Horner, Avril, and Sue Zlosnik. *Landscape of Desire: Metaphors in Modern Women's Fiction*. Hemel Hempstead, England: Harvester Wheatsheaf, 1990.

Howe, Florence, ed. *Tradition and the Talents of Women*. Urbana: University of Illinois Press, 1991.

Hughes, Robert. *Culture of Complaint: The Fraying of America*. London: Harvill, 1994.

Hull, Gloria T., Patricia Bell Scott, and Barbara Smith, eds. *All the Women Are White, All the Blacks Are Men, but Some of Us Are Brave: Black Women's Studies*. New York: Feminist Press, 1982.

Humphreys, Josephine. *Dreams of Sleep*. London: Collins Harvill, 1985.

———. *Rich in Love*. London: Collins Harvill, 1988.

Humphries, Jefferson, ed. *Southern Literature and Literary Theory*. Athens: University of Georgia Press, 1990.

Humphries, Jefferson, and John Lowe, eds. *The Future of Southern Letters*. New York: Oxford University Press, 1996.

Hunt, Marsha. *Free*. 1992. London: Penguin, 1993.

Hunter, Gordon, ed. *The American Literary History Reader*. New York: Oxford University Press, 1995.

Hurston, Zora Neale. *Their Eyes Were Watching God*. 1937. London: Virago, 1984.

Hurtado, Aida. "Relating to Privilege: Seduction and Rejection in the Subordination of White Women and Women of Color." *Signs: Journal of Women in Culture and Society* 14, no. 4 (1989): 833–55.

Inge, Tonette Bond, ed. *Southern Women Writers: The New Generation.* Tuscaloosa: University of Alabama Press, 1990.

Inscoe, John C., ed. *Georgia in Black and White: Explorations in the Race Relations of a Southern State, 1865–1950.* Athens: University of Georgia Press, 1994.

Jackman, Mary R., and Marie Crane. "'Some of My Best Friends Are Black . . .': Interracial Friendship and Whites' Racial Attitudes." *Public Opinion Quarterly* 50 (1986): 459–86.

Jacobs, Harriet J. *Incidents in the Life of a Slave Girl, Written by Herself.* 1861. Cambridge: Harvard University Press, 1987.

James, Stanlie M., and Abena Busia, eds. *Theorizing Black Feminisms: The Visionary Pragmatism of Black Women.* New York: Routledge, 1993.

Jameson, Fredric. *The Political Unconscious: Narrative as a Socially Symbolic Act.* London: Methuen, 1981.

———. *Signatures of the Visible.* New York: Routledge, 1990.

JanMohamed, Abdul R., and David Lloyd, eds. *The Nature and Context of Minority Discourse.* Oxford: Oxford Unversity Press, 1990.

Jewell, K. Sue. *From Mammy to Miss America and Beyond: Cultural Images and the Shaping of U.S. Social Policy.* New York: Routledge, 1993.

Johnson, Barbara. *A World of Difference.* Baltimore: Johns Hopkins University Press, 1987.

Johnson, Diane. *The Shadow Knows.* London: Bodley Head, 1974.

Jones, Anne Goodwyn. *Tomorrow Is Another Day: The Woman Writer in the South, 1859–1936.* Baton Rouge: Louisiana State University Press, 1981.

Jones, Anne Goodwyn, and Susan V. Donaldson. *Haunted Bodies: Gender and Southern Texts.* Charlottesville: University Press of Virginia, 1997.

Jones, Gayle. *Liberating Voices: Oral Tradition in African American Literature.* Cambridge: Harvard University Press, 1991.

Jones, Libby Falk, and Sarah Webster Goodwin, eds. *Feminism, Utopia, and Narrative.* Knoxville: University of Tennessee Press, 1990.

Jones, Suzanne W. "Dismantling Stereotypes: Interracial Friendships in *Meridian* and *A Mother and Two Daughters.*" Manning 140–57.

Jordan, June. *Technical Difficulties: Selected Political Essays.* London: Virago, 1992.

Jordan, Rosan A., and Susan J. Kalcik, eds. *Women's Folklore, Women's Culture.* Philadelphia: University of Pennsylvania Press, 1985.

Jordan, Shirley M., ed. *Broken Silences: Interviews with Black and White Women Writers.* New Brunswick, N.J.: Rutgers University Press, 1993.

Joseph, Gloria I., and Jill Lewis. *Common Differences: Conflicts in Black and White Feminist Perspectives.* New York: Doubleday Anchor, 1981.

Kaplan, Carla. "Recuperative Reading and the Silent Heroine of Feminist Criticism." Hedges and Fishkin 168–94.

Kincaid, Nanci. *Crossing Blood.* New York: Avon, 1992.

King, Florence. *Southern Ladies and Gentlemen.* 1975. London: Black Swan, 1989.

King, Katie. *Theory in Its Feminist Travels: Conversations in U.S. Women's Movements.* Bloomington: Indiana University Press, 1994.

King, Richard H. *A Southern Renaissance: The Cultural Awakening of the American South, 1930–1955.* New York: Oxford University Press, 1980.

———. *Civil Rights and the Idea of Freedom.* New York: Oxford University Press, 1992.

———. "Politics and the Fictional Representation: The Case of the Civil Rights Movement." Ward and Badger 159–76.

King, Richard H., Sharon Monteith, and Nahem Yousaf. "Interview with bell hooks." *Overhere: Reviews in American Studies* 11, no. 1 (summer 1991): 1–16.

King, Richard H., and Helen Taylor, eds. *Dixie Debates: Perspectives on Southern Cultures.* London: Pluto Press, 1996.

Kirby, Jack Temple. *Media-Made Dixie: The South in the American Imagination.* Rev. ed. Athens: University of Georgia Press, 1986.

Klein, Michael, ed. *An American Half Century: Postwar Culture and Politics in the U.S.A.* London: Pluto Press, 1994.

Kolodny, Annette. *The Land before Her.* Chapel Hill: University of North Carolina Press, 1984.

Kovel, Joel. *White Racism: A Psychohistory.* 1975. London: Free Association, 1988.

Kreyling, Michael. *Inventing Southern Literature.* Jackson: University Press of Mississippi, 1998.

Kubitschek, Missy Dehn. *Claiming the Heritage.* Jackson: University Press of Mississippi, 1993.

Ladner, Joyce. *Tomorrow's Tomorrow: The Black Woman.* New York: Doubleday, 1970.

Lauber, Lynn. *21 Sugar Street.* New York: W. W. Norton, 1993.

Lauret, Maria. *Liberating Literature: Feminist Fiction in America.* London: Routledge, 1994.

Lentricchia, Frank. *Criticism and Social Change.* Chicago: University of Chicago Press, 1983.

Lerner, Gerda, ed. *Black Women in White America: A Documentary History.* New York: Vintage, 1973.

Levy, Helen Fiddyment. *Fiction of the Homeplace: Jewett, Glasgow, Cather, Porter, Welty, and Naylor.* Jackson: University Press of Mississippi, 1992.

Lorde, Audre. *Sister Outsider: Essays and Speeches.* Freedom, Calif.: Crossing Press, 1984.

————. *A Burst of Light.* London: Sheba Feminist Publishers, 1988.

Lugones, Maria C., and Pat Alake Rosezelle. "Sisterhood and Friendship as Feminist Models." Weiss and Friedman 135–45.

Luttrell, Wendy. "'Becoming Somebody': Aspirations, Opportunities, and Womanhood." Young and Dickerson 17–35.

Machor, James L., ed. *Readers in History: Nineteenth-Century American Literature and the Contexts of Response.* Baltimore: Johns Hopkins University Press, 1993.

MacKethan, Lucinda. *Daughters of Time: Creating Women's Voice in Southern Story.* Athens: University of Georgia Press, 1990.

Mae, Verta. *Thursdays and Every Other Sunday Off: A Domestic Rap.* New York: Doubleday, 1972.

Magee, Rosemary M., ed. *Friendship and Sympathy: Communities of Southern Women Writers.* Jackson: University Press of Mississippi, 1992.

Manning, Carol S., ed. *The Female Tradition in Southern Literature.* Urbana: University of Illinois Press, 1993.

Marable, Manning. *Race, Reform, and Rebellion: The Second Reconstruction in Black America, 1945–1990.* Jackson: University Press of Mississippi, 1991.

————. "Race, Identity, and Political Culture." Dent 292–302.

————. "Malcolm X and the Crisis in Black America." Klein 192–205.

————. *Black Leadership.* New York: Columbia University Press, 1998.

Marable, Manning, and Leith Mullings. "The Divided Mind of Black America: Race, Ideology, and Politics in the Post–Civil Rights Era." *Race and Class* 36, no. 1 (1994): 61–72.

Marcus, Jane. "Invisible Mending." Asher, DeSalvo, and Ruddick 381–95.

Marshall, Paule. *Merle and Other Stories*. London: Virago, 1983.

Mason, Julian. "Kaye Gibbons [1960–]." Flora and Bain 156–68.

McCullers, Carson. *The Member of the Wedding*. 1946. London: Penguin, 1987.

McEwen, Christian, and Sue O'Sullivan, eds. *Out the Other Side: Contemporary Lesbian Writing*. London: Virago, 1988.

McKay, Nellie Y. "Acknowledging Differences: Can Women Find Unity Through Diversity?" James and Busia 267–82.

McLaurin, Melton. *Separate Pasts: Growing Up White in the Segregated South*. Athens: University of Georgia Press, 1987.

Melosh, Barbara, ed. *Gender and American History since 1890*. New York: Routledge, 1993.

Messent, Peter. *New Readings of the American Novel: Narrative Theory and Its Application*. London: Macmillan, 1990.

Michie, Helena. *Sororophobia : Differences among Women in Literature and Culture*. New York: Oxford University Press, 1992.

Miller, Nancy K. *Subject to Change: Reading Feminist Writing*. New York: Columbia University Press, 1988.

Mitchell, Margaret. *Gone with the Wind*. 1936. London: Pan, 1974.

Moers, Ellen. *Literary Women*. London: Women's Press, 1978.

Mogen, David, Mark Busby, and Paul Bryant, eds. *The Frontier Experience and the American Dream: Essays on American Literature*. College Station: Texas A&M University Press, 1989.

Monteith, Sharon. "Critical Interrogations of Self and Culture: bell hooks's Strategies on Gender and Race." *Overhere: Reviews in American Studies* 11, no. 1 (summer 1991): 138–49.

———. "Writing for Re-Vision." *New Formations: A Journal of Culture/Theory/Politics* 20 (summer 1993): 173–80.

———. "Across the Kitchen Table: Establishing the Dynamics of an Interracial Friendship." *Overhere: Reviews in American Studies* 14, no. 2 (winter 1994): 19–34.

———. "Liberating Voices, Telling Stories." *Overhere: Reviews in American Studies* 14, no. 1 (summer 1994): 62–77.

———. "On the Streets and in the Tower Blocks: Ravinder Randhawa's *A Wicked Old Woman* and Livi Michael's *Under a Thin Moon*." *Critical Survey* 8, no. 1 (1996): 26–36.

————. "Between Girls: Kaye Gibbons's *Ellen Foster* and Friendship as a Mono-logic Formulation." *Journal of American Studies* 33, no. 1 (1999): 45–64.

————. "Theorizing Women's Friendship: Interracial Friendships in the American South." *Women: A Cultural Review* 10, no. 2 (1999): 139–50.

Moody, Ann. *Coming of Age in Mississippi.* 1968. New York: Bantam, Doubleday, Dell, 1976.

Moraga, Cherrie, and Gloria Anzaldua, eds. *This Bridge Called My Back: Writings by Radical Women of Color.* Boston: Persephone Press, 1981.

Morgan, Robin, ed. *Sisterhood Is Powerful: An Anthology of Writings from the Women's Liberation Movement.* New York, Vintage, 1970.

————. *The Word of a Woman: Selected Prose, 1968–1992.* London: Virago, 1993.

Morrison, Toni. *Sula.* 1973. London: Picador, 1991.

————. *Beloved.* 1987. New York: Plume, 1988.

————. "Unspeakable Things Unspoken: The Afro-American Presence in American Literature." *Michigan Quarterly Review* 38, no. 2 (1989): 1–34.

————. *Playing in the Dark: Whiteness and the Literary Imagination.* Cambridge: Harvard University Press, 1992.

————. "Recitatif." In *Ancestral House: The Black Short Story in the Americas and Europe,* ed. Charles H. Rowell, 422–36. Boulder, Colo.: Westview Press, 1995.

————, ed. *Race-ing, Justice, En-gendering Power: Essays on Anita Hill, Clarence Thomas, and the Construction of Social Reality.* New York: Pantheon, 1992.

Moylan, Tom. *Demand the Impossible: Science Fiction and the Utopian Imagination.* New York: Methuen, 1986.

Nicholson, Linda J., ed. *Feminism/Postmodernism.* New York: Routledge, 1990.

Noble, Allen G., ed. *To Build a New Land: Ethnic Landscapes in North America.* Baltimore: Johns Hopkins University Press, 1992.

Noble, Donald R. "The Future of Southern Writing." Rubin et al. 578–88.

Noble, Jeanne. *Beautiful Also Are the Souls of Our Black Sisters.* London: Prentice Hall, 1978.

Oates, Joyce Carol. *Because It Is Bitter and Because It Is My Heart.* 1988. London: Picador, 1992.

O'Connor, Pat. *Friendships Between Women: A Critical Review.* Hemel Hempstead, England: Harvester, 1992.

Olsen, Tillie. "O Yes." 1956. In *Tell Me a Riddle,* 48–71. New York: Laurel, 1979.

Omi, Michael, and Howard Winant. *Racial Formation in the United States from the 1960s to the 1980s.* New York: Routledge, 1989.

Otto, Whitney. *How to Make an American Quilt.* 1991. London: Pan, 1992.

Parker, Patricia. *Literary Fat Ladies: Rhetoric, Gender, Property.* London: Methuen, 1987.

Patai, Daphne. "Beyond Defensiveness: Feminist Research Strategies." Barr and Smith 148–69.

Peeples, Edward H. "Richmond Journal: Thirty Years in Black and White." *Race Traitor: Journal of the New Abolitionism* 3 (spring 1994): 34–46.

Petry, Ann. *The Street.* 1946. London: Virago, 1986.

Phillips, Anne. *Engendering Democracy.* Oxford: Polity Press, 1991.

Phillips, Frank Lamont. Review of *Loving Her,* by Ann Allen Shockley. *Black World* 24 (September 1975): 89–90.

Pilkington, Tom. "A Twisted Family Feud." News World Communications Inc.: *World and I* 10, no.1 (1995): 330.

Plain, Belva. *Crescent City.* 1987. London: Harper Collins, 1993.

Polk, Noel, ed. Special Issue on Ellen Douglas. *Southern Quarterly* 33, no. 4 (summer 1995).

Porter, Judith. *Black Child, White Child: The Development of Racial Attitudes.* Cambridge: Harvard University Press, 1971.

Porter, Nancy. "Women's Interracial Friendships and Visions of Community in *Meridian, The Salt Eaters, Civil Wars,* and *Dessa Rose.*" Howe 251–67.

Pratt, Minnie Bruce. "Identity: Skin Blood Heart." Bulkin, Pratt, and Smith 11–63.

Prenshaw, Peggy Whitman. "Southern Ladies and the Southern Literary Renaissance." Manning 73–89.

———, ed. *Women Writers of the Contemporary South.* Jackson: University Press of Mississippi, 1984.

Pryse, Marjorie, and Hortense J. Spillers, eds. *Conjuring: Black Women, Fiction, and Literary Tradition.* Bloomington: Indiana University Press, 1985.

Radway, Janice. "The Utopian Impulse in Popular Literature: Gothic Romances and 'Feminist' Protest." *American Quarterly* 33, no. 2 (summer 1981): 140–62.

———. *Reading the Romance: Women, Patriarchy, and Popular Literature.* London: Verso, 1987.

Rawlings, Marjorie Kinnan. *Cross Creek.* 1942. London: Fontana, 1984.

Raymond, Janice. *A Passion for Friends: Toward a Philosophy of Female Affection.* Boston: Beacon Press, 1986.

Reed T. V. *Fifteen Jugglers, Five Believers: Literary Politics and the Poetics of Ameri-*

can Social Movements. Berkeley and Los Angeles: University of California Press, 1992.

Reynolds, David. "White Trash in Your Face: The Literary Descent of Dorothy Allison." *Appalachian Journal: A Regional Studies Review* 20, no. 1 (summer 1993): 356–66.

Rich, Adrienne. *On Lies, Secrets, and Silence: Selected Prose, 1966–1978.* London: Virago, 1980.

———. *Of Woman Born: Motherhood as Experience and Institution.* London: Virago, 1986.

———. *Blood, Bread, and Poetry: Selected Prose, 1979–1985.* London: Virago, 1987.

———. *What Is Found There: Notebooks on Poetry and Politics.* New York: W. W. Norton, 1993.

Riley, Denise. "Does a Sex Have a History? 'Women' and Feminism." *New Formations* 1 (spring 1987): 35–46.

Rhodes, Jewell Parker. *Magic City.* London: Headline, 1997.

Roberts, Diane. *Faulkner and Southern Womanhood.* Athens: University of Georgia Press, 1994.

———. *The Myth of Aunt Jemima: Representations of Race and Region.* New York: Routledge, 1994.

Roediger, David R. *Black on White: Black Writers on What It Means to Be White.* New York: Schocken, 1999.

Rollins, Judith. *Between Women: Domestics and Their Employers.* Philadelphia: Temple University Press, 1985.

Romines, Ann. *The Home Plot: Women, Writing, and Domestic Ritual.* Amherst: University of Massachusetts Press, 1992.

Rorty, Richard. *Contingency, Irony, and Solidarity.* New York: Cambridge University Press, 1989.

Rubin, Lillian B. *Just Friends: The Role of Friendship in Our Lives.* New York: Harper and Row, 1985.

Rubin, Louis D., Jr., Blyden Jackson, S. Moore Rayburn, and Lewis P. Simpson, eds. *The History of Southern Literature.* Baton Rouge: Louisiana State University Press, 1985.

Salisbury, Mark. "Get Out of My Face." *Empire,* July 1993, 74–78.

Sanders, Dori. *Clover.* New York: Fawcett Columbine, 1990.

Sartre, Jean-Paul. *Being and Nothingness: An Essay in Phenomenological Ontology.* Trans. Hazel E. Barnes. London: Routledge, 1993.

Scharf, Lois, and Joan M. Jensen. *Decades of Discontent: The Women's Movement, 1920–1940*. Westport, Conn.: Greenwood Press, 1983.

Schlesinger, Arthur. *The Disuniting of America: Reflections on a Multicultural Society*. New York: W. W. Norton, 1992.

Schultz, Elizabeth. "Out of the Woods and into the World: A Study of Interracial Friendships Between Women in American Novels." Pryse and Spillers 67–85.

Scott, Anne Firor. *The Southern Lady: From Pedestal to Politics, 1830–1930*. Chicago: University of Chicago Press, 1970.

Sedgwick, Eve Kosofsky. *Between Men: English Literature and Male Homosocial Desire*. New York: Columbia University Press, 1985.

Seidel, Kathryn. *The Southern Belle in the American Novel*. Tampa: University of South Florida Press, 1985.

Selway, Jennifer. "All in the Family." *Observer Review*, November 30, 1995.

Shelnutt, Eve. "A Contemporary Southern Writer's Predicament: Removing the Rose-Colored Glasses." *Southern Quarterly* 30, no. 1 (fall 1991): 52–57.

Shipler, David K. *A Country of Strangers: Blacks and Whites in America*. New York: Vintage, 1998.

Shockley, Ann Allen. *Loving Her*. 1974. Tallahassee, Fla.: Naiad Press, 1986.

———. *The Black and White of It*. Tallahassee, Fla.: Naiad Press, 1987.

Shoemaker, Jan. "Ellen Douglas: Reconstructing the Subject in 'Hold On' and *Can't Quit You Baby*." *Southern Quarterly* 33, no. 4 (summer 1995): 83–98.

Shohat, Ella, and Robert Stam. *Unthinking Eurocentrism: Multiculturalism and the Media*. New York: Routledge, 1994.

Showalter, Elaine, ed. *The New Feminist Criticism: Essays on Women, Literature, and Theory*. London: Virago, 1986.

———. *Sister's Choice: Tradition and Change in American Women's Writing*. Oxford: Clarendon Press, 1991.

Shreve, Anita. *Women Together, Women Alone: The Legacy of the Consciousness-Raising Movement*. New York: Viking, 1989.

Shreve, Susan Richards. *A Country of Strangers*. London: Sceptre, 1990.

Simpson, Lewis P. *The Dispossessed Garden: Pastoral and History in Southern Literature*. Mercer University Lamar Memorial Lectures 16. Athens: University of Georgia Press, 1975.

Small, Stephan. *Racialised Barriers: The Black Experience in the United States and England in the 1980s*. London: Routledge, 1994.

Smith, Beverly. Review of *Loving Her*, by Ann Allen Shockley. *Gay Community News*, November 16, 1978.

Smith, Barbara, and Beverly Smith. "Across the Kitchen Table: A Sister-to-Sister Dialogue." Moraga and Anzaldua 113–27.

Smith, Lee. *Oral History.* New York: Putnam, 1983.

Smith, Lillian. *Strange Fruit.* London: Cressnet Press, 1945.

———. *Killers of the Dream.* New York: W. W. Norton, 1949.

Smith, Valerie. "Split Affinities: The Case of Interracial Rape." Hirsch 271–87.

Smith-Rosenberg, Carol. "The Female World of Love and Ritual: Relations Between Women in Nineteenth-Century America." Abel and Abel 27–55.

Snead, James. *Figures of Division: William Faulkner's Major Novels.* New York: Methuen, 1986.

———. *White Screens, Black Images: Hollywood from the Dark Side.* New York: Routledge, 1994.

Sollors, Werner. *Beyond Ethnicity.* New York: Oxford University Press, 1986.

South, Cris. *Clenched Fists, Burning Crosses.* New York: Crossing Press, 1984.

Spelman, Elizabeth V. *Inessential Woman: Problems of Exclusion in Feminist Thought.* London: Women's Press, 1988.

Stallybrass, Peter, and Allon White. *The Politics and Poetics of Transgression.* London: Methuen, 1986.

Stam, Robert. *Subversive Pleasures: Bakhtin, Cultural Criticism, and Film.* Baltimore: Johns Hopkins University Press, 1989.

Steele, Shelby. *The Content of Our Character.* New York: St. Martin's Press, 1990.

Steinem, Gloria. *Outrageous Acts and Everyday Rebellions.* London: Flamingo, 1984.

Stowe, Harriet Beecher. *Uncle Tom's Cabin.* 1852. New York: Signet, 1966.

Styron, William. *The Confessions of Nat Turner.* London: Panther, 1968.

Sundquist, Eric J., ed. *New Essays on "Uncle Tom's Cabin."* Cambridge: Cambridge University Press, 1986.

———. *To Wake the Nations: Race and the Making of American Literature.* Cambridge: Harvard University Press, 1994.

Takaki, Ronald. *Iron Cages: Race and Culture in Nineteenth Century America.* New York: Oxford University Press, 1990.

Tallack, Douglas. *Twentieth-Century America: The Intellectual and Cultural Context.* Harlow, Essex: Longman, 1991.

Tate, Linda. *A Southern Weave of Women: Fiction of the Contemporary South.* Athens: University of Georgia Press, 1994.

Taylor, Gordon O. *Studies in Modern American Autobiography.* London: Macmillan, 1986.

Taylor, Helen. *Gender, Race, and Region in the Writings of Grace King, Ruth Mc-Enery Stuart, and Kate Chopin.* Baton Rouge: Louisiana State University Press, 1989.

———. *Scarlett's Women: "Gone with the Wind" and Its Female Fans.* London: Virago, 1989.

Thornton-Dill, Bonnie. "Race, Class, and Gender: Prospects for an All-Inclusive Sisterhood." *Feminist Studies* 9, no. 1 (Spring 1983): 131–50.

Todd, Janet. *Women's Friendships in Literature.* New York: Columbia University Press, 1980.

Todorov, Tzvetan. *Mikhail Bakhtin: The Dialogical Principle.* Translated by Wlad Godzich. Minneapolis: University of Minnesota Press, 1984.

Tucker, Susan. *Telling Memories Among Southern Women: Domestic Workers and Their Employers in the Segregated South.* Baton Rouge: Louisiana State University Press, 1988.

Turner, Patricia A. *Ceramic Uncles and Celluloid Mammies: Black Images and Their Influence on Culture.* New York: Doubleday, 1994.

Tyler, Anne. *A Slipping-Down Life.* 1970. London: Vintage, 1990.

———. *The Clock Winder.* London: Vintage, 1972.

———. *Searching for Caleb.* 1976. London: Chatto and Windus, 1990.

Ude, Wayne. "Forging an American Style: The Romance Novel and Magical Realism as Response to the Frontier and Wilderness Experiences." Mogen, Busby, and Bryant 50–64.

Urgo, Joseph R. *Novel Frames: Literature as a Guide to Race, Sex, and History in American Culture.* Jackson: University Press of Mississippi, 1991.

Voight, Cynthia. *Dicey's Song.* 1982. London: Collins, 1984.

Wald, Priscilla. *Constituting Americans.* Durham, N.C.: Duke University Press, 1995.

Walker, Alice. Review of *Loving Her,* by Ann Allen Shockley. *Ms.,* April 1975, 120, 124.

———. "One Child of One's Own: A Meaningful Digression Within the Work(s)—An Excerpt." Hull, Scott, and Smith 37–42.

———. *Meridian.* 1976. London: Women's Press, 1982.

———. *The Color Purple.* 1982. London: Women's Press, 1983.

———. *You Can't Keep a Good Woman Down.* London: Women's Press, 1989.

———. *The Temple of My Familiar.* 1989. London: Penguin, 1990.

Walker, Margaret. *Jubilee.* 1966. London: Hodder and Stoughton, 1967.

Walker, Melissa. *Down from the Mountaintop: Black Women's Novels in the Wake of the Civil Rights Movement, 1966–1989.* New Haven: Yale University Press, 1991.

Ward, Brian, and Tony Badger, eds. *The Making of Martin Luther King and the Civil Rights Movement.* London: Macmillan, 1996.

Ward, Carol M. *Rita Mae Brown.* New York: Twayne, 1993.

Ward, Kathryn B. "'Lifting As We Climb': How Scholarship by and About Women of Color Has Shaped My Life as a White Feminist." Young and Dickerson 199–217.

Warren, Kenneth. *Black and White Strangers: Race and American Literary Realism.* Chicago: University of Chicago Press, 1993.

Warren, Robert Penn. *Segregation: The Inner Conflict in the South.* 1956. Athens: University of Georgia Press, 1994.

Watters, Pat. *Down to Now: Reflections on the Southern Civil Rights Movement.* Athens: University of Georgia Press, 1993.

Waugh, Patricia. *Metafiction: The Theory and Practice of Self-Conscious Fiction.* London: Routledge, 1984.

Webster, Yehudi O. *The Racialization of America.* New York: St. Martin's Press, 1992.

Weed, Elizabeth, ed. *Coming to Terms: Feminism, Theory, Politics.* New York: Routledge, 1989.

Weiss, Penny A., and Marilyn Friedman, eds. *Feminism and Community.* Philadelphia: Temple University Press, 1995.

Weisser, Susan Ostrow, and Jennifer Fleischner, eds. *Feminist Nightmares, Women at Odds: Feminism and the Problem of Sisterhood.* New York: New York University Press, 1994.

Wells, Rebecca. *Divine Secrets of the Ya-Ya Sisterhood.* New York: Harper Collins, 1996.

Welty, Eudora. *Delta Wedding.* 1946. London, Virago, 1986.

———. *"The Bride of Innisfallen" and Other Stories, 1949–1955.* New York: Harvester, 1977.

West, Cornel, Jorge Klor De Alva, and Earl Shorris. "Our Next Race Question." *Harper's,* April 1996, 55–63.

Westling, Louise. *Sacred Groves and Ravaged Gardens: The Fiction of Eudora Welty, Carson McCullers, and Flannery O'Connor.* 1985. Athens: University Of Georgia Press, 1990.

———. *The Green Breast of the New World: Landscape, Gender, and American Fiction.* Athens: University of Georgia Press, 1998.

Williams, Patricia J. *The Alchemy of Race and Rights*. London: Virago, 1993.

————. *The Rooster's Egg: On the Persistence of Prejudice*. Cambridge: Harvard University Press, 1995.

Williams, Sherley Anne. *Give Birth to Brightness*. New York: Dial Press, 1972.

————. *Dessa Rose*. 1986. London: Futura, 1988.

Williamson, Joel. *A Rage for Order: Black-White Relations in the American South Since Emancipation*. Oxford: Oxford University Press, 1986.

————. *William Faulkner and Southern History*. New York: Oxford University Press, 1993.

Willis, Susan. *Specifying: Black Women Writing the American Experience*. 1987. London: Routledge, 1990.

Wilson, Harriet E. *Our Nig*. 1859. London: Allison and Busby, 1984.

Wilson, Midge, and Kathy Russell. *Divided Sisters: Bridging the Gap Between Black Women and White Women*. New York: Doubleday, 1996.

Woodson, Jacqueline. *I Hadn't Meant to Tell You This*. New York: Delacorte Press, 1994.

Wright, Richard. "The Ethics of Living Jim Crow: An Autobiographical Sketch." In *Uncle Tom's Children*, 17–53. New York: Harper and Row, 1965.

Yaeger, Patricia. *Honey-Mad Women: Emancipatory Strategies in Women's Writing*. New York: Columbia University Press, 1988.

Yellin, Jean Fagan, ed. *The Abolitionist Sisterhood: Women's Political Culture in Antebellum America*. Ithaca, N.Y.: Cornell University Press, 1994.

Young, Gay, and Dickerson, Bette J., eds. *Color, Class, and Country: Experiences of Gender*. London: Zed, 1994.

Young, Iris Marion. "The Ideal of Community and the Politics of Difference." Nicholson 300–323.

Zagarell, Sandra A. "Narratives of Community: The Identification of a Genre." *Signs: Journal of Women in Culture and Society* 13, no. 3 (1988): 498–527.

Index

Carraway, Nancie, 171

Cass (white character), 75–101; community of, 81–89; Huck Finn and, 79; setting of friendship for, 75–81; sisterhood and, 97–100; social development of, 94–96; structuring narration of, 90–94; tradition of, 77

characterizations, clichéd, 105–6, 116–17, 204 (n. 21). *See also* stereotypes

characters: archetypal, 20, 42, 102–33; confidante role of, 41; pairing white/black, 38, 39; racial equality in, 77; utopian, 39

characters, African American, 64, 65, 76

characters, black: depicting, 45, 49; narrative voice of, 89–90; redemptive, 42; romanticizing, 46; self-abnegation of, 152–53; servant role of, 138, 150; status of, 173–74; structuring friendship of, 61, 77; violence and, 191 (n. 21); white writers and, 8

characters, black girl: Manichean opposition and, 52–53; racial roles of, 54; structuring friendship of, 56, 60–61; structuring narration of, 50–51, 58–65

characters, black women: depicting, 173–76; domestic role of, 102–12; domestic status of, 109–10; household roles of, 134; oppression of, 111–12; servant role of, 204 (n. 21); sexuality of, 149;

white protagonist and, 127, 140–41, 144

characters, white: black writers depicting, 4; critique of, 48; moral power of, 144; privileged status of, 173–74; structuring friendship of, 42, 61; white writers depicting, 10. *See also* protagonists, white

characters, white girl: Manichean opposition and, 52–53; structuring friendship of, 56. *See also* protagonists, white girl

characters, white women: black domestic and, 118; black women and, 127, 129; black writers depicting, 45; employer role of, 102–12; employer status of, 109–10; oppression by, 111–12; southern ladyhood and, 158–60

characters, women: relationship models of, 43–44; southern model of, 77; structuring friendship of, 9–10

Chase, Richard, 78–79

Childress, Alice, 37

Christian, Barbara, 45–46

cinema. *See* media

civil rights legislation, 83–84, 137

civil rights movement: Douglas's use of, 113; Gibbons's use of, 70; influence of, 18, 102, 103–4; preoccupations with, 7; white sisterhood and, 5

Civil War motifs: in *Body of Knowledge,* 158; in *Copper Crown,* 168; in *Ellen*

Foster, 70; in historical romances, 189 (n. 36)

Clayton, Jay: on community models, 172; on *Ellen Foster,* 70–71, 73, 189 (n. 35); on popular culture, 23

commonality: vs. complementarity, 43; vs. complexity, 26; between white and black women, 182 (n. 64); of women in *Copper Crown,* 91–92, 100–101. *See also* racial differences

community: archetype of, 168; *Body of Knowledge* and, 137–39, 165–66, 168; connectedness in, 169; contemporary fiction and, 17–18, 24; *Copper Crown* and, 81–89, 98–99, 101, 168; feminist dream of, 74; interracial friendships and, 3, 167; models/ideas of, 170–72; preoccupations with, 7, 8; white women writers and, 27

connectedness: in *Copper Crown's* structure, 93; in mistress/maid relationships, 111–12; between white and black women, 118–21

consciousness raising, 31

Copper Crown (Herzen, 1991), 75–101; setting and focus of, 75–77; sisterhood in, 96–101; structure of community in, 81–89; structure of friendship in, 89–96; themes and images of, 77–81

Cornelia (white character), 113–33; narration and critiques of, 116–21; structuring friendship of, 122–31

critiques: of black influence on fiction, 47; of *Can't Quit You Baby,* 195–96 (n. 33); of contemporary southern fiction, 11–15; of friendship, 28; within narration, 117–18; and theoretical debates, 22. *See also* feminist critics

culture: etymology of, 192 (n. 25); female, 83; nature paired with, 75; popular, 2, 23; southern, 90. *See also* southern context

Davis, Angela, 80

Davis, Thadious, 34, 179 (n. 38)

Davis, Thulani, 48, 53

Dawson, Carol: *Body of Knowledge* by, 135–66; influences of, 137–38; language structure by, 158–66; mammy-child paradigm by, 148–54, 162; open-ended structure by, 167; structure of narrations by, 141–48, 154–58

de Beauvoir, Simone, 29

Deep South Evangelism, 137

DeMott, Benjamin, 7, 21–22, 176

"dialogic communitarianism," 18

"dialoguing," 33

differences, racial. *See* racial differences

domestic role: *Body of Knowledge* and, 134–66; *Can't Quit You Baby* and, 113–33; formulations of, 102–12

doubling device, 93, 98, 100

Douglas, Ellen: *Can't Quit You Baby* by, 113–33; exploring southern myths by, 46–47; metafictional devices used by, 116–21;

Douglas, Ellen (*continued*)
reconfiguring race relations by,
112–16, 169–70; structure of
dialogue by, 129–33; structuring
narration by, 121–29

eco-feminism, 78, 92
eco-utopianism, 77–81, 98
Ellen (white character), 53–73;
growth of, 69–73; Huck Finn
and, 65, 70; identity of, 65–69;
monologue of, 61–65
Ellen Foster (Gibbons, 1987), 51–73;
ambiguities in, 73; bildungsroman
and, 69–73; binary oppositions
in, 54–55; black/white identity
in, 65–69; individualism vs.
friendship plot in, 72; social
geography of race in, 53–58;
structural racial separation in,
60–65
Ellison, Ralph: on "American" literary
tradition, 64; on influence of
blacks, 47; on "mutual loneliness,"
51; on segregation "breaks," 20; on
white Americans' focus, 123
employer/housekeeper formulations:
in *Body of Knowledge,* 135–66; in
Can't Quit You Baby, 113–33; in
contemporary fiction, 102–12;
in southern fiction, 134
empowerment, 5, 63, 194 (n. 11). *See
also* power, racial
environment. *See* nature
equality: civil rights movement and,
18; *Copper Crown* and, 83–84,

86, 96, 97; *Ellen Foster* and, 69–
71; illusion of, 21; interracial
friendship and, 4; true friendship
and, 186 (n. 49); white vs. black
writers and, 77
erotic attachments, 95–96, 172–75
ethics, 23–24

families, southern, 136–47, 180
(n. 42)
family secrets, keepers of, 134–139,
140–166 passim
Faulkner, William: *Absalom, Absalom!*
by, 5–6, 10–11, 157–58, 165;
anthologies of, 179 (n. 25);
influence of, 14, 136, 157–59, 190
(n. 14); *Requiem for a Nun* by, 10–
11, 199 (n. 2); *The Sound and the
Fury* by, 155, 163; standard of,
201 (n. 27)
fear, 29, 35, 49. *See also* racial
attitudes
female subjectivity, 43–44, 185–86
(n. 48)
femininity, scripts of, 82
feminist collaboration, 178 (n. 11)
feminist critics: individualism and, 2;
literature and, 22; psychoanalytical
criticism and, 44; sisterhood
paradigms and, 177 (n. 10); theory
and, 24
feminist politics: characterizations
from, 116; fiction and, 74;
friendship-based, 36; narration
influenced by, 126
feminist principles: *Copper Crown*

and, 81, 83–84, 101; friendship and, 28; influence of, 7, 18, 41; sisterhood motifs and, 8; utopian, 85–87, 189–90 (n. 1); women's connections and, 33–34, 172. *See also* eco-feminism

fiction: alliances/differences in, 33; American polarizations and, 46; character types in southern, 49; childhood relationships in, 52–53; contemporary southern, 11–15; hopes and achievements in, 21; interracial friendships in, 2–3, 8–22; mistress-maid formulations in, 103–12; morality and, 23; racism in, 182 (n. 2); social change in, 24; social ills and, 7; theme of "convergence" and "counterpoint" in, 89–92; theories/models of friendship in, 29–49 passim; theory interfacing with, 183 (n. 8); utopian, 38–41, 74–101 passim

Fiedler, Leslie, 42–43, 65, 78

film. *See* media

Fister, Charles, 46–47

Fowler, Connie May: *Before Women Had Wings* by, 39, 55, 63, 69, 75; *River of Hidden Dreams* by, 75–76; *Sugar Cage* by, 9, 13

Fox-Genovese, Elizabeth, 37–38, 85

Frankenberg, Ruth, 53–54

Friedman, Marilyn, 5

friendship, Aristotle's views on, 29

friendship, interracial: adolescent, 51–52, 56, 58, 60; childhood, 50–73; contemporary fiction and,

13–14; contradictory models of, 167–76; fiction and theories on, 22–26; historical tensions in, 5–8; interdependency in, 64, 136–37; lesbian, 172–75; literary structures of, 8–22; literary use of "convergence" and "counterpoint" to explore, 89–92; media and fiction and, 2–3; mistress-maid formulations of, 102–33; paradigms of, 9–10; structure undermining, 61; true, 186 (n. 49); white vs. black writers on, 3–4; women writers on, 1–27. *See also* mammy-child relationship

friendship, political, 30

friendship, women's, 28–49, 41–45

"friendship plot": bildungsroman vs., 71; *Ellen Foster* and, 53, 66, 72; popularity of, 1–2; undermining, 176

Gardiner, Judith Kegan, 43–44

Gates, Henry Louis, Jr., 8

ghost relationships: *Body of Knowledge* and, 159–60; *Copper Crown* and, 82, 92, 101; Lillian Smith on, 148–49; literary friendships and, 190 (n. 13)

Gibbons, Kaye: childhood friendship novels by, 172; *Ellen Foster* by, 51–73; *On the Occasion of My Last Afternoon* by, 135–36, 151–52

Gilchrist, Ellen, 103, 107–12

Godwin, Rebecca T., 17, 135, 165

Golden, Marita, 4, 5

gothic qualities, 136–39, 159–60

Goyen, William, 79, 137

Grau, Shirley Ann: *The Keepers of the House* by, 13, 52, 134–35; *Nine Women* by, 105

Gray, Richard: on bildungsroman, 60; on black violence, 167; and southern context, 16; on southern writing, 147

Gwin, Minrose C.: and Faulkner's influence, 5–6; on kitchen metaphor, 119; on southern fiction, 10, 178 (n. 23); on women's readings, 45–47, 132

"gyn/affection," 36

Herzen, Lane von. *See* von Herzen, Lane

historical context: *Body of Knowledge* and, 137–39; *Can't Quit You Baby* and, 114; *Copper Crown* and, 81; novels structured by, 10; researching, 24–25; role in community of, 24; white vs. black and, 173–74

historical tensions, depicted, 5–8, 18

history, family: keepers of, 134–66; restructuring of, 142–48

Hobson, Fred, 14–15

Hollywood, 42–43, 191–92 (n. 24)

hooks, bell: on interracial friendship, 7, 171; on listening to black voice, 126; on race and class, 203 (n. 13); on racism and socialization, 114–15; reconfiguring race relations, 39

housekeeper role. *See* employer/housekeeper formulations

"ideal polity," 192 (n. 33)

identity: African American, 197 (n. 42); of characters, 35, 54, 98; derogatory names and, 56, 188 (n. 16); *Ellen Foster* and, 61, 65–69, 73; leitmotif, 43; literary exploration of, 25; moral, 3; politics of, 46; racial, 48; southern childhood and, 53–58; southern women's, 25

imagery and symbolism, 90

individualism, 2, 72, 172

integration, racial, 5–8, 17, 97

Irish, 76, 105

Jones, Anne Goodwyn, 29

Joseph, Gloria, 33

Keepers of the House, The (Grau, 1964), 13, 52, 134–35

King, Martin Luther, Jr., 146, 176, 187 (n. 2)

King, Richard H., 16, 39, 145

kitchens: metaphoric use of, 102–33 passim, 196 (n. 36, n. 37); in southern context, 47

Kreyling, Michael, 15

Ku Klux Klan, 80, 89

land, the, 75–76, 192 (n. 35)

landscapes, 74–77

language, *Body of Knowledge* and, 144, 154–55, 158–66

nature: *Copper Crown* and, 76, 92;
culture paired with, 75; ecocriticism and, 190 (n. 3); Faulkner
and the depiction of, 190 (n. 14)
"networking," 33
Noble, Donald, 17
novels. *See* fiction

O'Connor, Flannery, 45, 127
O'Connor, Pat, 32–33, 34, 183
(n. 11)
oral history, 145, 147–48
oral traditions, 29, 121–22

paradigms, interracial: breaks in, 19–
20; challenging, 9–10, 22–23, 177
(n. 10); changing, 167–76; maid-
mistress, 102–33; mammy-child,
137, 148–54; postcolonial, 35;
traditional, 48
paradigms, literary: binary
oppositions, 54–55; black women
writers of, 39; friendship, 10; racial
integration and, 61
parody, 141, 158–62
pastoral setting, 74–81, 90
pathetic fallacy, 92
patriarchal family, 17–18
patriarchy: *Copper Crown* and, 80–
81, 191 (n. 21); ladyhood and,
159; women's friendships and,
28–29
political bonds, 3, 21
political determinations: *Can't Quit
You Baby* and, 116; influence of, 9,
31–32; polarizing identities by, 46.

See sociopolitical determinations
politics, feminist. *See* feminist politics
polyphonic structure, 9
power, racial: *Body of Knowledge* and,
142; *Copper Crown* and, 87–89;
domestic relationship and, 111–
12, 144; white writers and, 174.
See also empowerment
protagonists, white: black servant to,
150, 204 (n. 21); black woman
aiding, 140–41; depictions of
black and, 6, 43; homogeneity of,
97–98; idioms deployed by, 5;
paranoia of, 105
protagonists, white girl: *Ellen Foster*
and, 65–69, 72; identity of black
vs., 54; maturation format of, 70;
narrations of black vs., 50, 60
psychoanalytical models, 43–44
psychosocial models, 44–45

race: *Body of Knowledge* and, 136,
148; *Can't Quit You Baby* and, 116–
21; class and, 36, 85, 88, 184
(n. 24); contemporary fiction and,
11, 13, 17; contemporary writers
and, 14; ethnicity and, 33; fiction
structured around, 8; friendship
theory and, 32, 183 (n. 11);
nomenclature for, 179–80 (n. 39);
perceptions of, 2; sex and power
in, 87–89; southern literature and,
29; U.S. and, 171–72; whites vs.
blacks and, 178 (n. 16); writing
and studies about, 7
race relations: *Body of Knowledge* and,

148–54; *Can't Quit You Baby* and, 124–25; *Copper Crown* and, 77, 100; depicting harmonious, 167–76; effect of 1960s, 47; *Ellen Foster* and, 67. *See also* power, racial

racial attitudes: *Copper Crown* and, 87–88, 96; *Ellen Foster* and, 69–73; social geography and, 53–58; writing structured by, 8, 19–20

racial differences: contemporary novels and, 8; *Copper Crown* and, 89–94, 99–100; forging alliances across, 33; utopian fiction and, 185 (n. 35); writing about, 183 (n. 11). *See also* commonality

racial geography: Lillian Smith's 1940s, 56–58; white women and, 53–54

racial guilt: *Copper Crown* and, 79, 81, 88; mammy role and, 151; the South as a crucible of, 3; young writers and, 14

racial "other": domestics and, 120; *Ellen Foster* and, 61–64, 172; paradigm of, 35; power and, 174

racial responsibility, white, 4. *See also* political determinations

racial tensions: *Copper Crown* and, 80, 82–83; writing about, 5–8

racism: *Copper Crown* and, 96; fiction and, 175, 182 (n. 2); U.S. definition of, 184 (n. 21). *See also* anger

Ransom family (white characters): calamities of, 138–39; secrets of, 140; sexuality of, 139–40

rape, interracial: *Copper Crown* and, 87, 88–89; lynching and, 193 (n. 38). *See also* violence

Raymond, Janice: on "gyn/affection," 36; on homogeneity, 97–98; on race victimization, 91

readers: access to characters by, 50; biracial experience and, 45; black characters and, 61; Dawson's narrative and, 138, 143, 152–53; Douglas's narrative and, 123–26; identity and, 132; interracial fiction and, 48; slave narrative and, 52

Reconstruction period: *Copper Crown* and, 79, 80; interracial friendships during, 191 (n. 17); *Jubilee* and, 169

recovery, collective, 24

relationships, cross-racial. *See* friendship, interracial

ressentiment, 129

Rich, Adrienne: on "disloyalty to civilization," 82; on interracial friendships, 39; on literary mother-daughter role, 148–49; on political correctness, 174–75; on race, 32–33, 47

Roberts, Diane: on Aunt Jemima stereotype, 149; on cultural images, 200 (n. 26); on the Faulknerian narrator, 163; *The Myth of Aunt Jemima* by, 10–11, 178 (n. 23); on white guilt, 151

romance, eco-utopian: *Body of Knowledge* and, 136–37; *Copper*

romance (*continued*)
   Crown and, 77–81, 101; feminist, 92

Rorty, Richard, 23, 24

Rubin, Lillian B., 30–31

Russell, Kathy, 35

segregation, racial: childhood friendships in, 53–58, 73; *Copper Crown* and, 96; depicting tensions of, 5–8; images of servant in, 150; mistress-maid relations in, 102–12; writers and, 20

self, sense of: *Body of Knowledge* and, 154, 156; *Ellen Foster* and, 70, 73; reading fiction and, 45–46

sexual miscegenation, 134

sexuality: black mammy's, 149; *Body of Knowledge* and, 139–40; *Copper Crown* and, 87–89

Shockley, Ann Allen: as black woman writer, 4; "friendship plot" by, 1; *Loving Her* by, 173; reviews of novel by, 204 (n. 21)

Shreve, Susan Richards, 58–60

"sister-friends," 1, 2

sisterhood: *Copper Crown* and, 74–101 passim; discrepancies in, 184 (n. 29); *Ellen Foster* and, 71–72; feminist theory and, 33–34; motherhood vs., 44, 148, 184 (n. 28); motifs of, 8; utopian ideas of, 36–38, 167–76; white vs. black, 5

slavery: images of women and, 150; interracial friendships during, 5;

trope of, 6; writing about, 52, 191 (n. 20)

Smith, Lillian: on black domestics, 138, 154, 200 (n. 16), 201 (n. 29); on democracy and discrimination, 48–49; on "disloyalty to civilization," 82; on memory and relationships, 145; on segregation, 56–58, 96; on southern "ghost relationships," 148–49; on white men's exploitation, 88

Snead, James, 201 (n. 29)

social consciousness: *Can't Quit You Baby* and, 116–17; *Copper Crown* and, 85; *Ellen Foster* and, 70; fiction initiating, 2; fiction raising, 18, 20–22; theories/fiction raising, 31–32

social values/ideals, 23, 181 (n. 55)

sociopolitical determinations: contemporary fiction with, 22; *Copper Crown* and, 83–84, 94–96; interracial friendships and, 53–58, 71; novels influenced by, 9. *See* political determinations

solipsism, white, 47

sororophobia, 37

southern context: *Can't Quit You Baby* and, 127; childhood interracial friendships in, 51–54; choice of, 16–17; contemporary writers and, 53–54, 172; *Copper Crown* and, 99; kitchen in, 47, 119; literary interracial friendships in, 2–3; novels structured by, 10, 179 (n. 38); *placeness* of, 20; researching, 24–25; U.S. vs., 6

Viola (black character) (*continued*)
language structure of, 162–66; as
metaphoric housekeeper, 140–41;
as metaphoric safe deposit box,
144–46; narration of, 142–48;
sexuality of, 139; structural status
of, 137; twentieth-century mammy
role of, 148–54

violence: *Body of Knowledge* and, 138;
Copper Crown and black/white,
80–82, 86, 88–89; lynching and
womanhood in black/white, 193
(n. 38)

voice, black vs. white: in
bildungsroman, 50; in *Body of
Knowledge,* 136–37, 138, 152–53;
in *Can't Quit You Baby,* 126; in
Copper Crown, 89–90; in *Ellen
Foster,* 58–65

von Herzen, Lane: *Copper Crown* by,
75–101; models by, 169; narrative
strategies by, 89–94; sisterhood/
community used by, 81–89;
sociopolitical forces used by, 94–
96; southern focus of, 75–77;
success of sisterhood by, 96–101;
themes and images by, 78–81

Walker, Alice: and *The Color
Purple,* 4, 104, 170; on Flannery
O'Connor's fiction, 45; and *Jubilee,*
169; and *A Letter of the Times,*
173–74; on "machete of freedom,"
171; and *The Temple of My Familiar,*
188 (n. 20)

Walker, Margaret, 8–9, 169

Wells, Rebecca, 1

Westling, Louise, 74, 77

"whiteness": anxiety and, 49;
derogative term for, 56, 188
(n. 16); presumption of, 47

Williams, Sherley Anne, 4, 80, 82, 97

Wilson, Midge, 35

"woman-centered" approach, 83–84,
119

womanism, 192 (n. 33)

women: category of, 22; commonality
of, 26, 182 (n. 64); differences of,
34; friendships between, 28–49.
See also characters, women

women, black: fiction and, 38;
representations of, 193 (n. 41);
studies of domestic, 150. *See also*
characters, black

women, white: black injustices and,
96; dominant narration of, 98;
requirements for, 47; self and racial
geography in, 53–54. *See also*
characters, white; protagonists,
white

women's suffrage, 5, 81

World War, First, 44, 139, 168

writers, black, 48, 49, 198 (n. 55);
black characters by, 46; black
domestics by, 103–4; interests of
contemporary, 14; racial equality
by, 77; tradition of, 34

writers, black women: assumption
for, 7–8; black women characters
by, 5; interracial friendship by,
4; paradigms by, 39; white
womanhood by, 45